THE SIEGE OF
KHE SANH:
AN ORAL HISTORY

ERIC HAMMEL

WARNER BOOKS

A Warner Communications Company

WARNER BOOKS EDITION

This Warner Books Edition is published by arrangement with Crown Publishers, Inc., 225 Park Avenue South, New York, New York 10003

Cover design by Don Puckey
Cover photo by DAVA

Warner Books, Inc.
666 Fifth Avenue
New York, N.Y. 10103

A Warner Communications Company

Printed in the United States of America

First Warner Books Printing: June, 1990

10 9 8 7 6 5 4 3 2 1

THIS BOOK IS DEDICATED TO
THE MEN WHO ENDURED THE SIEGE OF KHE SANH,
TO THEIR SURVIVORS AND LOVED ONES,
TO THOSE WHO SUCCORED THEM,
AND—MOST OF ALL—TO THOSE
WHO DIED AS A RESULT OF THE SIEGE.

GUIDE TO TERMS
AND ABBREVIATIONS

A-1	Douglas Skyraider propeller-driven attack bomber
A-4	Douglas Skyhawk jet attack bomber
A-6	Grumman Intruder jet attack bomber
AK-47	Soviet-pattern 7.62mm assault rifle
AN/TPQ-10	Ground-based aircraft radar guidance system
Arclight	B-52 high-altitude bombing program
ARVN	Army of Republic of Vietnam
ASP	Ammunition Supply Point
ASRT	Air Support Radar Team
B-52	Boeing Stratofortress jet heavy bomber
BGen	Brigadier General
C-123	Fairchild Provider medium cargo transport
C-130	Lockheed Hercules medium cargo transport
C4	Plastic explosive
Capt	Captain
CH-46	Boeing Sea Knight medium cargo helicopter
CH-53	Sikorsky Sea Stallion heavy cargo helicopter
Chicom	Chinese Communist (used for NVA hand grenade)
CIA	Central Intelligence Agency
CIDG	Civilian Irregular Defense Group
Claymore	U.S. directional antipersonnel mine
CN	Teargas
CO	Commanding Officer

COFRAM	Controlled Fragmentation Munitions (Firecracker)
Col	Colonel
Comm	Communications
CP	Command Post
CS	Teargas
DMZ	Demilitarized Zone
Duster	U.S. Army tracked 40mm gun carrier
EC-121	Lockheed Super Constellation electronics warfare aircraft
EOD	Explosive Ordnance Disposal
Exec	Executive Officer
F-4B	McDonnell Phantom jet fighter-bomber
1stLt	First Lieutenant
FOB	Forward Operating Base (Special Forces)
Gravel	Pressure-detonated explosive device
GySgt	Gunnery Sergeant
H-34	Sikorsky Sea Horse medium transport helicopter
H&I	Harassment-and-Interdiction
H&S	Headquarters-and-Service
HM3	Hospital Corpsman 3rd Class
HMC	Chief Hospital Corpsman
HN	Hospitalman
Hooch	Living quarters
HST	Helicopter Support Team
Huey	Bell UH-1E light attack/transport helicopter
KC-130	C-130 fuel tanker variant
KIA	Killed In Action
KSCB	Khe Sanh Combat Base
LAAW	U.S. light antitank assault weapon
LAPES	Low Altitude Proximity Extraction System
LBJ	President Lyndon B. Johnson
LCpl	Lance Corporal
Lt	Lieutenant
LtCol	Lieutenant Colonel
LtGen	Lieutenant General
LZ	Landing Zone
M-16	U.S. 5.56mm rifle
M-60	U.S. 7.62mm machine gun

M-79	U.S. 40mm grenade launcher
MACV	Military Assistance Command, Vietnam
Maj	Major
MCHD	Marine Corps Historical Division
Med	Medical (e.g., 3rd Medical Battalion)
MGen	Major General
MGySgt	Master Gunnery Sergeant
MIA	Missing In Action
NOD	Night Observation Device
NVA	North Vietnamese Army
Ontos	U.S. tracked 106mm recoilless rifle carrier
PAVN	People's Army of Vietnam (NVA)
Pfc	Private First Class
PT-76	Soviet tracked amphibious reconnaissance vehicle
Puff	Minigun-armed C-47 airplane
Pvt	Private
R&R	Rest and Rehabilitation (i.e., leave)
RPG	Soviet-pattern 40mm rocket-propelled grenade
S-3	Operations Officer
2ndLt	Second Lieutenant
SFC	Sergeant First Class
Sgt	Sergeant
SgtMaj	Sergeant Major
SKS	Soviet-pattern 7.62mm bolt-action carbine
SSgt	Staff Sergeant
TOT	Time On Target (artillery technique)
UH-1E	Bell Huey light attack/transport helicopter
USA	U.S. Army
USAF	U.S. Air Force
USAID	U.S. Agency for International Development
USMC	U.S. Marine Corps
USN	U.S. Navy
USS	United States Ship
VC	Viet Cong
VT	Variable Time (artillery airburst fuse)
WIA	Wounded In Action
Willy-Peter	WP (i.e., waterproof)

PHONETIC ALPHABET

Alpha	November
Bravo	Oscar
Charlie	Papa
Delta	Quebec
Echo	Romeo
Foxtrot	Sierra
Golf	Tango
Hotel	Uniform
India	Victor
Juliet	Whiskey
Kilo	X-Ray
Lima	Yankee
Mike	Zulu

Khe Sanh • Quang Tri
Hue •

THAILAND

LAOS

Danang •

I CORPS

Qui Nhon •

II CORPS

CAMBODIA

Nha Trang •
Dalat •

Cam
Ranh
Bay

III CORPS
• Bien Hoa

Saigon

My Tho •

Can Tho •

IV CORPS

| 0 | | 50 Miles |
| 0 | | 50 Kilometers |

© F. F. Parry (used with permission)

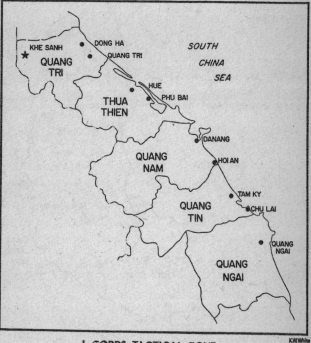

KW.White

I CORPS TACTICAL ZONE

NORTHERN QUANG TRI PROVINCE

E.L. WILSON

KHE SANH VALLEY

LOCATION OF OUTPOSTS

E.L. WILSON

KHE SANH COMBAT BASE

1/9

DROP ZONE

L/3/26

RED SECTOR

H & S CO

1/13 HQ

FOB—3

155mm PROV BTRY

4.2 MTR BTRY

A BTRY 105mm

AIR FREIGHT

CHARLIE MED

1/26

HELO REVETMENTS

GREY SECTOR

FSCC

CONTROL TOWER

BLUE SECTOR

1/26

WATER POINT

CP

26th MARINES

B BTRY 105mm

C BTRY 105mm

MAIN AMMO DUMP

1/26

1/26

1/26

1/26

37th ARVN RANGER BN

E. L. WILSON

881 SOUTH

January - April 1968

NVA TRENCHES and SPIDER HOLES

Downed H-34

WIRE MINES

RP26 LZ 105's

Ammo Bunkers 81mm Mortars

TRENCHLINE

WIRE MINES

TRENCHLINE

LZ

TRENCHLINE

TRENCHLINE

TRENCHLINE WIRE MINES

MG MG

MG RP26

106 RR 106 RR MG

MG

MINES WIRE

GATE

60mm Mortars

TRAIL

N

BGen. Harry Jenkins, USMC

RP — COMMAND POST   MG — .50-CAL or M-60 MACHINE GUN
LZ — LANDING ZONE   106 RR — 106mm RECOILLESS RIFLE
T — TRENCH TO BUNKER   ≣ — 105mm HOWITZER

THE EASTER OFFENSIVE

April 14, 1968

N

INITIAL CONTACT
ENEMY OUTPOSTS
0545

881 N

881 S

1:25.000

0   500   1000

Marine Corps Gazette (used with permission)

PART ONE

THE SIEGE

February 8–March 31, 1968

"They have us just where we want them."

Prologue

It is difficult for participants and historians alike to pinpoint the date on which the Siege of Khe Sanh actually began. Over the years—right after the siege, in fact—survivors and chroniclers began speaking and writing of a 77-day siege, but the beginning and end dates shift wildly from account to account. No *credible* combination of beginning and end dates comes to 77 days.

For practical purposes, the struggle for Khe Sanh—but not the siege itself—began on January 2, 1968, when a squad-sized reaction force from Lima Company, 3rd Battalion, 26th Marines (3/26) apprehended and killed five senior North Vietnamese Army (NVA) officers who were surveying Lima Company's lines. No doubt, the dead NVA regimental commander and his senior staff were preparing to assault Lima Company's position, which guarded the western end of the Khe Sanh Combat Base (KSCB).

A direct result of the killings in the wee hours of January 2 was the reinforcement of the two-battalion Marine force (1/26 and 3/26) at Khe Sanh by another Marine battalion (2/26) and a third 105mm artillery battery. Also, vigilance was heightened. As a result of increased patrolling, the defenders were able to detect the movement of elements of several fresh NVA regiments into hidden bivouacs around the combat base. An all-out entrenchment program was initiated by the defenders, who expected a massive ground assault by what they determined to be two fresh NVA divisions—two divisions against three reinforced battalions!

What the patrols and aerial surveillance missed entirely was the emplacement—over the border, in neighboring Laos—of many batteries of 152mm and 130mm artillery. Closer in, the NVA set in an impressive array of lighter artillery and 122mm and 140mm rockets. To directly defend the artillery emplacements against air attack and down incoming transport and cargo planes, the NVA set in many 37mm automatic antiaircraft cannon and .51-caliber antiaircraft machine guns.

The big show started on the night of January 20, 1968, with a regimental assault on Hill 861, which was held by one Marine infantry company—Kilo Company, 3/26. A simultaneous assault had been planned to go in against Hill 881 South (881S), but that bastion's defenders—India Company and two platoons of Mike Company, 3/26—had unwittingly spoiled the plan by sweeping onto neighboring Hill 881 North (881N), from which another NVA regiment was to jump off. It was a good thing the Marine supporting artillery—bolstered by Army 175mm guns many miles away, at Camp Carroll and the Rock Pile—had only one hill to support, for it took every available artillery tube to protect Kilo Company's otherwise untenable position.

On the morning of January 21, as Kilo Company licked its wounds and the NVA regiment charged with taking Hill 861 slunk into the jungle, all the NVA artillery and rockets arrayed on the Khe Sanh plateau and in Laos opened fire for the first time—on the combat base itself. The defenders and hundreds of headquarters and support personnel were knocked for a loop. If the NVA had followed up with a coordinated infantry assault, they might just have overrun the combat base. As it was, they overran the Huong Hoa District Headquarters in neighboring Khe Sanh Village—the first Republic of Vietnam government center to fall in the entire Vietnam War. Engrossed in the defense of their own base, the Marines neither sallied to reinforce the defenders of the ville while they might still have turned the tide, nor were they able to muster the troops to take back the fallen government center.

As the fourth and last fresh Marine battalion (the 1st Battalion, 9th Marines—1/9) arrived to guard a major approach into the combat base, the heavy shelling continued and serious close-in harassment began. The NVA antiaircraft array revealed itself as a massive aerial transport effort was layed on to get building materials, food, and ammunition to Khe Sanh, whose runway was not entirely within the defensive entrenchments. NVA snipers began taking a toll and close-in forward-observer teams controlling all manner of weapons from 60mm mortars to 152mm guns made movement anywhere in the combat base or the defended hills an iffy proposition.

Though sweeps and even movement to reconnoiter the enemy positions pretty much ended in the hills, the Marines defending the combat base itself were still able to reconnoiter and, to some degree, sanitize the immediate environs of the combat base. But "breaking out" was not the plan the senior commanders had in mind. Mindful of their ultimately more massive retaliatory potential—air power, mainly—the Marine commanders decided that the battalions defending Khe Sanh were safe enough underground and that serious Communist assault could be beaten back by supporting arms. Indeed, a strategy known as the "set-piece strategy" took hold. The "sitting ducks" inside the combat base were perceived by their highest commanders to be staked bait. As long as they were there to be attacked and pummeled—as long as the NVA allowed themselves to be tethered *around* the combat base, superior American air power and artillery could kill more of them than there were Marines in Khe Sanh to kill or maim. The terrible ordeal of positional, attritional warfare became, in the minds of the Marine commanders, the best means at hand for breaking the backs of two crack NVA divisions.

So, the Marines sat and took what the NVA had to dish out because doing so kept the NVA tethered to a locale within which they were obliged to die beneath the weight of the best retaliatory effort the Americans could dish out. Attritional warfare.

Using seismic sensors planted by aircraft, the Marines were able to track an NVA regiment as it moved on the nights leading up to the February 5 night attack against Echo Company, 2/26's newly established position on Hill 861 Alpha (861A). Still mindful of the need to grab a position dominating and overlooking the juicy combat base, the NVA did what was expected of them and ran pell mell into one of the scariest artillery interdictions set up in the Vietnam War. Though the lead NVA assault battalion nearly overran poor Echo Company, the precisely controlled American artillery cut it off from its supports and just butchered the two follow-on battalions. Echo Company suffered, but it appeared that another crack NVA regiment had been reduced to ineffective status.

Two nights later, on February 7, the NVA took their best shot to draw a large Marine unit into the open. Using PT-76 lightly armored amphibian reconnaissance vehicles—easily mistaken for tanks—for the first time in the Vietnam War, the NVA overran the Lang Vei Special Forces Camp, nine long kilometers west of the Khe Sanh Combat Base, on National Route 9. The Green Berets pleaded for the relief the Marines had promised in brighter days, but the Marine commander refused to send a company or a battalion off into the jungle at night, for he believed and was probably right that a much larger NVA force lay in wait. The Special Forces camp was overrun and a force of Green Beret volunteers from Khe Sanh rode out in the morning in Marine helicopters to gather in the survivors. It was a grim chapter that, even today, colors relations between Marines and Green Berets.

At Khe Sanh, the big news out of Lang Vei was contained in one of the last radio messages from the defenders—"Tanks in the wire!" That took everyone's breath away, for no serious effort had been expended to defend the combat base against a weapons system the Communists had never before used in South Vietnam.

On the night of February 8, an NVA battalion attempted to pluck an easy prize right from under the nose of the

Marine battalion (1/9) guarding a position known as the Rock Quarry, a little hill complex only a kilometer up the road on the best military approach to the combat base itself. Tiny Hill 64 was manned by a single reinforced platoon of Alpha Company, 1/9, and it was prime to be plucked. Somehow, the NVA battalion failed in its bid to seize Hill 64. A few survivors of the otherwise obliterated platoon hung on until morning, when the rest of Alpha Company sallied from the Rock Quarry and chased the last of the NVA from Hill 64.

The failed NVA assault on Hill 64 on the night of February 8 was the last of its kind. As the gunfire and grenade detonations died over Hill 64, the ordeal of Khe Sanh was set to enter its second, grimmer phase. The NVA divisions had given their all to dominate the Khe Sanh Combat Base by seizing the dominant high ground, and they had been rebuffed at every turn, had suffered insupportable casualties, had gained nothing.

As the sun rose over Khe Sanh, as 1/9 resecured Hill 64, the two NVA divisions arrayed on the Khe Sanh Plateau backed off from the assault and set themselves to the grim task of waging an attritional battle. The Siege of Khe Sanh—what everyone had been calling the struggle for nearly three weeks—truly began after the failed attempt to overrun Hill 64.

On February 8, 1968, the defenders of the Khe Sanh Combat Base and its outlying hill positions still faced their gravest ordeal and greatest casualties—the worst of the random maiming and killing lay before them.

Chapter 1

Hill 881S

Capt BILL DABNEY
India Company, 3/26 ——————————————

Hill 881S was the only outlying Khe Sanh Combat Base position not assaulted by infantry on the night of January 20–21.... Hill 861 got hit, the Khe Sanh ville got hit. Everything I heard about around there got hit that night, except 881S, and we were the most exposed. I was convinced... that we were not assaulted only because we'd been patrolling aggressively for a month out to the limit of our prudence and had developed our own intelligence as a result of those patrols and had acted on it within the limits of our capabilities. I believe that the India Company recon-in-force to 881N on January 20 ran into the NVA battalion that was designated to attack us that night. We could not destroy it, but we found and fixed it in the subsequent fire fight and hit it with supporting arms. Although it may not have decimated the battalion, it probably discouraged it. Thereafter, although I was prohibited from patrolling off the hill—and could not have done so had I been permitted, because I didn't have sufficient force to both extricate a patrol in trouble and hold the hill, and reinforcement from Khe Sanh was not possible—we used what we had learned from that point forward. We intimately knew the ground around us. I mean that seriously. We knew every valley, every fold in the ground. Every trooper on that hill had made patrols around that hill several times out to about four kilometers. One platoon was out almost every day. And often a squad or so down on the other side at the same time. . . .

We found that the NVA moved in close to Hill 881S at night to avoid the B-52's, artillery, etc., so we had a regular hose-down program of our own involving indirect-fire weapons only, including 60mm mortars, and fougasse. . . . Occasionally, on signal, the hose-down involved the simultaneous throwing of a grenade by every man on the lines, which was about 300 men. Sometimes, if something was going on around us, every man would pick a grenade up, pull the pin, and throw the damn thing as far as he could at the same time. That kept them off. We had plenty of grenades by that time. Easy to deliver. Every man had a case of them. We reacted to every movement, we reacted to every noise, even every smell, with massive volumes of indirect fire. Always, and unless we had immediate and fleeting targets of opportunity, we used exclusively non-organic supporting arms. We had enough problems with resupply as it was. We didn't use anything of our own if we didn't have to.

In the daytime on 881S, unless we had reduced visibility, we had about two guys per platoon on watch plus our observation posts. Everybody else slept. There were three reasons. One, daytime is when we got indirect fire and snipers, and people who were up took hits. We reduced casualties that way. Two, we didn't have much water, and if we worked the men in the daytime, we used a lot of water because it was hot. Two canteens per man per day took a whole helicopter for 400 men, and we didn't want to call any more helicopters up there than we had to because those guys in the birds were taking hits. Third, there wasn't any reason for more men to be up. The NVA didn't attack in the daytime. They came at night if they were coming at all.[1]

LCpl WALT WHITESIDES
Tactical Air Control Party _____

Early in February, the new 3/26 communications officer sent a radio up to Hill 881S for us to use for calling in fixed-wing air strikes. Khe Sanh was getting beautiful fixed-wing support—sorties every five to ten minutes during daylight hours were normally controlled by an aerial observer against known targets. If we had a target of opportunity, we could divert a strike by getting on the net and talking to the aerial observer. I never heard of a tactical-air-control operator's being turned down on a target of opportunity. The four of us on Hill 881S probably ran over 300 air strikes among us.

HM3 DAVID STEINBERG
India Company, 3/26 _____

The jets were constantly bombing around Hill 881S, working the hills around us with 500-pound bombs. One day it was green, and the next it was blown away. The hill was so high that, often, the jets were working below us.

LCpl WALT WHITESIDES
Tactical Air Control Party _____

One morning, LCpl Toby Jackson and I were staring through a spotting scope toward Hill 881N. Toby noticed a glint on the forward slope of a little hill between 881S and 881N, and closer examination revealed that it was an NVA soldier, probably the forward observer we had been hunting for. I quickly contacted Captain Dabney, and he arranged for the 60mm mortars to mark the position with white-phosphorus rounds while Toby was arranging for an air strike. Within minutes we were ready, and the mortars dropped a white-phosphorus round within 50 meters of the NVA soldier's position. The poor guy evidently wasn't too well set in because he immediately set to with his entrenching tool to deepen his hole. The two jets swooped in and he quickened his digging. On the second pass, one of the jets dropped two

250-pound bombs almost on top of him. I could see the guy rise with the bomb cloud. We gave the pilots "One confirmed," and the grunts around us cheered.

☆

Capt BILL DABNEY
India Company, 3/26 _____

What was the importance of 881S? What advantage would it have given to the North Vietnamese?

Any good artillery piece—antiaircraft artillery, 37mm, or even a 100mm gun—could have posed serious problems for any takeoffs coming west out of Khe Sanh, especially the C-130s making their paradrops off the west end of the runway. . . . Looking out the east side of 881S, you looked virtually down the runway, just a few degrees off it, about seven or seven and a half kilometers away.

Other than giving Khe Sanh its best forward observation post, I'm not sure that there accrued any significant advantage for us to hold it, but it was, I think, damned sure useful to keep *them* from holding it, because, with decent antiaircraft capabilities, and they had those, they could have done some serious damage to Khe Sanh because they'd have had no real problem looking right into the nose of the airplane coming off that runway or making . . . drops to the west end. Also, from 881S, we gave their rocket sites, all within two kilometers of us, a lot of trouble. We used to hose them down with M-60 machine guns and 106mm recoilless rifles.[2]

☆

MEDEVAC AND RESUPPLY

LCpl WALT WHITESIDES
Tactical Air Control Party _____

Hill 881S was attacked for the first time with mortars on the afternoon of January 22. The initial fire was fairly accurate, and one H-34 helicopter was shot down in the landing zone. The India Company senior corpsman, HM3 Robert Wickliffe, a Naval Reservist from Louisiana, was killed in the landing zone while helping to evacuate a casualty. Also, one of the members of the helicopter support team was critically wounded in the landing zone. It became apparent that the landing zone on the top of the hill was a registered target and that alternate landing zones would have to be established.

Eventually, we located two alternate landing zones. One was outside the wire on the Khe Sanh (east) side of the hill, and the other was in the saddle between the India and Mike company positions. Soon, Captain Dabney assigned the tactical-air-control radio operators with bodyguards for whenever we went into one of the landing zones. These individuals were to lie on top of us in the event the landing zone received incoming. We eventually had holes dug in the landing zones so the radio operators could jump in the hole and wait out the incoming. Landing helicopters became one of the most dangerous jobs on Hill 881S. LCpl Toby Jackson and I were the only two out of seven air-control and helicopter-support Marines who were not killed or wounded during the siege.

The routine for landing a helicopter went something like this: We would get word that a helo was coming in and what the cargo was. If it was an external load, it would usually be dumped on the main landing zone on top of the hill. Internal cargo, such as troops, would require the helo to land. Medevacs and troops going out would also require a landing. The birds would usually stick around for medevacs if the zone was well organized and if they didn't have to wait too long. They had about thirty seconds on the ground before incoming started landing in the zone. They could gain three to five more seconds if the mortar tubes were not registered right on the zone we selected.

The tactical-air-control operators decided which zone was to be used. Medevacs and troops would assemble in the trenchline near the zone. The operators would then occupy both zones, and when the helicopter was making a final approach, the lucky one would pop a colored-smoke grenade to indicate the selected zone. Up until that time, both zones would receive some enemy .51-caliber fire, which was not meant to hit the tactical-air operator but just get zeroed in so it could hit the helo. When the helo landed, the grunts would fire their weapons in the general direction of Hill 881N, where the NVA had an artillery forward observer.

When the helo landed, the tactical-air operator would direct the outgoing Marines onto the helo and steer the arriving replacements in the general direction of the trenchline. The helo would take off and the tactical-air operator would jump into his hole and wait for the incoming to stop.

This procedure worked fairly well unless the helo went into the wrong zone or if the troops got lost or delayed getting on or off the bird, or if the bird stayed too long. I believe that three helicopters were shot down during my stay on the hill, from January 20 until February 9.

The thing that bothered people the most, I think, was the fact that if you were wounded, you had no assurance that you would be evacuated rapidly. There were several reasons for this. First, the weather often prevented helicopters from landing. Second, even if the birds got in, they sometimes left prior to getting all the casualties aboard.

☆

Pfc MICHAEL LEE
Helicopter Support Team _____

I had been in Khe Sanh about three to four days when the Helicopter Support Team (HST) guy on 881S started calling down for relief. I talked it over with my commanding officer [of Alpha Company, 3rd Shore Party Battalion], and volunteered to go up to Hill 881S.

As I waited on the landing zone for the CH-46 to pick me up, I was sitting facing the control-tower bunker. All of a sudden, a couple of guys were waving their arms and yelling at me. I looked over my left shoulder and saw a 122mm rocket coming right at me. I thought, "Oh shit! This is it!" The rocket landed about ten feet behind me. The concussion lifted me up and really rattled my brain. Some people came running over. They thought I got hit. For some reason, not one piece of shrapnel touched me. About five minutes later, my bird came in. I got on it and was on my way to 881S, to replace the HST guy up there. The ride was really beautiful!

As we came up the hill, it really looked small! As the aircraft was coming in for a landing, the whole hill erupted in gunfire. I learned that was to keep the NVA down. The crew chief let the ramp down before we were down. As he did that, my pucker factor went sky-high. I went running down the ramp and I passed the guy I was replacing. The one thing that sticks in my mind was how scared he was. The aircraft was up and going before a couple of mortar rounds hit near the landing zone. There was only one landing zone on the hill for passengers. After I got in the trench, I was taken up to the command bunker to meet Captain Dabney.

After I was shown the three landing zones on the hill (the east end, the top, and the saddle), I was assigned to a bunker on the north side, in approximately the middle of the hill. There were two grunts there with a .50-caliber machine gun. We were facing 881N. They told me about the sniper over there called "Luke the Gook." Shit, he was everywhere.

My job was to direct the resupply and medevac birds to their respective landing zones. I would have to stand out in the open to direct the aircraft. During resupply, the whole hill would fire downslope to keep the NVA from firing at the resupply birds.

The medevacs were the worst! Captain Dabney had a policy of having the least wounded men carry the front of a stretcher on the bird. That's if there were two men wounded. When someone got hit, I would get the word from the corpsman as to the priority—routine, priority, or emergency. The routines [mostly KIAs] would generally have to wait until resupply came in. Priority—if there were aircraft in the area, they had the choice of coming in or not. Emergency— everyone dropped what they were doing, be it any type of helicopter. The worst were the emergencies. When I called down to Khe Sanh with an emergency medevac, aircraft would be given my call sign and contact me. We generally had fixed-wing aircraft and gunships on station for fire suppression.

I would direct the bird in and the casualty would be

carried on. Then the bird would get out there ASAP. We always took incoming mortars when this happened. You could see the strain in the faces of everyone. It got so you didn't pay any attention to it. Every time I would hear "Corpsman!" I would think "Shit!" because it meant another medevac.

HM3 DAVID STEINBERG
India Company, 3/26 _____

Replacements would jump off the helos, and supplies would just fall off. A couple times we even got the gunners off the helicopters because the crew chiefs would get so panicked they just shoved everyone off. We welcomed the gunners to the hill; we gave them shovels and put them to work.

Anytime we got resupplied was the time for a corpsman to worry. We got three or four mortar rounds in every time a chopper came in. Almost every time, we had casualties. Most of them were new guys who were getting off the chopper. They didn't know where the hell they were or what to do. They'd just stand there. Unless they got down, they were sure to get hit by the mortars of the .51-caliber rounds from the guns that had us zeroed in.

One time, I heard "Corpsman, up!" and I went over the top of the hill to the landing zone. I was treating one guy after the next. They were green, they'd just gotten off, and the chopper was leaving. It was sheer frustration, trying to get to their chest wounds. Their canvas backpacks had real thick straps on them, and I was spending too much time laying on my belly or back, trying to cut the packs off them so I could work, just so I could start to treat them. When I finished and went back to the trench line, my platoon commander came up and said, "My God, Doc! You're hit!" I was just covered with blood, but none of it was my own.

On two occasions I was treating someone when the Marine next to me, the guy helping me, got hit. I figured if I was going to go, it would be while I was doing my job, but I never thought too much, other than doing what I had to do. How do you let down your buddies?

☆

Pfc MICHAEL LEE
Helicopter Support Team _____

About the worst time I had was an afternoon I was bringing in a resupply at the saddle. I had two CH-46s, with gunships escorting. As I was directing the first CH-46 in, I noticed a winking light in the valley to the south. It was a heavy machine gun firing at the bird. The prick almost got me! I couldn't move until the bird dropped his net, as he was on his final approach. I told the pilot he was taking incoming, and he replied "Affirmative," that he could see tracers going by me. At that point, I almost pissed my pants. As soon as the bird dropped his net, I dived for the trench. I called the command post and told them I had a machine-gun position sighted. The gunships wanted the target marked, so I shot a magazine of tracers at it. They couldn't see them, so the 81mm mortars put some white-phosphorus rounds in the general area. From there, I directed the gunships on it.

Cpl TERRY STEWART
Mike Company, 3/26 _____

The few times that our resupply was lost at the bottom of the hill was a real heartbreaker to us. We just sat there and watched as our mail was blown to hell by friendly bombers. But we all knew that there were some things that would surely survive. And obviously some did. It wasn't uncommon for Charlie, who frequently communicated to us via some kind of speaker system or bullhorn, to mention names of the guys on the hill, and sometimes the names of their family or friends. This was naturally to demoralize us, but Charlie could never know what assholes Americans can be. None of their unsavory remarks ever bothered anyone, and I cannot recall anyone ever being brought down by this tactic. Most of us would laugh or toss off insults at the antagonizers.

One net drop did not land on top of the hill or go over the

side. The heavy net landed on top of one of our positions
and crushed two Marines. It was gruesome.

SUPER GAGGLE

Col FRANK WILSON
Marine Air Group 36 _____

It was the consensus of the helicopter group commander and
his pilots that the resupply of the vital hill outposts would
not long survive under the increasing enemy antiaircraft fire
and the resulting rapid rise in the attrition of the helicopters.
The UH-1E Huey gunships, though doing a valiant job, did
not posses the heavy volume of fire required to keep the
helicopter lanes open.

The solution was basically [that] all helicopter flights to
the hill outposts would be escorted by strike aircraft in order
to provide suppressive fires. Under the direction of the
Commanding General, 1st Marine Aircraft Wing, Marine
Air Group 12, and Marine Air Group 36 coordinated an
effort which came to be known as the Super Gaggle.

In this classic example of helicopter escort operations,
involving split-second timing, and coordinated by an airborne tactical air coordinator, six to eight CH-46s of Marine
Medium Helicopter Squadron 364 would depart Dong Ha
carrying external sling loads of cargo, proceed "in the
soup" to an orbit point southeast of Khe Sanh, and await
the arrival of the strike jets of Marine Air Group 12. On
signal from the airborne tactical air coordinator, the CH-46s
would start an approach to Khe Sanh, preceded by the
Marine Air Group 12 Skyhawks, which would commence
devastating attacks around the hill objectives and, at the
same time, smoke the surrounding ridgelines. As the CH-46s
drove toward the hill outposts, they were joined by Huey
gunships of Marine Observation Squadron 6, which would
make continuous strafing attacks on the terrain within the
helicopter lanes. These low-level attacks not only gave the
helicopters a fighting chance to reach the objective hilltops
and drop their external loads, it gave them some measure of
protection during those critical moments when they were

most vulnerable, i.e., when they hovered over the outposts or landed momentarily to pick up casualties or discharge reinforcements. During this phase of the mission, the jets usually laid a smoke screen, making long, shallow passes as they sprayed the North Vietnamese emplacements with clouds of teargas and chemical smoke. After their crop-dusting runs, the Skyhawks covered the withdrawal of the helicopters with more high explosives. Such tactics not only reduced the number of American casualties, they took a heavy toll of enemy gunners.[3]

Maj JIM STANTON
26th Marines Fire Support Coordination Center _____

The Super Gaggle was designed to flood the air with CH-46s bringing supplies to the hill outposts. They came in from all points of the compass at once, a sort of airborne time-on-target mission. They landed, discharged their cargoes and passengers, and got the hell out. We covered it with fire, coordinated to hit every intelligence target we knew about with air and artillery. The NVA never figured out how to counteract the Super Gaggle. There were too many targets at once, and too much going on.

HM3 DAVID STEINBERG
India Company, 3/26 _____

You'd look up in the sky and see around a dozen CH-46s; out in the distance, in a circle, chasing tails. Then, all of a sudden, fighter-bombers came in to strafe and bomb the hills below us. After they were done dropping their bombs and strafing the hills, we would line up and shoot into the valley—firing full M-16 clips and throwing hand grenades. All of a sudden, we would hear the *whup-whup-whup-whup* of the choppers. One chopper would land in the saddle. Then, as soon as we heard the *boomp* of the incoming mortar, it would lift off and fly to one of the other landing zones and all the other choppers would come in at the various zones.

Capt BILL DABNEY
India Company, 3/26 _____

For just about one minute, you could get in with external
loads coming in echelons of four or five birds at once. We
could get in ten helicopter loads on the hill in one minute
and get the birds the hell out of there and into smoke where
the NVA couldn't see to shoot.[4]

EVERYDAY LIFE

LCpl WALT WHITESIDES
Tactical Air Control Party _____

By the first week of February, life on the hill had become a
dreary, fearful routine. We were still constantly on alert for
an attack, and we were usually short of consumables,
mostly water. We had a fair supply of C-rations, and
plenty of ammunition. One had the feeling that he was
living in a bull's-eye, and that his time was numbered.
The lines were probed at night, but there was no serious
attempt to breach them. During the day, Captain Dabney
put out listening posts on the southern and eastern
approaches to the hill.

Capt BILL DABNEY
India Company, 3/26 _____

After you've had enough of that stuff shot at you—rockets,
artillery, it doesn't really make a hell of a lot of difference,
with the exception of mortars—a man who's been around
awhile and has been lucky can tell you where the round is
going to hit when it goes off, when he hears the tube pop.
Most of us who were on 881S got to the point where we
could hear the damned round, either rocket fire, the
rocket motor, or the artillery-tube pop. We knew whether
the round was going to land near us or not. You get so
you can tell within a few hundred meters where it's going
to land, by the sound of the tube pop. There is a certain
specific, unique sound to it, if the tube is oriented
directly on you.[5]

Pfc JIM PAYNE
Charlie Battery, 1/13 _____

I perceived incoming on that hill as a single, dreaded being
that I desperately tried to avoid. Incoming was a hooded
gray ghost in a long, flowing robe. Incoming was a slow-
moving shadow that drifted hauntingly over the 881S hilltop,
ever-searching. Incoming was faceless, but I could almost
hear it whisper,"Where are you, Marines? Where are you?"
Incoming was piss-taste-in-the-mouth fear. If it found you,
incoming was indiscriminate, unnegotiable death.

Capt BILL DABNEY
India Company, 3/26 _____

We got a message once—relayed to us by Battalion, ostensi-
bly from Regiment—which specifically said, "Hey, we
want you to overhead everything, every fighting hole up
there, to withstand 82mm mortars." Great idea, I guess. I
sent a message back down saying, "One, we have no
capability up here, no timbers, no engineer support, no
nothing—we've got only barbed-wire stakes. Two, nobody
is shooting at us with 82mm mortars. They're shooting
120mm mortars at us, and I don't have capabilities to stop
that with overhead without something like concrete or heavy
timber." Nothing we could do to stop that. We got a lot of
delay-fuse 120mm. They'd go three or four feet into the
deck before they would detonate. And what little we had—
logs and things—we had to use for our ammo bunkers.
God! We had 1,500 rounds of 105, 2,000 to 3,000 rounds
of 81, perhaps 1,000 rounds of 106 and 3.5-inch rockets,
plus grenades and demolitions. They'd have blown the top
off the hill if they had hit into one of those bunkers. The hill
was only 75 by 150 meters on top![6]

HM3 DAVID STEINBERG
India Company, 3/26 _____

Our C-rat meal was supposed to be one-third of our daily
requirement. We usually got one C-rat per *day*, but some-

times one C-rat had to last three days. If you got lucky and
saved a can of peaches until you came up with a piece of
pound cake, you could probably trade it for twelve cans of
boned chicken.

Cpl TERRY STEWART
Mike Company, 3/26 _____

We had a code of honor on the hill—you NEVER touched
another man's food or water. The code was violated once.
The culprit, a lance corporal, helped himself to his partner's
C-rats. It wasn't much—a can or two of something—but
the thief was awarded an Article 15 punishment, and for
many months after we were off the hill, the men of the
platoon did not forget what he had done, or ever forgive
him. It was serious.

If food was a major concern, water was doubly so. Here
is where we were most careful and protective. It wasn't
really critical, at least to the point that we ever really went
without, but what we had was just enough, and if we were
unable to get more, we would surely have been in serious
trouble. There were times, quite often, that we rationed both
food and water: one C-ration per day and two B-1 cans of
water.

Water was delivered in the most unusual manner. Birds
could not land on the hill, so it was necessary to literally
drop supplies in large cargo nets suspended from the bellies
of the birds. In this way, the birds could fly over the hill and
simply release the net full of supplies so that it would land
on top of the hill. There were times when a pilot's timing
and aim were not so hot, when all our chow, water, ammo,
and, most important, our mail, sailed by over our heads and
tumbled down the slope into injun country. When this
happened, jets were immediately called in to drop napalm
and bombs on the precious cargo to ensure that the enemy
did not benefit from the mishap. Even when the supplies
landed on the hill, the jarring impact precluded any sensible
means of delivering water. The C-rats were in cases and
cans that were quite tough and able to survive the fall very

well. Ammo came in cans and boxes that were designed to sustain heavy abuse. But water cans just couldn't take the drop. The problem of how to get us water was solved by partially filling plastic bags, like those used in cafeteria milk machines, with water and then stuffing the bags into artillery powder shipping canisters. This worked exceedingly well and there were side benefits. The canisters, once emptied of their precious cargo, could be used as piss tubes and crap tubes.

☆

Cpl TERRY STEWART
Mike Company, 3/26 _____

Stop and consider over 400 men stranded on a wasted hilltop and forced to live in the narrow, restricted confines of a simple trench system. Where do you construct heads? How do you construct them, camouflage them, and fortify them so that they can be safely used? It would have been a real mess if we'd just used catholes in the trenches. The trench would have filled up eventually, and the almost-daily rains would have had the place a real joy to live in—for a bunch of hogs.

For crappers and piss tubes, we buried the artillery powder canisters in which our water arrived—just deep enough to hold them. When they were full, we put the locking tops back on. The full canisters were kept in a shell crater on the very top of the hill at first, but soon there were too many there. One night, an 82mm mortar round found its way into the stack and it rained a most foul and disagreeable barrage down upon us. It was decided that the system must change.

Someone got the bright idea to just roll them over the edge of the hill. He explained, after nearly everyone stated that it was a bad idea because Charlie would get them, that it was okay for Charlie to have them. "Picture it," he told us. "Here comes Charlie, crawling several hundred meters from his protective cave to the bottom of our hill. He's braved mortars, artillery, and the most fearsome bombing in the history of warfare to get close to us, probe us, and pick up anything that he could find along the way. Now, near the bottom of the hill, these poor bastards find a gold mine. These tubes represent so many possibilities: live artillery shells, perhaps food, maybe they know about how our water's delivered, or maybe the tubes can be filled with earth and used to reinforce their bunkers. The Charlies risk life and limb to drag as many canisters back to their cave as possible, and when they arrive there, they very proudly present them to their first sergeant. He's a real hard-dick, but this time he is pleased with his two shitbirds and praises them for their find. After having the canisters dragged to his own tiny room in the back of the cave, the first sergeant opens one.''

☆

LCpl WALT WHITESIDES
Tactical Air Control Party _____

After a while, LCpl Terry Smith and I moved to a separate bunker on the northeast corner of the landing zone. The bunker was on the edge of what had evidently once been a gun pit. We had our communications gear and everything in there, and it was pretty comfortable. However, Captain Dabney had the idea that the gun pit would be a pretty good place to put a water trailer, which would greatly alleviate the water shortage on the hill. The pit was below the skyline and on the reverse slope from an enemy 120mm mortar. It was well protected from incoming rounds, as most of them either landed on top of the hill, on the forward slope, or in the landing zones. Since this seemed to be a reasonable request, and since Captain Dabney was a captain and I was a lance corporal, I agreed that if he could get the water trailer to the hill, I would get it off the helo and into the gun pit.

Everything was working pretty well in the planning stage until a CH-53 showed up—unannounced—with the water trailer externally loaded.

The pilot flew around while we tried to identify the zone

for him without marking it. This gave NVA mortar crew plenty of time to prepare, and they took full advantage of it. Next, after identifying the zone, the pilot announced that he couldn't drop the water trailer there because of the ground effect. I thought he was just being uncooperative. We argued for a while, and finally he said he was going to set the water trailer down on the landing zone. He also wanted us to unhook it because he wanted his slings back. I guess they were running low on nets and slings because we were then returning them at our leisure. We were not mentally prepared to unhook the slings in the landing zone, but one of the HST men said he would do it. Naturally, the slings did not unhook easily, and the HST man was wounded in the attempt, so we had to call in another helo to evacuate him. The same round that punctured the HST man also punctured the water trailer, and most of the water ran out before it could be saved. We continued to get our water in external loads of five-gallon cans and in bags loaded into 105mm shell canisters.

HM3 DAVID STEINBERG
India Company, 3/26 ⎯⎯⎯⎯⎯⎯⎯⎯⎯⎯⎯⎯⎯⎯⎯

We got water sometimes by laying out plastic tarps during the night and licking them off in the morning.

Chapter 2

Cpl DENNIS SMITH
Bravo Company, 1/26 _____

February 8, 1968

Dear Mother,

Two years ago today I went to boot camp. If I hadn't re-enlisted upon completion, I would be home today. It hurts.

I'm sending you my income tax thing because I don't know what to do with it.

It's been a while since we've received any mail. Ammo and food have priority on the planes that resupply us. There are about 200 people waiting at Phu Bai for transportation to Khe Sanh.

Remember the shooting galleries at the fair? I feel like one of those little ducks that move back and forth and get shot at. I ride in a jeep all day, all over the base, picking up gear and delivering it to our three platoons. Bravo Company is spread out around the perimeter. We never know when to expect incoming (except when a plane lands; we always catch it then), or where the rounds will land. Too many times they have landed too close.

☆

Sgt FRANK JONES
26th Marines Scout-Sniper Platoon _____

On February 8, I was over by the helo pad with some buddies, drinking whiskey with dehydrated orange juice. I wrote a letter to my wife and went outside to put it in a mail bag. I was outside by the sandbag wall when three Marines carrying C-rations on their shoulders walked by. I didn't hear the rocket come in, but the next thing I knew, it seemed like everything had shifted down to slow motion, and it got real hot. I had a pain and pressure in my head I had never felt before, and it seemed like my body was jelly. I didn't even hear the explosion. The rocket hit about thirty feet from us. Those three guys in front of me absorbed most of the shrapnel. I came to on the ground. The concussion had knocked me out, and I had blood on my leg. My helmet had a big dent in it. I crawled over to this guy who was lying there on his back. His helmet chinstrap was buttoned and the helmet was filled up with this thick purple liquid. He was dead, and so were the other two guys. I got taken over to Charlie-Med and had the wound on my leg cleaned up and dressed. Then I returned to duty.

FEBRUARY 9

LCpl DAN ANSLINGER
3rd Marine Division Air Section _____

Because of the Lang Vei attack and problems evacuating survivors, one of the division air officers had to fly to Khe Sanh to help sort things out, and he took me with him. It was different there than it had been during my last visit, the first few days of the siege. The place was like a junkyard, and everything standing looked like it was falling apart as a result of the shelling. Some of the confidence and cockiness I had noticed a few weeks before seemed to be gone, and everyone was pretty grim, apparently wondering who would be next after Lang Vei.

I didn't have any bowel movements at all during the few days we were there because there was no way I was going outside to the shitter. I was within a few weeks of rotating home.

☆

Cpl DENNIS MANNION
Charlie Battery, I/13 (Hill 861) _____

February 9, 1968

Dear Joe,
    This day just ain't a good one for me. This morning a guy I became pretty good friends with took an 82mm mortar round right in his foxhole. Just blew him away. Not too pretty. But if you're gonna go, that's the best way. Quick.

PAY RUN

LCpl PHIL MINEER
Bravo Battery, I/13 _____

What the hell we needed money for up there was beyond me, but Lieutenant McGrath got picked to make the pay run down to Danang. I went as his shotgun, his bodyguard. We went to take a C-123 out.

When we got near the runway, we did what everyone called "the Khe Sanh shuffle." You looked the way you were going, and you never went more than fifty meters in one shot. It was a half-slouch combined with the opposite of being cross-eyed: One eye always looked where you were going and the other always looked at an alternate route, where you would go if the rounds came in. When we got to the runway, we found a little trench and hid out there. The C-123 came in, made its swing, and kept moving. There were about a dozen body bags laid out that had to go on the plane, so they got the plane to slow down. When they got all the bodies on the plane, everyone who was waiting in the trench jumped on.

1stLt FRED McGRATH
Bravo Battery, 1/13 _____

The plane was loaded with montagnards from Lang Vei. They seemed in good spirits and were happy to be flying out. The pilot wasted no time in getting off the ground, but he had a full load and he could not climb as rapidly as he would have liked.

LCpl PHIL MINEER
Bravo Battery, 1/13 _____

It was eerie as hell going down the runway, hearing the engines race in the C-123's effort to get off the ground. It was very slow. I looked at the lieutenant and saw that he had that thousand-mile Khe Sanh stare. He was looking at me, but he was looking beyond me. I felt the plane lift off, so I put my thumb up—"We're off the runway and we're almost out of here." But the lieutenant held up his finger—"No, wait. We're not out yet." And then here comes Luke the Gook. I could hear the *dat-dat-dat-dat* of the gun and *shwee-shwee-shwee-shwee* as the rounds went through the fuselage.

1stLt FRED McGRATH
Bravo Battery, 1/13 _____

Bullets began striking the plane everywhere. Riding where we were—sitting on the deck on pallets and seabags—we could feel the bullets impact.

LCpl PHIL MINEER
Bravo Battery, 1/13 _____

They hit near the rear ramp and blew out a hose filled with pink hydraulic fluid. This created some concern among the crewmen, who didn't know if they could get the landing gear down. I didn't give a shit. I really didn't. If the C-123 had to come in on its belly, at least it would come in at Danang, and not Khe Sanh.

1stLt FRED McGRATH
Bravo Battery, 1/13 _____

But we gained altitude, gained the cloud cover, and got out of range. Just when the flight became routine, those montagnards caused a mild sensation. One asked me for a match. I gave him a book of C-ration matches, thinking he knew what he was doing. He struck one, but for some reason the whole book ignited. So we had this small ball of flame flying around the inside of the plane. The crew chief rushed over and stomped it out. That's all he needed!

LCpl PHIL MINEER
Bravo Battery, 1/13 _____

When we finally did come into Danang, they had foam on the runway, a dozen fire trucks, and hundreds of Air Force guys watching. The Air Force guys had Bermuda shorts on and Coke bottles in their hands. The crew chief lowered the landing gear manually with a crank and we got down okay, but they made a big deal out of it.

1stLt FRED McGRATH
Bravo Battery, 1/13 _____

When we arrived in Danang, we had to exit from the side hatch. The bullets had severed the hydraulic line that controlled the rear ramp. The pilot walked around his aircraft and counted seventeen holes. I am certain he considered himself lucky. So did I.

LCpl PHIL MINEER
Bravo Battery, 1/13 _____

I was wearing all my gear—flak jacket, diaper, pistol, field transport pack, and my M-16. One guy said to me, "Jesus

Christ! You're *pink*!'' That was the red Khe Sanh mud that had dried on me. "Where you been," he went on, "in a *war*?" It was a different world in Danang.

Those Air Force guys treated me good that night. I had a *rack*—a *real* rack—and a *real* mattress on a spring frame. And *real* sheets! They got me hot chow.

1stLt FRED McGRATH
Bravo Battery, 1/13 _____

The war had a different face in Danang. Since we had landed near the Air Force terminal, I decided to grab chow at the Air Force compound adjacent to the terminal. I approached the gate guard, not expecting any problem, even though I was pretty scruffy-looking. He noticed the .45 strapped to my leg and halted me. "No weapons inside the compound, sir." Surely you jest! Same war, right? Wrong! Since there was no way I was going unarmed anywhere, I asked directions to the nearest Marine Corps installation.

LCpl PHIL MINEER
Bravo Battery, 1/13 _____

During our three-day stopover in Danang, the lieutenant and I bought a duck and started fattening him up with C-ration crackers so we could cook him on Easter. Also, before we left Khe Sanh, I had been authorized to purchase some beer if I could. I got the beer, but by the time the lieutenant and I were ready to go back to Khe Sanh, the only way in was by chopper, and even then they were reluctant.

I talked an Air Force pilot into taking us and the duck and our pallet of beer back to Khe Sanh on his CH-53 helicopter. This guy had never flown combat before, just transport in and out of Danang. As we were coming in, I tried to tell the crew chief to tell the pilot to get down to treetop level, but they stayed up high. I kept trying to explain to the crew chief that the higher you fly, the better the bead they can get on you. Well, sure as shit, we took ground fire. A round going through the side of the CH-53 is like punching your

finger through a piece of aluminum foil. But we made it in,
the beer made it in, the duck made it in, and the payroll
money made it in.

The payroll was all in military payment certificates,
which looked like Monopoly money. That led to some heavy
card games for the next few days. We built the duck his own
bunker, but he got blown up just before Easter. That pissed
a lot of guys off. There were feathers everywhere, but *no
meat*!

☐

FEBRUARY 10

Pfc LIONEL TRUFANT
106mm Platoon, 3/26 _____

Five of us, all new 106mm gunners, were in the transit hut
in Phu Bai when a Marine who had just rotated from Hill
861 came through. The guy was shattered. He looked like a
shattered person. His nerve was gone. He was smoking a
cigarette, shaking. He told us about what was happening up
there. He mentioned how Hill 861 was almost overrun, how
they were getting hit with artillery, how the NVA were
probing their lines. He mentioned how his company had lost
so much manpower. And he told us it was a hell of a trip
just getting out of there. That really shocked us.

We worked in supply for a few days, until they found an
airplane that could take us to Khe Sanh. We went down to
the airstrip, but we couldn't get out because the airstrip was
getting hit too hard. The second day, we got on the aircraft,
a C-130. We were standing facing the rear. Behind us was an
internal load on a pallet on rollers. We were in full gear—
helmet, willy-peter bag, rifle, pack. There were mostly Marines, but also a few Navy, a few Army, and a few Air Force.
We took off and flew over Khe Sanh, but we couldn't land. The
airstrip was getting hit too hard, so we flew back to Phu Bai.

We had to go out the next day, February 11. That
morning, we went back out. While we were waiting at the
airstrip, we heard a shot. A guy had shot his finger off. We

knew he wasn't going to Khe Sanh. They loaded us on the plane and we flew out. It was the same situation as the day before. We were packed in the front of the plane, all dressed in full gear, and we had an internal load in front of us as we faced the rear.

I was close to a window. When we flew over Khe Sanh, it looked like a giant anthill to me. I could see all the trenches. It looked *dirty*.

The crew chief gave us instructions. He said, "This is how we're going to land. When the aircraft lands, we're going to open up the back and release the internal load. When I give the signal, all of you roll out. You jump out and run."

The word came down from the pilot that we were going to land but that the airstrip was under attack. I could envision in my mind a machine-gun nest firing at the aircraft, shooting at us when we got off the plane.

When the plane landed and the back door opened up, I came to realize how the airstrip was getting hit. I saw two well-placed artillery rounds hitting the runway. Next thing I knew, the internal load was released. But nobody waited for the crew chief to give us the word to jump out. Everybody just went hauling out of the back. It was just like jumping off the back of a pickup. The plane was still moving. I jumped off and hit the ground flat. My rifle went one way, the magazines went another way, and my willy-peter bag went a third way. My helmet was still on my head because I had it strapped on.

I picked up my rifle, I picked up my willy-peter bag, and I grabbed about two magazines. All I could see was people running to the side. Some guy was hollering, "Come on! Come on!" So I just started hauling ass—ran and ran until I found a hole. I jumped in, but I must have tripped over someone, because I went flying into the hole. I was scared as hell.

The incoming kept coming in. Then, all of a sudden, everything stopped. Some guy came down, looked in the hole, and said, "All right, you guys, get outta there." So we got out. When I came out of that hole, everything was in a normal state. I saw a guy driving a jeep and other people jogging from place to place.

On our way to check in, another Marine and I had this great debate about the incoming sound and the outgoing sound. He said it sounded the same way it had sounded at Phu Bai, and I said it sounded different. Soon we had an answer. More incoming started. I told the other guy, "Get your ass down," and we jumped into the nearest hole.

We reported in to the 106mm Platoon commander at the 3rd Battalion headquarters, and they sent us out to Lima Company, which was holding the western end of the perimeter. There were three Marines manning the gun, and two more of us made a five-man crew.

To our left were the Special Forces and Vietnamese strike troopers. Ahead of us to the right was 1/9, on a hill outside the perimeter. To our right rear was the drop zone. The main reason our 106 was there was to protect the road leading from 1/9 to the Special Forces area. To the left of our position was a Marine-manned .50-caliber machine gun, and just to our rear was an Ontos position. The Ontos had six 106s on it. To our right was a hole manned by two M-79 grenadiers, and the hole to the right of that had an M-60. We were in a reinforced strongpoint, guarding the road. Just in our hole itself, the five of us had the 106mm recoilless rifle, an M-60 machine gun, our five personal M-16 rifles, and one .45-caliber pistol.

When I got to the gun, our living bunker was sitting on top of the ground. It had three layers of sandbags and pallets on top and three layers of sandbags all the way around. There was only one small trench, which had the 106 in it. Starting right away, we dug deeper trenches, dug the living area into the ground, and put in a separate bunker for the M-60 machine gun.

Cpl WILLIAM ROBERTSON
Logistics Support Unit _____

On February 10, a Marine Corps KC-130 fueler was coming in. We heard it and saw it circling around. Then we heard the antiaircraft fire. The KC-130 came around and touched down on the runway, and probably made it a hundred feet when the tires on the right side of the plane blew out. The pilot held it on the runway a long time—I don't know how he managed to do it, but he kept it straight for, it looked like, almost all the way. We thought he was going to make it, but finally the front end got away from him.

1stLt NICK ROMANETZ
Charlie Company, 1/26 _____

Suddenly it veered off to the right and burst into flames. The whole airplane was not initially engulfed.

Cpl WILLIAM ROBERTSON
Logistics Support Unit _____

The plane went off the runway and broke in half. It was carrying six rubber fuel bladders of helicopter fuel.

1stLt NICK ROMANETZ
Charlie Company, 1/26 _____

I sat and watched people start coming out of the hatches over the flight deck. Crash vehicles arrived and started foaming the plane down, but it kept burning more and more.

Cpl WILLIAM ROBERTSON
Logistics Support Unit _____

In no time flat, that plane looked just like molten liquid. There was molten aluminum running down the ditch beside the runway. This was right next to the concrete bunker I lived in.

1stLt NICK ROMANETZ
Charlie Company, 1/26 _____

As soon as it started burning, it drew a crowd. Boy, did it draw a crowd. My concern was that the enemy was going to pop a few mortar rounds in on us. Apparently they had a few 60mm mortars dug into the ground in front of my position, and it would have been easy for them to cause casualties. Fortunately, we didn't take any incoming.

The KC-130 was apparently hit by machine-gun rounds and set afire before it touched down on the runway. The pilot and copilot escaped, but six crewmen and passengers were incinerated.

FEBRUARY 11

Sgt FRANK JONES
26th Marines Scout-Sniper Platoon _____

I was going back to the Blue Sector the night of February 11 and I found one of my buddies, Cpt Dennis Keefe, sitting out on a water can in front of his bunker, polishing his boots. I asked him what he was doing and he told me he was getting ready to go home on a thirty-day leave because he had just extended his tour six months. We laughed about it, that it would probably be over by the time he got back. I told him, "Take it easy and have one for me." As I turned to walk away, I heard a round coming in. When it went off, I fell and a lot debris and dirt came down on top of me. I turned to check on Keefe, but he was gone. The rocket had hit right where he was sitting. We never found a part of him. No boots, no body parts—nothing

FEBRUARY 12

Cpl WILLIAM HUBBARD
Echo Company, 2/26 _____

My buddy, Corporal Houska, and I went down through the trenches every day to try to get a helo out of there, so we could go home. Our time was up. But the only thing going out was wounded; they had priority. It took twenty-three tries. Finally, on the twenty-third day, February 12, we made it down to the end of the runway. I had my seabag with me. Until I started trying to get out of Khe Sanh, I hadn't seen it in the thirteen months and twenty days I'd been in-country. I didn't even remember what was in it, but it was my only connection with The World. Houska had his, too. When we got to the end of the runway, there was a little Army helicopter hovering there. The pilot was looking out the other side, so me and Houska started waving and yelling. He looked down and shook his head; he couldn't take us. But we had his attention, so we threw our seabags down. We even dropped our rifles. Less weight, less room. He set the helicopter down as close to us as he could, and we jumped in. As he went up as high as he could go, right over Khe Sanh, Houska and I ripped off our flak jackets and sat on them. We didn't want to catch a live one in the nut sack that late in the game. We rode on out of there, straight to Dong Ha, stayed the night, got as drunk as we could get, and went to Phu Bai the next day. Then we went to Danang, waited at the airport, got on the biggest plane I had ever seen in my life, and flew home. It took us twenty-five hours.

HM3 BILL GESSNER
Delta Company, 1/9 _____

12 February

Dear Dad:

Enclosed is my W-2 form. I would like you to square my income tax away, if you would.

I have a project for you and I wish you would get it accomplished as soon as possible. Our captain is leaving the company soon and we want to give him a plaque. I'll describe it and then draw it. We would like a metal heart (a large one) on shellacked wood. In the center of the heart, a Marine Corps emblem (anchor and globe) in the center (engraved) above the emblem: "CAPT SCHAFER CO OF DEATH DEFYING DELTA." Beneath the emblem put: "THE HEART OF ONE-NINE." At the base of the heart put "67–68." And on a piece of metal on the back put "From the Docs of D 1/9." I would like

you to get this done and send it to me as quickly
as possible. We have a $50 reserve, which is the
most we can spend. Do the best you can, please.
Take what it costs out of my money and I'll replace
it next month.

FEBRUARY 13

Capt KEN PIPES
Bravo Company, 1/26 _____

The troopers of the 37th ARVN Ranger Battalion had not
been paid for several months, and, most important, the Tet
Offensive was centered around the towns, villages, and
hamlets from which most of the troopers had been recruited.
They did not know the effect that the NVA Tet Offensive had
on their families and loved ones.

On numerous occasions, we assisted each other by fire
and collective action. Marines and corpsmen made volun-
tary nightly trips to the ARVN lines to carry wounded
ARVN Rangers to the Regimental Aid Station.

Sgt FRANK JONES
26th Marines Scout-Sniper Platoon _____

We were taking fire from an NVA recoilless rifle until
finally Colonel Lownds told the ARVNs to put a stop to
it.

26th Marines Command Chronolgy _____

At 1300, a six-man patrol form the 37th ARVN Ranger
Battalion ambushed a five-man recoilless-rifle site. Results
of the contact: 2 NVA KIA (confirmed), 1 57mm recoilless
rifle captured.

Capt KEN PIPES
Bravo Company, 1/26 _____

The ARVN lieutenant leading the patrol was severely wounded
and isolated from the other ARVNs. When his troopers took

casualties trying to get to him, he killed himself with his pistol so they would stop trying. That's unbelievable leadership.

☆

Cpl DENNIS MANNION
Charlie Battery, 1/13 (Hill 861) _____

February 13, 1968

Dear Joe—
   Gooks have slacked off the last couple of days.
We (861) have taken no, zip, none, zero rounds
in over three days. Quite a switch! It almost scares
you worse than when they throw 'em in. You
wonder what those sneaky fucks are doing.

FEBRUARY 14

Pfc JIM PAYNE
Charlie Battery, 1/13 (Hill 881S) _____

I was assigned to an India Company squad that was preparing to fire suppression for an incoming chopper operation. The squad occupied a stretch of trenchline on the south side of 881S, facing the hostile 689 ridgeline, a thousand yards distant. Minutes after we arrived, we could hear the choppers approaching the hill from the north and east. About that time, the squad opened up with heavy rifle fire on the distant ridgeline to the south.

While we were putting out rounds, I could hear loud chopper noises above and behind us in the direction of the landing zone. These sounds were followed by rotor noises rising up and moving away, indicating that the choppers had had a successful trip and getaway. At that point, the lieutenant leading the squad ordered us to cease fire. While the squad was still standing in the trenchline, I heard the *ka-rumph, ka-rumph* of incoming mortar rounds impacting behind us, up the hill. Someone shouted, "Innn-coming!"

As the squad scattered, the incoming rounds blew a heavy

wooden cargo skid into the air, and it came down with
tremendous force on my helmet, knocking me senseless and
center-punching me straight down onto the trench floor.

I ended up on my back with the cargo skid across my
face. I couldn't hear, I couldn't move, I was just laying
there, staring up at the bright yellow sun through a narrow
crack in the skid. I thought I was dead. It was sort of like
the last moments of a living brain inside a dead body, taking
turns watching the sun and a brilliant white ball ricocheting
around inside my skull. Death was saying, "See, I'm not so
bad. Just lay back and let me take you away." Life was
saying, "Oh . . . fuck!"

After about thirty seconds, I started to hear noises and
see shadows. Two Marines were stooping over me, and
one of them lifted the wooden skid off my face and said,
"You all right, Marine? You all right?" After I regained
full consciousness and stood up on shaky legs, one of the
Marines handed me my rifle and patted me on the back.
The thought of rejoining the living world was momentarily exhilarating.

FEBRUARY 15
HURRIED DEPARTURES

Pfc MICHAEL LEE
Helicopter Support Team (Hill 881S) _____

The landing support company sent me up a teammate to
hook nets and help with medevacs. We would alternate
directing in the aircraft. On February 15, we both got hit as
we were bringing in a resupply on the eastern landing zone.
Apparently the NVA sent rounds on all three zones at the
same time. My teammate and I were standing in a shallow
crater after the aircraft dropped the net and left. A 120mm
mortar round hit a few feet to my right. I saw a big burst of
dirt and felt a bang like a baseball bat had hit me in the right
arm and went through my flak jacket. My teammate was hit
in the stomach. I called for the corpsman and we dragged
him to the trench. His intestines and all were bulging out.
The corpsman tucked it all inside again and put a big com-

press on his stomach. They looked me over and put a couple of compresses on. No big deal.

I got on the radio and called my own medevac in. My teamee was a priority and I was a routine. The aircraft that had just left called back and said he would come and get us. I went back to our bunker to get our personal gear. Someone had already stolen both of our cameras and wallets.

The CH-46 came back and I took the front of the stretcher. As I went up the ramp of the 46, an updraft caught the aircraft and took it up about ten feet. The guy on the back let go, and so did I. The stretcher went up and my teamee hit the ground. I could see that it hurt. After another try, we got on the aircraft and were on our way to Khe Sanh. We landed and I walked off. From there, I was medevacked to Dong Ha. After I recovered in March, I was sent back to Khe Sanh.

☆

Cpl WILLIAM ROBERTSON
Logistics Support Unit _____

I was supposed to have left Khe Sanh on January 22. I had my seabag packed and I was ready to leave for the rear, Phu Bai. But, since the ammo dump blew on January 21, I had to stay. My relief had arrived two or three days before the dump blew, but he was killed by an artillery shell on January 24.

A CH-53 helicopter came in on February 15. We were unloading loose 155mm white-phosphorus rounds off the back of it. We were just rolling them off when three mortar or rocket rounds came in. Next thing I knew, Corporal Baker and I were airborne. Our rifles were sitting up against a stack of ammo next to the runway, and we were gone. The next place the helo set down was Dong Ha. There was nothing else going back to Khe Sanh that afternoon, so Baker and I spent the night at the ammo dump at Dong Ha with some of our friends. In a way, this was a relief. Water had been rationed at Khe Sanh, and the only thing we used it for was to drink and maybe to shave with. I had not had a bath since January 21. Both of us got everything clean except our boots and our covers. Everything else we got from friends and put on clean. That's the only time in my life I ever wore someone else's underwear. We threw our other clothes away and stayed in the shower a long time. We even ate at the mess hall!

The next morning, we were unable to get back because fog had Khe Sanh closed in. That afternoon, we were fixing to get on a helicopter to go back when the base colonel came through. He almost had a kitten because neither Baker nor I had a weapon. I think he was ready to court-martial us until he found out how we got there. Then he held the helicopter up and sent his driver over to the armory. He got two shotguns and two boxes of ammo for us. The colonel told us to turn it all over to Colonel Lownds as soon as we got back. He wished us good luck.

Until we got back, we had been unable to tell anyone at Khe Sanh where we were. All they found when they went looking for us were our rifles. They had a pretty good idea we had left on the CH-53, but they had no idea why or where—if we had decided we had had enough and just gotten on the helicopter and left or what. I can imagine the expressions on their faces when they came up looking for us and only found our rifles.

☆

1stLt JOHN KAHENY
1/26 Combat Operations Center _____

My father was very ill, and I had a suspicion that he would not live six months until the end of my Vietnam tour, so I had to get home to see him. For whatever reason, there was a delay in my orders, but on February 15 we got a message through to Division Headquarters, and they replied, saying that my orders were at Phu Bai and that I had to pick them up within two days or they would be canceled. I went over to the battalion command post to see Lieutenant Colonel Wilkinson, our battalion commander. As I walked in the door, he turned to me and said that something tragic had just happened. SgtMaj James Gaynor, the battalion sergeant major, and Capt David Ernst, the Charlie Company commander, had both been seriously wounded by a rocket that had hit the Charlie Company command post. He said, "You're the next-senior lieutenant. Do you want to take Charlie Company?" I told him then that my orders had been approved and were down at Phu Bai, and that if I didn't act I would not be able to get my 30-day leave. He was aware of my father's illness and patted me on the back and said, "Why don't you go on home." He indicated to me that I would probably be able to get another rifle company sometime after my return to the battalion. With that, I went back to my bunker, packed my gear, said a few quick good-byes, and went down to the airstrip.

At that time, the only way to get out was to hop one of the medevac choppers and help tend the wounded. Most of the helicopters went to the Delta-Med aid station at Dong Ha. So I went down to Charlie-Med, which was right next to the airstrip, and waited for a helicopter to arrive. During the wait, I heard that Captain Ernst was going to lose his arm and the sergeant major was in very serious condition.

The basic scenario was that the choppers would send word that they were on the way in. Four or so Marines, acting as stretcher bearers, would take each wounded man and race out across the airfield to the helicopters, which would not necessarily stop because of the mortar and recoilless-rifle fire. They only stopped at that point when the stretcher bearers were getting the wounded aboard.

I waited for quite a long time. I went up to the helicopter pad to run an errand and there met Lieutenant King, who had come off Hill 881S. He was on his way to Graves Registration with the remains of a Marine from India Company, 3/26. All he had was a small willy-peter bag because the Marine had been hit directly by an enemy mortar. As I started talking to Lieutenant King, both of us were called back down to Charlie-Med because the helicopter was on its way. I was assigned to help with Sergeant Major Gaynor.

The sergeant major and I had lived together in the battalion alternate command post for the previous month or so, and I had gotten to know him fairly well. He evidently had been in the Air Wing most of his time in the Marine Corps, and this was going to be his twilight cruise before his retirement. He had made a request to be able to serve his last tour with the grunts because he had never served with the infantry and felt that one could not be a retired sergeant major of Marines without having so served. He was injured doing what he did best, which was visiting the troops on the line. I thought highly of the man, and it was very difficult for me to go down there and see him as badly wounded as he was. But I took one end of the stretcher and we raced out to a CH-53 that was coming in and got him aboard.

It was quite dark by then. We barely got out of Khe Sanh while there was enough light.

Captain Ernst was next to me. I lit a cigarette for him. I had in my hand the IV bottle for the sergeant major, who was resting on my lap. It was kind of eerie because, as we got closer to Dong Ha, he became grayer and grayer. I think that he passed away sometime on the way into Dong Ha, but I'm not sure; the corpsman still wanted to work on him.

When we hit the ground at Dong Ha—which was still in the throes of the Tet Offensive—artillery rounds were coming in. Lieutenant King and I, and the other people aboard the chopper, ran down the runway with the stretchers and met up with some ambulances. Since we had to spend the night there, we were all told to go help out at Delta-Med. Everyone there pitched in without distinction of rank. I worked in the triage center until late that evening, mopping and sweeping all the blood and gore and debris and bandages.

It wasn't until years later that I learned that Sergeant Major Gaynor had indeed passed away that evening.

Chapter 3

RESUPPLY

There would have been no Khe Sanh Combat Base—no "set-piece" strategy—without one of the biggest aerial resupply efforts in history. The effort was enormous. While it strained and stressed the capacity of air-cargo units throughout the western Pacific and Vietnam, the massive airlift barely made good the daily use of supplies by the troops and the daily loss of supplies to enemy fire. The effort is more remarkable in that it took place entirely within the period of the Tet Offensive, when U.S. military units throughout Vietnam were under unremitting pressure. Throughout February, most aerial resupply missions were flown through dense fog or enemy fire—or both.

☆

Maj TOM COOK
26th Marines Assistant Logistics Officer _____

I was assigned as assistant logistics officer. My duties consisted of the ordering and allocation of materials required for construction and fortification and the ordering and allocation of munitions.' That took up most of my time, particularly the ordering of the munitions. Every day, around 1800, I called Dong Ha on the land line and reported a long, long list of numbers, each corresponding to a particular item. I reported quantities on position, the quantities in the dumps, and the quantities that I thought were required. It took a tremendous amount of time to gather all this information every day. Probably I worked twelve hours a day on that aspect of my job. In addition, I had other little duties. From what I understand, when that report was received at Dong Ha, it was immediately forwarded to Saigon, to MACV Headquarters. From there, it was dispatched directly to the White House so that President Johnson and his staff could look at it, to make sure that Khe Sanh was not going to fall.

LtCol DICK ROMINE
Marine Medium Helicopter Squadron 165 _____

If we stayed high and made a steep approach to Khe Sanh we were not vulnerable to the surrounding enemy antiaircraft guns (mostly 12.7mm), which were predominantly to the west. I made most of my approaches from the east of the plateau, which was at about 1,500 feet. It took only one time to realize when you'd made a bad approach and flown over the wrong positions. The clatter of rounds got your attention. The guns were impossible to spot from the air. I later observed why. Those ingenious little bastards had most of their antiaircraft guns mounted on dollies or wheels at the entrances of small caves high on the hillsides. They probably tunneled through from the other side of the hills. They stuck the noses of the guns outside just long enough to take potshots at us and then pulled them back into concealment before we could see where this fire was coming from.

LtCol JOHNNY GREGERSON
Marine Air Support Squadron 3 _____

The majority of the cargo was lifted to the outlying outposts from a staging area at Dong Ha. It was difficult enough to sustain supply support at Khe Sanh itself without adding an additional problem of staging supplies and massing the helicopters necessary to resupply the outposts.[1]

1stLt FRED McGRATH
Bravo Battery, 1/13 _____

I watched a CH-53 attempt a takeoff. The pilot got it about fifteen or twenty feet off the deck, then it slammed down hard and burst into flames. The pilots and crew chief escaped, but that 53 was a pile of melted metal within ten minutes. No happy hour for them that night.

1stLt NICK ROMANETZ
Charlie Company, 1/26 _____

On February 5, a camouflaged Air Force C-130 landed from west to east, taxied to the turnaround ramp, which was outside the perimeter, shut down his engines, and sat there. It had apparently taken some fire coming in, and the pilot apparently was unsure of the worthiness of the aircraft. I have to hand it to the pilot; he just parked it out there instead of taxiing it inside the base. Standing there watching, we couldn't figure out why he did that. I kept thinking, Hey, pal, get your ass out of there. He was easily within range of bad guys who could come up the trenches and fire RPGs of 60mm mortars at him. No crewmen came out of the aircraft. We thought those guys were really going to get it. He must have sat there for about forty-five minutes before he cranked up the engines. It turned out that the reason he didn't bring the aircraft into the perimeter was that it was loaded with ammunition. I guess the pilot was worried that there would be a big explosion inside the base.

Maj JIM STANTON
26th Marines Fire Support Coordination Center _____

The NVA infiltrated in a man who sat about two hundred meters off the end of the runway. He was in a little vertical

hole, three feet across, just big enough for him to stand in
and with a round column of dirt in the middle to support a
.51-caliber machine gun. All the planes taking off and
landing had to survive a burst from that gunner. We couldn't
hit somebody in a hole that small.

LCpl PHIL MINEER
Bravo Battery, 1/13 _____

There was an NVA we called Luke the Gook. He had a
.51-caliber machine gun. I could almost see his position on
a big hill across from my gun, to the right. Luke took a shot
at every C-130 that came into Khe Sanh. Sometimes he'd
get a hit, and sometimes he missed. We knew exactly where
Luke was, so we shot at him with artillery pieces—pounded
the area all around him. We *had* to have hit him, but they
kept sending guys to replace him. Once we called in a
Phantom. It hit him with rockets, it hit him with machine
guns, it hit him with bombs. But Luke got the Phantom.
The jet started smoking and the pilot ejected. In fact, his
canopy came down right in our gun section and the pilot
came down right outside the wire. He was picked up by
some guys from 1/26. The plane went right into the side of
the hill; I think the pilot aimed it right at Luke the Gook.
Not long after that—*dit-dit-dit-dit-dit*—the .51 was back
again. We gave Luke a standing ovation and never bothered
with him again.

☆

Sgt DAVID MACH, USAF
29th Tactical Airlift Squadron _____

I was a loadmaster with the 29th Tactical Airlift Squadron
when we flew out of Clark Air Force Base, in the Philippines, and staged through Tan Son Nhut for fifteen days at a
time.

On the first mission we brought in five pallets of ammunition. I'll always remember them telling us we had five
minutes total on the ground. We landed, combat-offloaded
the five pallets, taxied ahead, stopped to pick up ten

wounded Marines, taxied to the runway, and took off just as the mortars started to hit the base.

My second mission was a couple of days later. Same as before—five pallets of supplies—but this time we had to be gone in three minutes. We combat-offloaded the pallets and stopped to pick up fifteen KIAs. I was trying to close the ramp as we were taxiing off, as the mortars were coming in. On the way back to Danang, I was sitting on the floor with those bodies around me. I was afraid to look at the toe tags because I might have known one of them. The smell was nauseating, as always.

☆

Within days of the total loss of the Marine KC-130 fueler on February 10, the Khe Sanh runway was closed to all C-130 traffic.

Col GEORGE KINNEY, USAF
834th Air Division Vice Commander _____

The C-123 pilots continued to land throughout the entire operation, although only when absolutely necessary. The [C-123s], needing only 1,400 feet of roll-out to slow sufficiently, were able to make the 90-degree turnoff to the offload ramp. But the C-130s had to go to the end of the runway to turn around, presenting inviting targets for enemy gunners.[2]

Maj TOM COOK
26th Marines Assistant Logistics Officer _____

Air drops became our main means of getting supplies. We were totally dependent on them. There was no way that the planes could land in sufficient numbers because of the mortar fire, rockets, and artillery that rained in if they tried to sit there long enough to unload anything. On the whole, the air drops were quite successful. We depended on them for artillery ammunition, small-arms ammunition, food— everything that had to come in there. The only thing we didn't depend on them for was water. (I have no idea why the water point was never contaminated by the NVA. It could have been, very easily. If it had been, we would have been out of business.)

MAJ MYLES ROHRLICK, USAF
834th Air Division _____

The drop zone was extremely small, only 300 yards square, and located outside the Marine defense perimeter. There was no room for it inside the camp. So we dropped only during daylight. At night the Marines withdrew to the camp proper and, essentially, gave up the drop zone to the enemy.

In the morning they would sweep it for mines and secure it for the day's use. And the equipment to recover the dropped supplies was limited. Rough-terrain forklifts and trucks were used to get the supplies to camp. The Marines and our combat controllers were always under enemy fire in the drop zone.[3]

LCpl ARMANDO GONZALES
Bravo Company, 1/9 _____

The supplies that were dropped fell between the Rock Quarry and the combat base, so 1/9 was responsible for sweeping the drop zone every morning for any type of booby traps or ambushes. We rotated platoons and companies every morning. We found booby traps a few times, and we lost a few guys in the process.

Maj TOM COOK
26th Marines Assistant Logistics Officer _____

We went out there every morning and waited for the air drop. We had a terrible time during the month of February because it was foggy nearly every day. We could hear the planes, but we couldn't see the parachutes until they broke out of the clouds, which was at about a hundred feet. At first, our security at the drop zone, which was a different platoon every day, was never properly instructed about what to do if they saw a pallet falling toward them. When they saw the parachutes, they would take off running. Since they usually ran with the wind, the parachutes would follow them. After a few days of that, we finally got the problem corrected by telling them each day to run into the wind.

LCpl ARMANDO GONZALES
Bravo Company, 1/9 ⎯⎯⎯⎯⎯⎯⎯⎯⎯⎯⎯⎯⎯⎯

Once in a while, the resupply aircraft overshot the zone and we literally had to blow up our own supplies with artillery. In a few cases, jets came in to blow it up to keep the NVA from getting it.

Through the latter half of February, most of the parachute drops were made through patches of dense fog. Often the crews of the cargo aircraft never saw the ground. The extreme visibility problem, combined with the need for pinpoint accuracy—the drop zone was extremely small— required sophisticated technical innovation. The result was the IMC—Instrument Meteorological Condition-technique.

Maj HENRY VAN GIELSON, USAF
834th Air Division ⎯⎯⎯⎯⎯⎯⎯⎯⎯⎯⎯⎯⎯⎯

There was ground radar close to the drop zone, so we combined two existing systems to develop [IMC]. Marine [ground controllers] positioned the aircraft over the threshold of [the] runway. . . . Then by using the Doppler [radar] to keep on course, and calculating the exact time it took (twenty to twenty-six seconds, depending on winds) to fly to the computed air-release point we were able to put bundles on the [drop zone].[4]

LtCol FRANK HAMMOCK, USAF
21st Tactical Airlift Squadron ⎯⎯⎯⎯⎯⎯⎯⎯⎯⎯⎯⎯

The weather had turned to instrument conditions over Khe Sanh. Cloud tops were from 4,000 to 10,000 feet and Khe Sanh was reporting cloud bases from "on the ground to indefinite."

We took on our load at Danang—32,000 pounds of artillery shells and a pallet of toilet paper. We got airborne and headed for Hue to set up holding pattern and wait our turn to start our run. As each airplane departed the drop zone, it would report being clear, and then the next airplane on the bottom of the holding stack would start its run. Taking a westerly heading from Hue and starting the let-down through heavy clouds, we headed toward a gap in the mountains that lined up with the drop zone. Charlie and the NVA owned the land on both sides of the gap for several miles. When at the planned altitude to pass through the gap, the airplane would be below the tops of the mountains around the approach path. As we reached the minimum altitude through the pass, we would hear the small-arms fire going through the skin of the airplane.

After I reached drop altitude and slowed the airplane to 130 knots, the navigator made Doppler contact and passed information to me. At that low altitude and low airspeed, the *thump-thump* of the artillery could be heard above the whine of the engines. The loadmaster finished his load check and was standing by the emergency load release—just in case. The countdown was in progress when, suddenly, the command "Green light" arrived. The load was released. I could hear the rumbling sound of the pallets as they started rolling toward the open tailgate of the airplane. I could also hear the impact of small-arms fire as it pinged through the skin of the airplane.

Things began happening very fast. I could feel the weight of the load on the controls shifting toward the tail, so I applied forward pressure on the wheel. The nose started to rise rapidly due to the shifting load, so I ran in all the forward trim available and applied power. I was no longer simply applying pressure to the wheel, I was manually pushing the wheel against the stop, but the nose was still rising. I had full throttle. The nose could not go up much more or the airplane would stall. At that altitude and airspeed, that could ruin my whole weekend. There was nothing more I could do except hold on, keep the pressure on the wheel, and hope the load cleared the tailgate.

Then the rumbling stopped and the nose pitched downward fast enough to lift me against my seat belt. I had to get the wheel back to neutral and the trim back to normal. I could still hear the ping of small-arms rounds hitting us as the airplane made it back to straight and level flight. The throttles were well forward to get all the airspeed that Hercules could handle. We started our climb-out in a wide turn to the left. I had not seen the ground through the fog yet, but our load was on the way to the drop zone. I waited for the Airlift Control Element to tell us about our drop. The call told us that we were only ten yards off the mark.

As I continued my climb-out, the copilot called to tell me that we were clear of the drop zone. I could hear the next airplane's call that it was starting its run. Meanwhile, my crew went through the usual post-drop checks. They found several holes from the ground fire, but no big deal.

When all the exacting work was finished, the inevitable joking started. The loadmaster was saying, "Man, did you see that second pallet start wobbling as it was rolling aft? I sure thought it would jam!" The laughter went through every crew member in turn. No one cared if it wasn't funny. As we were flying back, I thought of that load having toilet paper. I knew toilet paper was needed, but I wondered if we should have been endangering an airplane and crew to drop it.

A few days later, all air drops were stopped. We had dropped all the cargo chutes into Khe Sanh, and we had none to use. To get our chutes out of surrounded Khe Sanh, several fighter strikes were coordinated with a fast run-in by an Air Force helicopter to pick up the chutes and return them to Danang.

☆

Maj TOM COOK
26th Marines Assistant Logistics Officer _____

They decided to try the Low Altitude Parachute Extraction System—LAPES. The load would be palletized on rollers. The plane would come along the runway at about twenty feet and the crew pop a parachute, which would drag the load right out of the rear of the aircraft. At the same time the load was coming out, the aircraft would climb out. It seemed like a neat system,but it required too much coordination between the crew chief and the pilot.

A total of fifty-two LAPES and similar GPES (Ground Proximity Extraction System) missions were run in order to deliver outsized loads—mainly construction material—that could not be dropped safely into the tiny drop zone outside the combat base perimeter wire.

Sgt DAVID MACH, USAF
29th Tactical Airlift Squadron _____

On my fourth and final mission to Khe Sanh, the day started with us and four other C-130Bs going to Danang,where each picked up a single LAPES platform of supplies weighing about 25,000 pounds. The day was rainy and foggy, and it wasn't going to get any better. The five aircraft took off five minutes apart, but when we arrived we had to hold because of the weather. It was sunny and cool above the gray clouds.

There was a combat control team on the ground that talked us down. When it was our turn, we already had the ramp and door open for the drop. As we entered the cloud, it was dark gray behind the aircraft. At about a minute out, over the noise of our engines, we could hear the sound of the North Vietnamese shooting at us with antiaircraft guns. I asked the pilot if he could hear it on the flight deck, and he said he could. They tried but never hit us.

We broke out of the cloud at about one hundred feet and in line with the runway. The aircraft descended with landing gear down, similar to a landing approach. At three to five feet altitude over the drop zone, and on command from the navigator, the copilot started the process. I saw the green light as the copilot released the extraction parachute, which in turn extracted the supply load from the aircraft. In a second, the load was gone. When it left the aircraft, the load was traveling in excess of 100 miles per hour. Ideally, it landed rear end first, settled to the front, and slid on the ground. The last I saw of it, it was sliding down the runway, and then it was gone. Ideally, the extraction chute and the friction of the ground stopped the load within 200 yards. By then we were back in the clouds. I felt proud that we had sort of sneaked in, made our drop, and made it out without getting hit. However, I still carry a hollow feeling because I later learned that one of the LAPES loads dropped that day hit a bunker and killed at least one Marine in it.

1stLt NICK ROMANETZ
Charlie Company, 1/26 _____

One day, in the fog, I heard a C-130 making approaches and pulling out because he wasn't on line. Finally, listening to the pitch of the engines, I figured he was going to land. I thought it was still too foggy for him to try to land, but then I thought he must have been on a radar approach and in control. I was standing in my bunker with a Marine, in the trenchline not more than fifty or seventy-five feet away from the edge of the runway. We were watching Bunker 21, which was right on the edge of the runway. We knew from the pitch of the engines that the pilot was not right over the runway. Lo and behold, an Air Force C-130 came out of the fog, heading right for Bunker 21. He was off to the side of the runway by fifty or sixty feet. The pilot saw that he was heading into the bunker, which was a concrete two-story job with a .50-caliber machine gun in the second story. The pilot throttled up and tried to pull up, but his tail ramp was down because he was trying to make a skid drop. The tail ramp hit the top of the bunker just as he released his cargo, which was a load of airfield matting. It went tumbling down just to the right of the runway. The tail ramp collapsed a good part of Bunker 21, and a Marine manning the bunker was crushed. The tail ramp broke off from the C-130 and started tumbling right down toward my bunker. It landed in a hole about twenty-five feet away from us. It all took a matter of seconds, but it looked like it was in slow motion.

☆

1stLt PAUL ELKAN
Bravo Battery, 1/13 _____

A lot of ammo we got that way seemed to get banged up.
The brass got dented.

Cpl DENNIS SMITH
Bravo Company, 1/26 _____

One of the guys in my supply section was LCpl Virgil
Crunk, from Ohio. All he wanted to do when he got out was
drive a truck and listen to country music. He had an
uncanny way of finding anything he needed on that base. If
he couldn't make a trade or a deal for something, he stole it.
I never asked where things came from. He ordered his parts
for his jeep direct from Motor Transport and used their tools
to maintain it. He was the fastest jeep at Khe Sanh, proven
over and over on the airstrip against other drivers.

Virgil really proved his stuff during the worst of the shelling,
when the resupply planes couldn't even land. He would be
hanging around the airstrip, waiting for some supplies to be
skid-dropped, knowing that everyone else would have their
heads down because any aircraft *always* drew incoming rockets. In fact, we called the planes "mortar magnets." Great
sport for the NVA gunners. The planes would skim down the
runway with their rear doors open and pop a parachute to pull
their supply skids out on the run. Our job was to recover the
skids when they stopped sliding down the runway.

As soon as the cargo skid was pulled from a plane, Virgil
was out on the runway, throwing anything and everything
into his jeep trailer. Then he was out of there in the fastest
jeep at Khe Sanh. Once, as rockets were slamming into the
base, I watched him take a curve into our area so fast that
the trailer flipped over. He dragged it in upside down and
jumped into the hooch—laughing. Virgil was kind of hard
on jeep trailers.

Pfc LIONEL TRUFANT
106mm Platoon, 3/26 _____

The only chance we had to improve on our situation came
from the kamikaze truck drivers on the road from the drop

zone, which ran in back of our position. Guys driving the trucks couldn't hear the incoming, so they would just *drive*—take a chance. They couldn't hear so they would drive so fast that, a lot of times, extra pallets would fall off the trucks, break, and leave C-rats all over the deck. Hell, those guys weren't going to come back and get it, so we ran out, picked them up, and brought them back to our hooch.

Chapter 4

Maj ALEX LEE
Marine Corps Development Center (Quantico, Virginia)

There were photos in the press of Marines and corpsmen listening to long steel stakes driven into the ground with the purported (by the press, who put the troops up to that silly activity) purpose of listening to the tunneling by the NVA who were "expected" to blow up the combat base à la Petersburg.

Those photos and the resultant clamor from the ignorant resulted in some real scrambling on the part of the McNamara folks involved in sensors—the Defense Communications Planning Group, which was headquartered at the Naval Observatory. They were asked if their super-sophisticated sensors could detect tunneling. They ran some quick and dirty test and determined that the sensors could not, but that the AN/PSR-1 Seismic Intrusion Detector—one of my projects—could do a fair job. The device was not field-ready, but we had some in the shop at Quantico that I was testing.

I took part in the tests at Eglin Air Force Base, made my report, and, that weekend, went to get my car painted. On return to the house in early afternoon, my wife reported that I was "leaving again"—something I did regularly as I tested many items in Vietnam to work out bugs.

The Defense Communications Planning Group sent three Army officers. They were full-time participants in the sensor business and were prepared to talk to all the specialists in Vietnam and to help the Target Information Officer at Khe Sanh—Capt Harry Baig—integrate information being received (and improperly understood) from the large sensor-evaluation unit in Thailand [to which it was beamed directly from the sensors seeded around Khe Sanh]. I was sent along with my Seismic Intrusion devices to hunt tunnels and—most probably—to "speak Marine" to the officers and men of Colonel Lownds's 26th Marines.

We flew nonstop to Saigon, where the chairborne commandos were universally disparaging of the conduct of the Marines at the combat base—even though none of them had been there. After this nasty reception, we were given a VIP aircraft to the north, and went immediately to Khe Sanh in a CH-53. On about February 12, we flew into the combat base with General Tompkins and had his blessing to find the tunnels. We arrived amid a spate of incoming, and the accompanying Army officers were suitably impressed. This was their first taste of shellfire.

The sensor drops had taken place prior to our arrival, however, the entire effort was coordinated from Nakhon Phanom, in Thailand, and the Marines on site—Maj Jerry Hudson, the 26th Marines intelligence office, and Capt Harry Baig, the regimental target information officer—were not fully able to utilize the reports. In fact, the reports, knows as "Spotlights," were often confused with those we knew as "Usually Reliable Source," a cute way of saying that radio battalion monitor teams heard the bad guys announcing some move or other on their communications nets. Hudson and Baig just didn't understand what they had in the way of intelligence from the sensors.

At the combat base, we were greeted with open minds and very positive interest. Captain Baig was quick to under-

stand the fantastic value of the sensor evaluation reports
from Thailand. He was, at that time, using five-inch-by-
eight-inch cards to plot intelligence info on every grid
square he could reach with any of his supporting arms.

I was given free run of the combat base and permitted to
search anywhere and everywhere for proof of tunneling. I
began doing some careful research. To make a long story
short, I found that even if you went to bedrock below the
base, there was only the seismic energy of falling shells,
distant bombs, artillery firing, and mortars firing. The NVA
were prodigious diggers, completing in one night 1,700 feet
of stand-up trenches outside the base, but we found *no* signs
of the tunneling that was suspected.

Since we were without specified responsibilities, two of
the Army officers and I went throughout the base and
discussed with the people in the fighting holes the use of the
new small radars and night-observation devices (NODs),
both of which had just arrived, as integrated methods of fire
control. With the radar to detect movement, the NODs
could find the enemy. If used at dispersed sites, you could
cross lines on a map and get precise locations for time-on-
target shoots with artillery and mortars on site in the combat
base.

Pfc JOHN KONKO
Bravo Battery, 1/13 (Hill 558) _____

A major came up to me and handed me a radar receiver in a
black box along with a map and coordinates of sensors that
had been dropped from planes out in front of the hill I was
on, Hill 558. This was because I was a radio operator
forward observer. The major taught me the use of the
receiver and told me it was a secret device. Then he gave
me an incendiary device. In case we were overrun, I was to
destroy the black box and the map.

A sequence of numbers would light up on the black box.
These were the numbers on the map. By watching the box
for a length of time I could figure out where the enemy was
and what route he was taking past our sensors. According to
what set of numbers we had, there would be a B-52 strike.

Maj ALEX LEE
Marine Corps Development Center (Quantico, Virginia)

Capt Harry Baig and I happened to collaborate on one small use of the sensor one night. We found a seismic-energy signal of the enemy digging in along Route 9. The next day, our air reported only holes. The next night, there was more seismic data. Harry intuited antiaircraft. The next morning, the first air strike went in and found and destroyed several 37mm antiaircraft guns sited to fire zero-deflection shots down the long axis of the runway. Harry could see in his mind the thought processes of the enemy commander, and, so doing, he divined that cutting our air link was uppermost. Thus, from a bunch of semi-garbled messages from Thailand on seismic-energy bursts, Harry solved the equation and kept the air link open another day.

Capt HARRY BAIG
26th Marines Target Information Officer _____

Sensors were extremely useful intelligence indicators, but they were not good for targeting purposes. As we learned to employ them and to interpret the Spotlight reports [from Thailand] against the meaning of other intelligence, we found that their value increased. Two nights of heavy activity along infiltration routes often signified a probable attack on the third night, and appropriate area clearance fire would be discharged into the assembly and attack positions to break up the enemy formations. On one occasion, enemy digging in the vicinity of the sensors gave us the location of six 37mm antiaircraft guns. Truck convoys, moving toward known supply dumps, enabled us to estimate the rate of replenishment and dump status of enemy logistic agencies. The general locations of self-propelled guns were often betrayed by the sensors. Finally, and most important, sensors clearly showed the route pattern and density of traffic along major infiltration routes on a daily and nightly basis.[1]

Maj ALEX LEE
Marine Corps Development Center (Quantico, Virginia)

What was important about our team going to Khe Sanh was
the introduction for the first time of *real-time* sensor read-
outs. Army Maj Hy Stevens, who was with me, had some
readout receivers. We put Baig into *real time* vis-à-vis the
sensor data and helped him and, eventually, Colonel Lownds
understand what the sensors meant and what the evaluation
from Thailand was telling them regarding movement, targeting,
etc.

1stLt NICK ROMANETZ
Charlie Company, 1/26 _____

We were worried about night probes. After a while, we had
NODs and sniper scopes delivered. They worked pretty
good, but we never saw any bad guys. We rotated them
around the base; never got to keep them very long.

□

SSgt HARVE SAAL, USA
FOB-3 _____

It was common for us to monitor the team radios and listen
in on all the current events of the day. I could listen to a
large selection of active radio channels. It was just like
listening to a war program on NBC, except *we* were the war.

One day in mid-February, we overheard an American
reconnaissance aircraft analyzing a newly discovered convoy of NVA vehicles. They way they normally reported
convoys was to say something like, "I'll count off in tens."
However, this day, something big was obviously happening.
The pilot said something like, "Convoy spotted. I'll count
off in . . . like hell I will! Convoy vehicles too numerous to
count. I'm pulling out now!"

With that report, and through our intelligence sources, we
learned that the NVA were using abandoned buildings in
Khe Sanh ville to stockpile their munitions and repair parts.
The Vietnamese high command in Saigon refused our re-

quest to destroy the enormous store of war materials in Khe Sanh ville. They said that the town was very important to the Vietnamese people and must not be disturbed by us. Actually, the town was in extreme disrepair, and very few Vietnamese people lived anywhere in the near vicinity— only about fifteen, and that was before the siege began. They *all* deserted the area posthaste on January 21. The buildings that still stood were very old and ready to topple over. We felt that the only reason the NVA used these buildings was because of sanctuary offered by the high command in Saigon.

□

DUEL

1stLt PAUL ELKAN
Bravo Battery, 1/13 _____

We got hit bad one night in mid-February. We had H&I targets to shoot, but there was no comm to the guns because the lines had been cut. It was raining like hell: thunder, mud, dark, flashes, lightning, and explosions from incoming.

LCpl RAY NICOL
Bravo Battery,1/13 _____

Sergeant Arona, Private Smart, and Private Aguilar had just gone on duty to fire their shift when two big mortar rounds landed in the gun pit, one on each side of the gun. They blew out both tires and destroyed the sight. Arona and Aguilar were not too badly hurt—Arona was hit in both legs and Aguilar was hit in the legs and arms—but Smart had been hit in the face and the upper body. He was bleeding badly, and, because of the incoming, I couldn't get a corpsman out right away. Pfc Bill Chapman and I patched Smart as well as we could and waited for the corpsman.

1stLt PAUL ELKAN
Bravo Battery, 1/13 _____

We medevacked Private Smart in a jeep. His back looked like he had been whipped with a cat-o'-nine-tails. It was

shredded. He was shaking so hard from shock and the cold
that the jeep shook.

LCpl RAY NICOL
Bravo Battery, 1/13 _____

After Smart was taken to Charlie-Med, I was ordered to try
to find another gunsight and tires at the 155mm battery,
which was at the other end of the base. I dodged incoming
trying to see in the dark and managed to scrounge a sight,
but not tires.

1stLt PAUL ELKAN
Bravo Battery, 1/13 _____

The section chief on that gun, Sergeant Arona, fired all
night with just one other man. His ears were bleeding from
concussion, the gun's tires were flat, they had no gunsight,
and the section was down from five men to just three. I put
him in for a Bronze Star.

Pfc LIONEL TRUFANT
106mm Platoon, 3/26 _____

We didn't stay in our holes all day. The junior troops had
work details. We had to dig trenches—sometimes our own
trenches—and we had to constantly work on our bunkers.
Someone had to go get the mail, someone had to go get the
food, we had to re-lay comm lines whenever they were
destroyed, and we had to take care of basic necessities like
going to the shitter, or burning the shitter.

When we had to get the mail, we could take either of
two routes. We could go through the trenches, the long
way, or we could take the adventurous route, straight
across the open ground. Since I and one of my buddies
were the lowest-ranking personnel, we had that job a lot.
We made a game of it. Sometimes we went individually
and sometimes we went together. It was a game of
dodging the incoming. After a while, it became part of
our everyday existence.

I have never been in jail, but I can understand how a person in jail can become used to being there. Once you're there, once you get over your initial shock, you get to feel that you're not going to let it get you down. That's the way it was at Khe Sanh. There wasn't enough water, so we could not get clean. About all we could do was wash vital parts and brush our teeth. Taking a shit meant going out in the open and sitting on an open shitter. If we had built an outhouse, it would have been a target. To blend in better, we just sat on a one-holer in the open. Food was just basic C-rations.

☆

Cpl WALT WHITESIDES
3/26 Tactical Air Control Party _____

I was reassigned to the battalion command post from Hill 881S on February 9 and was meritoriously promoted to the rank of corporal soon after that.

At first, during the day, I was put on radio watch in the battalion command post, on the tactical-air-control net. This was really cushy duty as there was absolutely nothing for the radio operator to do there except monitor the net. At the time, we had no active role. At night, the operations chief would let me sleep, or we played cards. This lasted only a short while, until the communications officer figured out that we had no real role to play.

Suddenly, the communications platoon was required to man a section of the line behind the grunts. We had to connect our bunkers with a trenchline. I was put in charge of one section of the line. I also was put in charge of getting some covered trenches dug near the base helo pad, for troops who were waiting to leave or arriving on the birds.

I arranged for some grunts from Lima Company to do most of the digging.

Pfc LIONEL TRUFANT
106mm Platoon, 3/26 _____

On work details, we took turns listening for the incoming while the other people dug holes or trenches. One day, while we were digging a trench for H&S Company, I was listening when I heard the incoming. I told everybody to get down. The last person I saw before I went down was a private from Lima Company. The rounds hit as soon as I got down in the hole, and then I heard moaning. Someone was hit. My first thought was that it was the private I had seen in the open. I thought, Damn, I have to go out and get him. I stuck my head out of the hole and saw that it wasn't that Marine. Another Marine off to my side had gotten hit in the lower leg and knee. I went over to him, took his bandage off his helmet, opened it, and started wrapping it around the leg. While I was doing it, I had lots of things going through my mind: I had to listen for incoming, I had to stop the wounded man's blood, I had to watch him to make sure he didn't go out on me, and I had to figure out what to do if more incoming came in: Should I stay where I was, or pull the wounded man into the hole? Luckily, there was no incoming that minute. I called for a corpsman, and Doc came up and took him away. We got back to digging, more artillery came in, and I sounded off again, and everybody jumped back in the hole. It went on and on like that until we finished.

Cpl WALT WHITESIDES
3/26 Tactical Air Control Party _____

We got the trenchline done in a few days. The only problem was that the communications officer and I had an argument over which way the firing ports were to face. He had the strange notion that the ports should face the runway, *away* from the lines, as he thought the NVA would penetrate the lines a mile or so away and run across the runway to be stopped by troops fortunate enough to be in the two trenches with the firing ports facing inward. We had to take the roofs off the bunkers and redo the tops when he discovered that I had faced the ports 180 degrees from where he wanted them. I diplomatically solved the problem by putting firing ports on both sides, since the trenches were 100 to 150 yards inside the mainline.

1stLt NICK ROMANETZ
Charlie Company, 1/26 _____

We had homemade fougasse devices outside our wire. They were 55-gallon drums cut in half with napalm and thermite grenades or tripflares in them. The idea was that they would explode and create an additional obstacle for the enemy. I don't know if they would have burned a lot of people, but they probably would have added a lot to the confusion.

SSgt HARVE SAAL, USA
FOB-3 _____

I thought it appropriate to warn the elite NVA regiment in front of FOB-3, should they find themselves inside the FOB defenses. So I hand-printed a sign:

SIR CHARLES
IF YOU CAN READ THIS SIGN
YOU'RE ON THE WRONG SIDE OF THE WIRE!

☆

LCpl ARMANDO GONZALES
Bravo Company, 1/9 _____

Helicopter resupply runs always drew enemy incoming. They usually came in with slingloads of supplies, which they dropped off. Sometimes, for some reason, a helo would drop its sling and then climb without leaving, hovering right over our positions. That gave the NVA forward observers more to shoot at. The helos raised big dust clods, and they made a lot of noise. The NVA could sight in on the clouds, the noise, and the helos themselves.

One time I saw a crewman in one of the hovering helicopters leaning out to take pictures. A young Marine in my squad we had nicknamed Baby was killed by the incoming drawn by that chopper. I *know* he would have heard the incoming if the noise from the chopper's rotors hadn't drowned it out. When I saw Baby get blown away, the pilot and crew of the helicopter were as much my enemies as the NVA around us. I took a couple of potshots at the chopper. My only regret then—and now—is that those sons of bitches didn't pay for their ignorance the way Baby and other guys did.

☆

Sgt FRANK JONES
26th Marine Scout-Sniper Platoon _____

There was an NVA sniper outside the wire, at the east end of the base, who kept shooting at our guys. They couldn't find him. One evening, about dusk, when I was a little drunk, I told them I'd show them how to do it. I jumped up on the parapet of the trenchline and lit up a cigarette. A green tracer went whizzing by my face and I fell into the trenchline. They had told me he was about two hundred yards away, but I knew that he was seventy-five to one hundred yards away. We pulled a 106mm recoilless rifle around and ended that sniper's shooting at us anymore.

☆

LCpl CHARLIE THORNTON
Lima Company, 3/26 _____

After Lang Vei fell, I was trained to operate against tanks we expected to attack us. Although we never saw tanks at Khe Sanh, the flamethrower was used once for a rather bizarre purpose.

Capt DICK CAMP
3/26 Assistant Operations Officer _____

I overheard a Red Sector listening post call in to say they heard some movement in front of Lima Company and to ask for permission to open fire. The listening post was asked if they knew what the noise was coming from, but they said no. Permission to fire was granted. Of course the listening post knew what the target was. They just didn't want to tell anyone, in case permission to open fire was withheld.

Pfc LIONEL TRUFANT
106mm Platoon, 3/26 _____

We got attacked by a mad elephant. This big elephant came running toward the line, so everybody opened up on it. I think we all thought it was packed with explosives. Eventually we killed it, but then we had this problem with the carcass sitting out in front of our lines.

LCpl CHARLIE THORNTON
Lima Company, 3/26 _____

As the elephant lay there, the NVA discovered how to use the carcass as a shield and snipe at us during the day. We finally were sent out with the flamethrower and attempted to burn the elephant to eliminate the NVA snipers' shelter. All we succeeded in doing was singeing the hair on the elephant. I was extremely glad that an NVA tank was not our first target. We later exploded the elephant with C4 plastic explosives.

Cpl BERT MULLINS
Bravo Company, 1/9 _____

I had taken no extra clothes when we left Camp Evans for Khe Sanh on January 22 because we had been told we were going for only three days. When we finally received new clothes, I was able to get a new T-shirt. When I took the old T-shirt off, it was rotten. The collar stayed around my neck when it ripped free of the rest of the rotten fabric, which came to pieces.

LCpl CHARLIE THORNTON
Lima Company, 3/26 _____

The Marine Corps is not known for its high-tech weapons and supplies.Once we received a shipment of socks (a rare commodity) that were stamped on the heel U.S. ARMY REJECTS.

Chapter 5

1stLt NICK ROMANETZ
Charlie Company, 1/26_____

We had double rows of concertina with a minefield in between. We mapped out and marked a path through the minefield for the listening posts. On the morning of February 20, we couldn't bring in the listening post at first light because it was too foggy. After a while, the Marines in the listening post called and asked if they could send a man back for some chow. I said okay, and he came back. Then another guy called and asked if he could come back and take a crap. I said okay, and *he* came back. Then the third guy called and asked if he could refill the canteens. I said okay, and *he* came back. On the way, the third guy tripped a mine. As it turned out, the lance corporal in charge of the listening spot never took his guys through the second wire. Instead of being 600 meters in front of our lines, they were maybe fifty meters out. The guys who had been coming in had been walking back and forth through the minefield, but

it wasn't until the third guy came back that they found out.
That Marine had his foot blown off.

☆

SSgt HARVE SAAL, USA
FOB-3 _____

It became obvious to us that the Communist artillery gunners had a sense of humor. We were under an artillery and
rocket barrage that climbed to about 400 rounds. It lasted
about an hour. I looked up periodically from out of the
trench to keep abreast of the damage being caused by the
incoming and, during the course of my surveys, I started to
have some strange feelings—as though something that had
been there wasn't there. Then the answer became obvious.

There was some yelling from the place where the Seabees
had built three new aboveground latrines just before the
siege began. Only there weren't any latrines anymore. The
latrines had been the targets of the entire barrage!

The yelling was asking for help. I quickly moved to
where the nearest latrine had been, and found a wounded
Vietnamese interpreter. He was all scrunched down in a
half-barrel of dung. He was bleeding from a wound in one
leg. I got him into the trench and started cleaning the
wound. *Yech!* Then I heard laughter. My Special Forces
brothers in the trench next to me were laughing uncontrollably
over the spectacle.

☆

Cpl TERRY SMITH
3/26 Tactical Air Control Party (Hill 881S) _____

[SILVER STAR CITATION] Cpl Terry Smith observed a Marine helicopter in a zone on which he knew North Vietnamese
Army gunners had registered heavy mortars. He realized
that the aircraft would almost certainly be destroyed if it
remained in the landing zone, and attempted unsuccessfully
to contact the pilot by radio. Aware that enemy rounds were
probably already on the way, he restrained a Marine junior

to him from going out onto the zone and, leaving the safety
of his bunker, ran across the open ground, signaling manually
to the helicopter crew to take off immediately. As the
helicopter took off, and before Corporal Smith could reach
cover, he was . . . wounded by mortar fragments. . . .

Cpl WALT WHITESIDES
3/26 Tactical Air Control Party _____

I was getting a haircut from the communications platoon
barber when I heard that my best friend, Cpl Terry Smith,
had been wounded while guiding a helo on Hill 881S. I
remember saying, ''Good,'' when I realized that he would
be getting home because this would give him his third
Purple Heart. I regret ever saying that. Terry died of his
wounds.

FEBRUARY 21

Cpl DENNIS MANNION
Charlie Battery, 1/13 (Hill 861) _____

February 21, 1968

Hey Man—
   War still goes its shitty way. *Still* waiting for the
big gook attempt. My guess is they're building up
to a strength to carry on a big fight. (Their
resupply has got to be a bitch no matter how you
look at it.) But we're getting better, too. I'll go so
far as to say we're 100 percent better than we were
a month and one day ago—and that's a lot.
   Spent last three days building a new bunker—me
and three other guys. It's boss. About 10 feet "down
in" with a big fucking roof. Should take just about
anything. I hope it never comes to that. Boing!

FEBRUARY 22

Cpl DENNIS SMITH
Bravo Company, 1/26 _____

February 22, 1968

Dear Dad,
  Our little slant-eyed sniper took a few shots at
me with his .51 this afternoon as I was driving
around the strip to deliver water to a platoon from
Alpha Company that is attached to us.
  I'm about to write everything that happens here,
but if I filled my letters with such stories (as I
easily could) it would serve no purpose except to
increase the worrying at home. I just marvel each
night over the preceding day's near misses and the
fact that I am still able to mark off, with shaking
hand, one more day in my little calendar.
  We're down to two meals of C-rations plus one
canteen of water per man per day, but I'd go without a day's rations for each letter from home.

☆

26th Marines Command Chronology _____

Khe Sanh Combat Base and its outposts received a heavy
volume of enemy mortar, rocket, and artillery fire. Approximate incoming total: 270 rounds. Approximately
250 rounds of this fire came between 1200 and 1700.
Casualties from incoming: 7 friendly KIA, 24 friendly
WIA (medevacked), and seven friendly WIA (minor).

Lt RAY STUBBE
1/26 Battalion Chaplain _____

[DIARY ENTRY] Casualties started pouring in from 2/26.
There were seven KIA, one of whom was the 2/26 chaplain,
Lt Robert Brett. One of the corpsmen asked me to remove
the boots from an injured man lying on a stretcher moaning,

blood all over. The boots were caked with mud and blood, and my hands were red from both. The mixture began to dry, causing the skin to feel like it was shrinking, so I went to my hooch to wash my hands. All of a sudden, there was a large blast. A large piece of metal and other debris flew up in the air. A CH-53 helicopter had been hit.

LCpl RAY NICOL
Bravo Battery, 1/13 _____

A big helicopter loaded with medevacs was about fifty feet in the air, taking off, when a recoilless rifle round hit it. The helo bounced a lot when it hit the ground, but it didn't explode. The helo went down right behind my platoon area. When it hit, the big floppy rotor blades, which were still going, got caught on the ground and big pieces of them broke off and went whipping around. I heard that one of the blades sliced off the top of the cockpit. I do know that the pilot and copilot had their heads and upper parts of their bodies severed by something. The Marines in the back—the rest of the crew and the wounded—all got out more or less okay. The Graves Registration people eventually came by and took the bodies away.

Lt RAY STUBBE
1/26 Battalion Chaplain _____

[DIARY ENTRY] The pilot and copilot were killed— Capt William "Rex" Riley and 1stLt Carey Smith. Father Brett's clerk, Pfc Alexander Chin, was also killed. He had been wounded twice before.

1stLt NICK ROMANETZ
Charlie Company, 1/26 _____

Next day, a foggy, chilly morning, my platoon radioman went out to take a leak in the weeds. When he came back he told me he had found an arm. I went out there with him and, sure enough, there was a left arm, severed at the shoulder. It had a wedding band on the ring finger. I sent it to Graves Registration in a mail sack.

☆

Cpl ALLAN STAHL
Logistics Support Unit _____

I was with Force Logistics Support Group Alpha, at Phu
Bai, all ready to go home, when I decided to extend my tour
of duty. I wanted to get in a little excitement before I went
home. They sent me to Danang to pick up my orders, and
they in turn sent me to Khe Sanh on a courier run. I was to
stay at Khe Sanh to replace a communicator who had
rotated.

I got back to Phu Bai that morning, but it was the
afternoon before I eventually managed to get aboard a
CH-53 that was making a late run to Khe Sanh via Dong Ha
to pick up and deliver some essential artillery part. The part
wasn't ready, so we sat at Dong Ha for hours, waiting.
Then, just before dusk, they decided to go ahead and make
the run into Khe Sanh.

We were way up high, and then the CH-53 began to spiral
down. All of a sudden, I saw this landscape. We had been
flying in over dense vegetation, and suddenly we came over
a red plain. It was late afternoon, very sinister, and very
dark. It was also very quiet; we didn't take a single round.
There were large holes in the ground, and no one was
moving about. It was forbidding. The crew expected to get
shot at. The gunners were looking out over their guns. The
helicopter was spiraling in; I could hear it whistling down
through the air.

I had been briefed: when they opened the door I had to
get the hell out. I jumped out, but I had no idea where to
go. Two seconds later, the chopper took off. I couldn't find
a hole to jump into. All I could see was the air terminal. It
was aboveground, all sandbagged. It was stone silent. It was
eerie.

I had been a sort of professional courier for Force Logistics
Support Group Alpha for six months. I had been hopping in
and out of places worse than this appeared. But this was so

much bigger, and *quiet*. I was the only man I could see. I worried that I was facing a bunch of trigger-happy nuts.

As I began to walk, a couple of guys popped out of the ground. I asked where the Logistics Support Unit was, but they said they didn't know and then went on their own way. It was getting quite dark. Everything had wire around it. Only the roads were clear. I couldn't walk in a straight line because of the wire; I had to stick to the roads. There were little units here and there, hooches piled over with rubble, all kinds of crap. So there I was, walking along through my conception of hell. I began to realize that there were people around, but I couldn't really see any. It was like being alone, way out in the country, except there were no crickets chirping. I could hear my own feet pounding on the roadway.

I happened to be walking south or southeast when I saw boxes stacked up near a big hexagonal concrete bunker. I was looking for a supply unit, so I headed for the boxes. A couple of guys were near the boxes, so I asked them where the Logistics Support Unit was. They motioned me toward the concrete bunker.

The next shocker for me was when I threw back the poncho on the bunker door and broke through all the silence and eeriness outside. The lights were on, music was playing, there was a guy running the switchboard, and a few guys were sleeping in their racks. It was a whole different world inside there.

FEBRUARY 23
WATER DETAIL

Pfc ROBERT HARRISON
Alpha Company, 1/26 (Hill 950) _____

By February 22, our platoon outpost had been unable to get resupplied for over a week, and our water supply was nearly exhausted. I do not recall anyone being overly concerned, because of the large amount of C-rations we had on hand. Without water we could not shave and we could not have coffee. I do not consider this life threatening, and that is the way I felt at the time.

Our platoon commander, 1stLt Maxie Williams, radioed for and received permission from Battalion to send a detail out for water. Lieutenant Williams ordered Sergeant Zeiss to select a fire team from each squad, plus an M-60 machine-gun team, for the water detail. This meant that there would be about fifteen men for the detail. There was a feeling of apprehension mixed with excitement. No one questioned the order, but we did discuss it among ourselves. We came to the conclusion that the chances of making it down the hill undetected were not very good. If we were cut off from the hilltop position, rescue would be out of the question due to the fog and the lack of any sizable force close by.

I awoke in my bunker the morning of February 23 and got ready for the patrol—checked my rifle, magazine, ammo, etc. I stepped out of the bunker and noticed that the weather was still miserable, cold, and foggy. Visibility was about five meters.

Everyone on the detail wore a pack filled with empty canteens. We started to file out of the barbed-wire perimeter, trying to be as quiet as we could, but that was asking the impossible. Everyone kept catching clothes and equipment on the barbed wire, creating a lot of noise.

I watched as the point element moved out and disappeared into the jungle. The hill was covered by triple-canopy rain forest, so we were in dense foliage as soon as we cleared the perimeter. It was very muddy, and guys kept falling down, making a lot of noise. I kept thinking to myself, I hope the gooks aren't watching this trail. If they are, we've had it. One thing in our favor was the fog; it helped conceal our movement. It finally came my turn to move through the wire. I was the last man in the column, "tail-end Charlie." Sergeant Zeiss and the machine-gun team were toward the middle of the column and Cpl Thomas Birch's fire team was walking point.

The footing was difficult due to the muddy conditions. Guys kept falling down and making noise. Pfc Tony Weaver was in front of me. He turned around, looked at me, then rolled his eyes. I smiled and shrugged my shoulders. We continued to move down the trail. I turned around occasionally to check the rear of the column. Walking "tail-end Charlie" made me kind of nervous as to what was behind me, but it was not as bad as walking point. One thing that surprised me about the jungle was that it was quiet. There were no real animal sounds like you hear in movies. I guess the bombing and other activity around Khe Sanh scared off most of the wildlife.

I think we had gone about 200 meters when the pointman heard someone cough. He looked over to where the sound had come from and there stood close to a dozen NVA in a circle, shooting the breeze. As soon as he saw them, he opened fire with his M-16 and dropped a few of them. The rest of the NVA took cover and started to return fire. Corporal Birch was hit during the first moments of the fire fight. As soon as the firing broke out, the guys in front of me started to run down the trail. I followed as quickly as I could. Sergeant Zeiss was yelling to form on line. Everyone was in the prone position when Zeiss ordered, "Right front. Fire." Visibility was not too good due to the jungle growth and fog. I pointed my rifle in the general direction and began firing. I think the firing lasted three or four minutes. We finally gained fire superiority and were able to kill the rest of the NVA. The return fire slacked off and finally ended. Sergeant Zeiss ordered cease-fire.

Someone yelled, "Corpsman, up," but it was already too late for Corporal Birch. He had died in the first moments of the fire fight. Sergeant Zeiss ordered Corporal Brockway to send one of his men to help with Birch's body. I volunteered to go. I moved down the hill toward the point element. When I got there, I gave my rifle to the corpsman, Doc Richards, an ex-hippie from San Francisco. There were four of us to carry Birch's body. By the time I got there, Sergeant Zeiss had decided to try to get back within the perimeter as soon as possible. All thought of obtaining water was abandoned.

Sergeant Zeiss was on the radio to the platoon command post. He informed them of the contact and that we were returning to the hilltop position. The squad formed up on the trail and began to move out. We didn't mess with the NVA bodies by looking for souvenirs. That should tell how much of a hurry we were in. We started back up the trail we had come down. Some more firing broke out behind us, but it soon stopped. I don't know what that was all about.

Going back up the hill was worse than going down. We kept dropping the body due to the muddy conditions. I was carrying Birch by the arms and shoulder. Once I lost my grip and his head hit a large rock. I thought to myself, "That must have really hurt." Then I realized how dumb that was.

I kept thinking that we would be mortared, but it never happened. I was totally exhausted by the time we made the perimeter. Some guys came down from the trenchline and carried Birch the rest of the way in. We got through the barbed wire and into the trenchline with the rest of the platoon. Everyone was soaked and covered with mud. We took off our packs with the empty canteens in them. I got a surprise when I took mine off; there was a bullet hole through it—in one side of the pack and out the other. I hadn't even felt it.

We wrapped Corporal Birch's body in a poncho and put it in the ammo bunker. Lieutenant Williams seemed pleased with the kill ratio, but I considered the patrol a near disaster, and I think some of the other guys did, too. We did not really discuss the patrol among ourselves other than to say that we were lucky to make it back. I believe we did not want to make it seem like Corporal Birch had died for nothing, even though we failed to collect the water. The weather cleared three or four days after the patrol, making it possible for us to be resupplied. One thing is certain: no one died from thirst.

☐

RECORD INCOMING

1stLt FRED McGRATH
Bravo Battery, 1/13 _____

The sound of incoming is like no other in the world. We had ample opportunities to hear it, learn it, adjust to it, and finally to live with it. From descriptions of battles from World War II and Korea, we at Khe Sanh got an inkling of what our fathers experienced. It was a constant reminder that even though we were in a very picturesque mountain valley, somebody did not want us there. There were a lot of men who had fears of dying. And there were plenty of chances. Like the day and night the base took over 1,300 rounds of incoming.

HN ROD DeMOSS
26th Marines Regimental Aid Station _____

Another corpsman and I were topside at the entrance to our bunker,talking with a couple of guys across the road, when we heard *boomp*. We went below and soon we heard the round hit close. The two guys we had been talking to took a direct hit. All that was left was pieces of two bodies.

Cpl DENNIS SMITH
Bravo Company, 1/26 _____

First Lieutenant Kim Johnson was our 1st Battalion supply officer. He was handsome, even with glasses, tall, articulate, a practicing Mormon married to a former Miss Arizona who was going to school in Hawaii while she awaited his return. He had the option of running the supply end of things at Phu Bai—the battalion rear—but he sent his gunnery sergeant there instead so he could remain with his men. The guys at battalion supply noticed the funny underwear he wore—lower-body armor. He referred to it as "anti-mortar and -rocket skivvies." He would have quiet religious discussions with his men from time to time. They loved him.

The last week of February was the peak of the siege. On February 23 we absorbed the record for the whole siege— [1,307] rockets and artillery rounds in a 24-hour period. That afternoon, during the scariest barrage of rockets imaginable, LCpl James Jesse and I were in our house, hugging the sandbags, quietly acknowledging the absolute fear in each other's eyes. The explosions were constant as they mounted to a crescendo of head-splitting, knee-knocking sound. I can't adequately describe the terror I felt that afternoon. We should have been used to this, right?

Lieutenant Johnson was in his bunker, not far from mine, along with the battalion motor-transport officer. An explosion that knocked Jesse and me off our butts was a direct hit on the lieutenants' hooch. I looked out and saw the battalion supply men scrambling out of their holes, so, over Jesse's protests, I ran across the road to help. The supplymen all yelled at me, "Get back. We'll handle it. Go on!" There were four or five guys there already, throwing boards and sandbags aside like madmen, machines, so I went back. During the next lull, one of the supplymen came over to our hooch. He was the picture of dejection and despair. He told us that Lieutenant Johnson was dead from a broken back. There were no other visible wounds. The motor-transport officer had been carried to the aid station; his legs looked so bad that everyone thought he'd lose them.

When the supplyman left, I just sat there staring. Something inside me had snapped. Jesse said, "Smitty, you're pale and you're shaking. Have a Salem." Right there, I started up a four-pack-a-day habit. The incoming did not stop, but it became a little more irregular. I was still sitting and staring when my eyes went to a little leatherbound Bible I kept on a shelf. On an impulse, I flipped it open with my right index finger. I was numbly looking at the 91st Psalm, verse five. Then verses six and seven. I was not feeling any comfort. All I could think was, Why the lieutenant? Why *him*?

They had told us in boot camp not to make friends with anyone we went into combat with because if he was wasted you ran the risk of coming unglued and losing your battle effectiveness. Good advice, but impossible to follow. We depended on each other too much not to become friends.

Maj TOM COOK
26th Marines Assistant Logistics Officer _____

One of the incoming rounds hit the ammo dump and created a low-order explosion that set the dump on fire. The fire kept getting hotter and hotter, and finally the dump blew. I saw all that stuff going up in the air. It was one of the most amazing sights I had seen in my life, all those mortar rounds, hand grenades—you name it—just going up into the

sky. I stood there and watched, totally amazed. Then it
suddenly occurred to me that all that stuff was going to
come back down. As a matter of fact, it had already started
back down. I was about twenty or thirty yards from a
bunker. I took off running and just barely got in there when
I started hearing all that stuff hitting the ground. It blew
mortar rounds a mile from the dump. A helicopter pilot who
happened to be flying near Hill 881S at the time told me that
he thought it was an atomic blast because there was a
1,400-foot fireball.

26th Marines Command Chronology _____

> Enemy incoming caused a fire in ASP-1. Fire equipment
> responded, but at 1705, the ammo began to cook off. The
> fire destroyed 1,000 rounds of 90mm high explosive, 500
> rounds of 106mm Beehive, and 120 rounds of 90mm
> canister ammunition.

Maj TOM COOK
26th Marines Assistant Logistics Officer _____

We had to have EOD people come up from Danang and
clean the whole thing up. It was a mess. It made my job a
little tougher, too, because I had to get all that stuff
inventoried and reordered.

Pfc LIONEL TRUFANT
106mm Platoon, 3/26 _____

The rounds just kept coming in, kept coming in. There was
such a concentration of artillery hitting us! Usually, when
artillery came in, we just sat in our living bunker and played
cards. We just played chicken with the regular incoming,
sitting in the living bunker. When it got real heavy, we
would usually jump into the trenchline, which was a smaller
target. But that particular day, it was coming in so heavy
that three of us hid out in the machine-gun bunker, which
was tiny. We were just hugging the ground, afraid. I had
never smoked in my life, but that day I did. I did a lot of
praying, too.

Every once in a while, one of us had to stand up and look out to make sure Charlie wasn't coming. We *knew* this was Dienbienphu. This was the day. One time, when I was looking out of the hole, a round came in real close. Dirt and rocks and stuff pounded me right in the face. I thought I was hit. I felt my face and thought aloud, "Oh God, I'm hit." One of my buddies thought it was comical. "Damn," he said, "you ain't hit."

HN ROD DeMOSS
26th Marines Regimental Aid Station _____

Two Marines escorted a gunnery sergeant into the regimental aid station. He came in shaking, wouldn't talk, had both hands holding his helmet down on his head, and every time a round hit he would shake. He was, of course, suffering from shell shock, but it surprised me because here was this tough Marine gunnery sergeant—been through all kinds of shit—and this makes him crack. I realized then that shell shock can happen to anybody.

Lt RAY STUBBE
1/26 Battalion Chaplain _____

[DIARY ENTRY] Went by the new operating-room bunker, visiting all the wounded who kept coming in during the afternoon. One had a blast wound on his foot. He was in bad pain, even with morphine. Another said his legs hurt no matter where he put them. He was also in intense pain and was given an injection of morphine, but it still hurt him. The doctor said it was broken and would continue to hurt.

More and more incoming.

The 106mm recoilless rifle bunker near us, where I had slept on February 8, took a direct hit, and the trench adjacent to it, injuring one and killing four. I ran down there, through the internal barbed wire, with the Catholic chaplain. There were pieces of arms and bodies. One had no head; we couldn't find it. There were small pieces off flesh all over the place. I knew them all intimately. . . . I took this very hard, but couldn't cry. Parts of one man's body hung out as I held him in my arms, carrying him into the ambulance. A hand, an arm, a stringy piece of flesh intertwined with cloth and caked with mud. The 106mm recoilless rifle was completely untouched.

Returned to my bunker. The west wall, by my rack, was protruding in like it would collapse on my rack. Things inside had shifted.

We had taken in the following incoming today: 476 rounds of artillery, 42 rounds of 60mm, 372 rounds of 82mm, four rounds of 120mm, 437 rounds of 122mm, and five rounds of recoilless rifle. Total, 1,313. But Lieutenant Colonel Wilkinson reported (from the regimental briefing) a total of 1,407 rounds. Major Smith, CO of FOB-3, told me we had received 1,700 rounds of incoming, counting those that landed in his area.

1stLt FRED McGRATH
Bravo Battery, 1/13 _____

It was fortunate that the NVA gunners were short of fuses, because many rounds would have done considerably more damage if they had exploded. The rounds that were not fused were particularly eerie. They whistled. We knew they would not explode, but when they hit, they were like wrecking balls. No shrapnel damage, but what a hole! As it was, they dug up a lot of dirt and nothing more. When EOD dug them up, they found the lift lugs still in the rounds.

Bravo Battery pumped out over 1,250 rounds in reply. Bravo was really a battery and a half. That is, we controlled six 105mm howitzers of our own and three from Charlie Battery. So we combined our assets and created a nine-gun battery. During that very busy day and night, I had, at various times, five separate and distinct fire missions going simultaneously. To the everlasting credit of the Marine gunners on the line, they never missed a command or fired the wrong missions. In fact, Colonel Lownds personally came to our position the next day and thanked every Marine in the position for the superb fire support his regiment had received.

HN ROD DeMOSS
26th Marines Regimental Aid Station _____

One of my more gruesome duties was identifying and tagging bodies to be sent back home. I kept thinking to myself, This could be me. I was thankful it wasn't, but I felt bad because I knew this was someone who had a family or friend who would grieve over him, someone who had a girlfriend or wife back home. All I could do, though, was zip up the bag and try to make it through without ending up like that.

FEBRUARY 24

Capt EARLE BREEDING
Echo Company, 2/26 (Hill 861A) _____

They never stopped pecking away at us. It seemed like someone got hurt every time a round landed. On February 24, a Marine was out working on the wire when a mortar round came in and got him. LCpl Max Nelson, one of my radio operators, went out with the corpsman to pull the guy out of the wire. The next round got them. Then my exec, 2ndLt Ferdinando DiStefano, went out to pull Max out of the wire. The third round got him. The NVA always fired in threes. They should have known better. The first Marine died and Nelson and DiStefano were killed instantly, though there wasn't a mark on Max. The corpsman was badly wounded, but he survived. Another Marine was killed in another incident later that day. That's four KIAs just in one day.

Chapter 6

FEBRUARY 25
AMBUSH

2ndLt SKIP WELLS
Charlie Company, 1/26 _____

At first, we patrolled daily to keep the NVA from getting right on top of us and to cover the completion of the defensive wire and minefields. I can still recall putting up the last (outside) row of tanglefoot and double apron one afternoon under artillery and mortar fire.

We, and every other unit, took casualties during these daily patrols, and they were cause for a lot of soul-searching every third night before our patrol. But they did do what they were supposed to do. The NVA were not able to establish any real close-in positions.

Then in early February, the company commander told us that we would not run any more patrols, "on orders form Saigon." It was explained that the casualties were wearing us down and that the supporting arms were going to cover us. Even as a boot second lieutenant, I knew that was bullshit and that we would pay for it later.

MGen TOMMY TOMKINS
3rd Marine Division Commanding General _____

General Westmoreland has been criticized for tying the Marines at Khe Sanh to their perimeters. It wasn't Westmoreland, it was me. I told them that 500 meters was the absolute max. Five hundred meters, and no more. My whole plan for the defense of Khe Sanh was to make the enemy come to us.[1]

LtCol JIM WILKINSON
1/26 Commanding Officer _____

We never really stopped patrolling. We only curtailed the distance of the patrols. They had to be in visual contact with the perimeter line.

2ndLt SKIP WELLS
Charlie Company, 1/26 _____

The new Charlie Company commander called me to the command-post bunker about 1800, February 24, and gave me the order for a patrol we were to take out the next day in coordination with one from Bravo Company on the south side of the perimeter. The order was specific: only two squads with one machine-gun team. Bravo was to go at 0900 and we were to go at 1100. They would go south, then west, while we would go east of the east end of the airstrip and then south. The reason for the patrol was obvious. The NVA had closed in and constructed their own trenchlines, especially to the south and east. The position appeared to be the classic assault position.

We didn't have much time to get ready for that patrol. I picked the two squads and a machine-gun team based on who I felt was the best. I knew it would be a bad one and wrote a letter to my wife—in case. I tried to hide my feelings about the patrol, but I think they all knew it could be bad.

Capt KEN PIPES
Bravo Company, 1/26 _____

The NVA had several 60mm mortars fairly close to our lines that were dropping heavy on us. We figured the mortars were out along the access road that ran south and southeast in front of part of our company position on its way to the old garbage dump. We kept sending platoon patrols out to look for the mortars, but nothing turned up. We had to send patrols because the ground out there was rolling, undulating, and there was still plenty of high elephant grass. The B-52 strikes had burned off the grass and brush farther out, but we had a dead zone several hundred meters wide, beginning right outside our wire. We couldn't observe the mortars from our lines; we had to send people out to look for them. Second Lieutenant John Dillon led Bravo Company's 2nd Platoon out to look on February 23, but no contact was made and nothing unusual was observed.

Two heavily reinforced squads of Bravo Company's 3rd Platoon, about forty-three Marines commanded by 2ndLt. Don Jacques, were assigned to go back out on February 25 to try to find the mortars. When I briefed Don on the evening of February 24, I identified three checkpoints at which he was to call in to report. Most of his route would keep him under observation from the combat base, but he was sure to get out of sight a few times in that undulating ground. The idea was to make a quick sweep to find the NVA 60mm mortars and get right back into the perimeter near the FOB-3 sector. The patrol route was to be from the southeast corner of the base westward to the southwest sector, right in front of the Gray Sector.

LtCol JIM WILKINSON
1/26 Commanding Officer _____

All our patrols were carefully plotted in as to route and everything was approved by Regiment, including our fire-support plan in case the patrol ran into anything. The Bravo Company patrol was to follow a diamond-shaped route— Point A to Point B to Point C and then back in.

Cpl GILBERT WALL
81mm Mortar Platoon, 1/26 _____

The day started with me at Bravo Company's 2nd Platoon area. The 2nd Platoon commander, Lieutenant Dillon, told me to go to the 3rd Platoon command post, that I would be going out on patrol.

When I arrived, Lieutenant Jacques came out of his bunker and invited me in for breakfast and some coffee. Lieutenant Jacques and I had been to many patrols together and knew each other pretty well. He introduced me to the new platoon sergeant, a staff sergeant who asked me to call him Mac. I thanked them and started making jokes about them having such a late breakfast, because I had eaten hours ago. I started talking to some of the Marines on the line. Some I knew, but many were new.

Everybody was in a surprisingly good mood. They all were happy, loose, and relaxed. It was a nice day, and just to move out of base for a while gave me a good feeling.

I checked my gear. I had twenty-five M-16 magazines and nine hand grenades. Then I looked over my map and, following that, had my radioman get a radio check. Then I looked out at the area we would be patrolling. I knew the area very well because we had run many patrols there before.

Capt JIM LESLIE
26th Marines Assistant Communicator _____

Bravo Company had a platoon ready to sweep the perimeter as daylight was breaking. Our bunker was 20 meters inside the barbed concertina wire and I was going through my morning routine of washing my face and brushing my teeth on the pile of sandbags outside. I had a radio there so I could listen in on routine conversation. I switched the channel to Captain Pipes's frequency so I could monitor the station for any communication problems. The morning air was extremely heavy with fog, and I could barely see past our perimeter wire, which was only 20 meters away. I heard Captain Pipes request a delay in kicking off the sweep as the ground fog had not lifted. However, his battalion commander told him he had to get moving because they had coordinated artillery fire. Captain Pipes again requested a delay, but it was denied.

As the wind blew the fog around, I was able to catch glimpses of Marines as they slowly moved across the side of the hill between the Frenchman's plantation and our perimeter.

Cpl GILBERT WALL
81mm Mortar Platoon, 1/26 _____

We went out the south gate by the trash dump and moved down along the NVA trenches. Although I knew the NVA were watching us, I was still very relaxed. While we were walking along the trenches, I pinpointed them on my map for future use.

We followed the trench until it came to an end, then headed south away from the base. It was open—no cover at all—but the NVA never fired any mortars or sniped at us. We moved hundreds of meters away from the base.

I was a few meters behind the platoon radioman as we got closer to the treeline at the top of the hill. As the point and his backup moved for the treeline, two NVA jumped up and started running down the road. The Marines on the front were talking fast and loud; they looked confused.

Capt KEN PIPES
Bravo Company, 1/26 _____

I heard Don Jacques report that he had spotted two or three NVA and that he wanted to try to capture them. I wasn't sure at the time, but I had the impression that, by then, the patrol was quite far from its assigned route. If that was the case, I realized, then chasing the three NVA would take it even farther beyond supporting range, maybe as far as 700 meters from our wire.

Cpl GILBERT WALL
81mm Mortar Platoon, 1/26 _____

Lieutenant Jacques ended the confusion by shouting, "Let's go get them!" His pistol was in the air and his hand fell forward to signal "Charge!" Then he turned and looked at me and we both smiled at the same time. It was as if the same thought went through our minds: This is what we want.

We started moving after the two NVA, and the firing began. The Marines who went to the woods first were with the platoon sergeant. The NVA put some heavy fire on them.

Capt JIM LESLIE
26th Marines Assistant Communicator _____

All of a sudden, all hell broke loose with small-arms fire. My radio was buzzing with conversation. Someone reported, "We are taking heavy casualties."

Capt KEN PIPES
Bravo Company, 1/26 _____

They were ambushed. They walked into it, and it built quite suddenly.

1stLt ERNIE SPENCER
1/26 Intelligence Officer _____

I heard the whole thing on the radio. After Bravo took four casualties, I recommended that they get their dead and get out. They tried to fight. Attack.[2]

Cpl GILBERT WALL
81mm Mortar Platoon, 1/26 _____

Lieutenant Jacques and I went with a squad to the left of a little road that came out of the treeline. Marines were getting hit or taking cover as we moved between the trees.

I moved ahead of Lieutenant Jacques and to the left of the squad. Some Marines were moving on my left when the NVA opened up on us. We were right in front of the NVA trenches and bunkers. The air was filled with screaming, shouting, gunfire, and blood.

I hit the ground, looked at the NVA trenches, and started to return fire. Then I ran toward a large tree to my left. They were very close—close enough that I could see their faces clearly.

We were putting some heavy fire out. I took out my map to call a fire mission with the 81s. I wanted to call the mission in front of the squad that had gotten hit first. The visibility was bad because of the weather, but that was not my problem. The trees that were between us and the squad, which was on my right, directly in front of their trenches, were the real problem. I was confused; I didn't know where all the Marines were. I wanted to call the mission, but I was afraid of hitting my own people. I didn't want to get careless.

When my first round landed, I could not see it, but I heard it. Between ducking and returning fire with my M-16, I couldn't place exactly where my round hit. I checked the map and found grids I wanted; I was going to go with white phosphorus, but I changed my mind. I ordered a repeat. Then I couldn't even move because I was under too much fire; I was pinned behind the tree.

Suddenly a Marine was telling me to pull back. He opened fire along with the Marine to my left, and that took the fire off me. I moved back and to the right.

Marines were wounded and screaming for help everywhere. My second round had landed, I guess, in front of the Marines but behind the NVA trenches. I couldn't see it. I made a correction to move the 81s in front of us. Then the fight to my right stopped. I looked up. All the marines were dead.

Capt KEN PIPES
Bravo Company, 1/26 _____

Don Jacques had joined the company in December and had done very well in his first action, when his platoon had ambushed an NVA recon unit. He was learning how to lead troops, and his patrol included the company's most experienced platoon sergeant, SSgt George McClelland, and the most experienced squad leader, Cpl Kenneth Claire. From what we pieced together later, Corporal Claire immediately led his squad in an attempt to envelop the NVA ambush. However, as soon as the squad moved, it ran into even heavier fire coming from behind it. Corporal Claire and most of his men were killed. I told Don to disengage and get back to the perimeter the best way he could.

The minute the ambush closed, I requested permission from Battalion to send 2ndLt Peter Weise's 1st Platoon as a reaction force. Pete moved toward the wire between FOB-3 and the western edge of the Bravo Company sector. However, just as the 1st Platoon reached the Route 9 access road, it was subjected to extremely heavy small-arms, RPG, mortar, and machine-gun fire. Pete couldn't advance, but he was able to maintain his position about 50 meters outside the wire. From my observation post I could see that the NVA had preplanned—but had not fired in—60mm and 82mm mortar concentrations in the general area of the 1st Platoon's position. Several barrages from at least six mortars fell on the 1st Platoon position, but the platoon was able to maintain its position and provide covering fire for the proposed withdrawal of the 3rd Platoon patrol.

1stLt ERNIE SPENCER
1/26 Intelligence Officer _____

Bravo sent out another platoon to assist. It got chewed up by concentrated mortar fire from [the NVA]. Marines died trying to save dying Marines. That is our way. It separates us from everyone else. A Marine likes to know that someone will try to get to him, if he's down and can't get himself out. That's what Bravo Company tried. . . .[3]

Capt JIM LESLIE
26th Marines Assistant Communicator _____

I could see Marines running and falling, and corpsmen running, and stretchers flying. Men were screaming with pain. I didn't know what to do. I could not help as the area between our wire and the Marines fifty yards away was heavily mined. As some of the Marines crawled toward the fence, others were helping. I followed their path and helped some back to safety. I couldn't believe I was witnessing this massacre that close to our lines.

Capt KEN PIPES
Bravo Company, 1/26 _____

I requested assistance from our tanks and Ontos, and permission was granted. They provided excellent firepower, but their visibility was limited by the rolling terrain. I then asked that another company move out to break up the NVA ambush and blocking positions as well as to recover our WIAs and KIAs. This request was denied. I was extremely bitter at the time the denial came, but later reflection convinced me that this was a wise decision.

LtCol JIM WILKINSON
1/26 Commanding Officer _____

Had I based a decision to relieve them purely on emotion, pride, and guilt, I would not only have sent a unit out, I would have *led* it. I thought about grabbing some people, racing out there, and saving those Marines. But I decided, based on radio reports, that the heaviest casualties had already been inflicted and that, from a military commander's point of view, my mission was to protect Khe Sanh Combat Base. I was well aware of many episodes in Vietnam where commanders had sent a squad out to save a fire team, then a platoon to save the squad, then a company to save the platoon, and finally a whole battalion to save the company— all at enormous expense in killed and wounded Marines. It was a tough decision, not based on emotion. It was a hard decision.

Capt KEN PIPES
Bravo Company, 1/26 _____

My company artillery forward observer, 1stLt Hank Norman, and the artillery aerial observer overhead worked hard to get suppressive fire on the ambush site and suspected NVA mortar positions, and the 81mm forward observer with

Don Jacques, Cpl Gilbert Wall, also called in fire missions.
These fires, along with our own .50-caliber machine guns,
106mm recoilless rifles, and 60mm mortars undoubtedly
inflicted friendly casualties, but I feel it enabled the 3rd
Platoon patrol to break contact and return toward our wire.
In addition, the aerial observer controlled air strikes consisting
of napalm and rockets.

1stLt ERNIE SPENCER
1/26 Intelligence Officer _____

After hearing the radio reports from the patrol and the
backup platoon, we know only that we have taken a big hit
and that we are still taking. Charlie is now sending mortar
fire inside the wire. It is as though we are walking through a
tunnel. J.B. [LtCol Jim Wilkinson] and I are out in the
open, jumping over the trenchlines, but the doom that hangs
around us forms a tunnel that encloses and guides us to the
spectacle of the slaughter still going on.[4]

Cpl Gilbert Wall
81mm Mortar Platoon, 1/26 _____

I couldn't believe how many NVA were there. I threw a
grenade in their trench and killed three, but they filled the
spot in no time. The more we killed and got killed, the more
they came.

The screaming and shouting was so loud I couldn't hear
my own voice. I was terrified. I could see clearly the deep
trouble we were in. We just didn't have enough men to
match their firepower.

My third round landed. I didn't see it, but I heard it very
close and knew it had to be behind the NVA trenches, so I
decided to move it closer to us.

The Marine to my right got hit. My radioman, who was
behind a tree a few meters to my rear, put out a whole
magazine as I went for the wounded Marine. I bandaged the
wounded Marine and then moved back to the tree up front
on the left.

I was pinned. They were chewing the bark and I could

hear the bullets cracking the tree. I put my rifle around the tree and kept firing blindly. My rifle jammed, so I took the round out of the chamber. It fired three times and jammed again.

Some Marines moved to my left and took the fire off me. I looked around the tree. An NVA was looking at me. I shot him in the face. Then I turned left and noticed the Marine next to me had his ass in the air and his face in the ground. I reached over and pulled him. He was shot in the face. They had blown out the back of his head. I took his rifle and threw mine away. I was running out of ammo. A Marine showed up by the mound and asked me for some grenades. I gave him three.

I was told by Lieutenant Jacques to go back down a little hill. I jumped up and ran to him while the Marine was throwing the grenades. I told Lieutenant Jacques that I wanted to move the fire mission to their trench. The response I got was to pull back, get out of here, take the wounded, and leave the dead ones! "Chief," he told me, "get out of here. Every man for himself." Then Lieutenant Jacques started running up by the other Marines while he was shooting an M-79 at bunkers.

As another Marine and I fired, Lieutenant Jacques and the others ran out of the treeline. Then the other Marine took off, hollering, "Come on, let's get out of here." I started running to the left, through the trees, until I hit the road we had come in from originally. The NVA were firing at me constantly, but a little too high, which saved me.

I picked up two boxes of M-60 ammo when I started going down the little road. I was the last Marine to come out of the treeline. I could see the other Marines running down the hill. Some were helping the wounded and others were on their own.

As I moved out in the open area and started going down the hill, I heard a Marine calling me. He sounded very scared. He was lying by a tree. I guess he thought all the Marines were gone and he was left there all alone. He could see all the Marines running down the hill, and when he saw me running too, he got terrified and started screaming, "Marine, Marine, help me!"

I turned around and ran back for him. Just seeing me coming toward him brought a look of relief to his face. He was hurt badly, shot in three places, so I picked him up and started running down the hill. I was carrying the wounded Marine with one hand and firing blindly at the NVA bunkers with the other hand. In no time at all, the magazine was finished. I was out of ammo. Two Marines came running back to help us. They gave me some ammo and the wounded Marine's rifle, and took him with them.

For a while I was walking backwards and firing both rifles at the same time—until the magazines were finished. I returned one of the rifles to one of the Marines, reloaded the other one, and kept shooting while we moved slowly down the hill. I believe that my radioman and I, the two other Marines, and the wounded Marine were the last ones headed for the base.

By the time we got to the rice paddy at the bottom of the hill, some other Marines were halfway up the other side and some were still trying to move the wounded over the rice paddy. We waited for them to pass by and then got moving again.

Although we were not under fire at this time, the loud noise of continuous shooting never stopped. That was because the 1st Platoon was trying to come out and help us, but had walked into an ambush on the top of the hill by the base.

We were feeling a little relief because we were getting closer to the base when the Marines behind us ran into another ambush as they entered another treeline. We were all under their fire again.

Right in the middle of all the banana trees and high grass, there was this circular open area in which we were trapped. Bullets were flying all over the place. The cracking sound of AK-47s and M-16s was all I could hear. Wounded Marines were all I could see. The odor of blood and fresh grass was all I could smell.

I thought of calling a fire mission, so I lay down on my stomach to get the map out and realized that I had lost it. The fire mission was out of the question. The bullets were cutting the big leaves above my head to pieces. Everyone

was lying there, dead or wounded. There was no time to be
afraid of death.

I was still on the ground when I noticed a Marine who
was shot in the chest, wounded real bad. He was moaning
and obviously in deep pain. I reached him and put a
bandage on his chest, but he was bleeding too much and the
bandage didn't do much. I knew there was not much more I
could do for him. He was dying.

I saw Lieutenant Jacques, shot in the groin, lying on the
ground. I reached over and started putting a bandage on his
wide-open wound. All the blood went through the bandage
and ran down my fingers. He was hurt very bad and I
couldn't do anything more to stop the bleeding. He was
trying to talk to me, but I couldn't understand him. That
was when a couple of bullets hit my flak jacket on the
shoulder and knocked me on my ass. Another bullet went
between my arm and my ribs and left a hole in my sleeve.

Capt KEN PIPES
Bravo Company, 1/26 _____

Though I ordered the patrol to break contact and provided
what assistance I could, they could not move. As the action
continued to build, it became apparent that the survivors
would have to return singly or in pairs. As they left, Don
Jacques was hit in both femoral arteries. Don called me on
the radio to ask, "Why in the hell aren't you doing something to help us? Why are you leaving us out here to die?"

Cpl GILBERT WALL
81mm Mortar Platoon, 1/26 _____

I started moving Lieutenant Jacques to a safer place, where
there were not that many bullets flying in the air. I moved
him behind a small mound of dirt. Uselessly, I tried once
again to stop the bleeding, but soon I noticed a change in
the color of his face. It was turning white. His head fell
back, his eyes rolled back, and he died.

By this time, 1st Platoon had broken the NVA line and
was in our area. The shooting had stopped and the fight was

over. Marines came and took Lieutenant Jacques and the other wounded and dead bodies back to the base.

2ndLt SKIP WELLS
Charlie Company, 1/26 _____

We heard the fight start over the Bravo tactical net, which we monitored so we would have an idea what was going on. From the talk on the net, I knew they were in deep trouble. I didn't hear Lieutenant Jacques on the net, so I figured he had been hurt.

We moved through the trenchlines to just south of the airstrip, to where we were to move through the wire to the east. By 1100, when we started out from the airstrip, the Bravo patrol was already in very bad trouble. We had to use fire-and-movement tactics just to get through the gate in the wire. We had to leapfrog squads, then fire teams, to get outside the wire, and I had to call back for more machine-gun ammo before we even got out. Just as we were about to move farther east, I got the word on the radio to "get back inside the wire." As we were just about stopped anyway, it took a while to get enough fire out to move back. But, as we never got closer than about fifty yards to the first NVA trench or positions, we were able to get back. Also, we were still practically tied in to the perimeter, so our rear and right flank were secure. It took us until about dark to get back in.

Capt KEN PIPES
Bravo Company, 1/26 _____

The survivors, most of them wounded, continued to come in for quite a while. In at least one case, 2ndLt Pete Weise, the 1st Platoon commander, went out in front of his platoon position to pull in a wounded machine gunner who couldn't get all the way in by himself.

Cpl GILBERT WALL
81mm Mortar Platoon, 1/26 _____

I was very tired and weak. My jacket and trousers were covered with blood. Flies were all over me. A Marine who was obviously a new boot kept hitting them. He looked like he felt sorry for me and was trying to help. I sat there for a while, thinking about all the Marines we had lost in that fire fight. Then I called Captain Pipes and asked him what he wanted me to do. He asked me to go back to the command post.

Capt JIM LESLIE
26th Marines Assistant Communicator _____

Our portion of the base was in chaos for a couple of hours, with wounded Marines and stretchers everywhere.

HN ROD DeMOSS
26th Marines Regimental Aid Station _____

[The Bravo Company patrol] got led into a trap and was chewed up and spit out by the NVA. We had heavy casualties that day, but what was so bad about it was that a lot of wounded men couldn't make it back on their own. I recall one Marine we were trying to patch up. He kept drawing maps of where some of these wounded were. He couldn't talk because the flesh under his chin was blown away and I think that his tongue was gone, too. This guy had to be in a lot of pain, but his main concern was for the guys who had been left behind. He was one of the heroes. Later that night, we could hear the cries of the ones who couldn't make it back.

Lt RAY STUBBE
1/26 Battalion Chaplain _____

[DIARY ENTRY] The casualties started coming in in pretty bad shape from Bravo Company. A man from 1/26 came to the [Charlie-Med] operating-room bunker with a list of twenty-six MIAs. He was checking to see if any had come to our triage, but there were none. Killed (missing): 27 Marines, including Cpl Kenneth Claire, the man who always used to yell like Tarzan on the hills, who had taken a whole loaf of bread and begun gnawing it like an animal, a man who enjoyed life and made us all happy.

1stLt ERNIE SPENCER
1/26 Intelligence Officer _____

Bravo's command bunker overlooks the entire scene. It is barren, desolate terrain—red dirt with mortars hitting. Marines carrying others, dragging, crawling. This is a live show. This is no fucking Hollywood epic. This is the real thing. Those are Marines getting hit. . . .

As Ken looks back at J.B. and me, his face seems like a mask that is melting. The sorrow flows from his eyes in dry tears that seem to pass out and over his cheeks and chin like wax running down a candle. We stand together beside his bunker as the wounded stream in.

J.B. is crushed. Like a coach who knows· the game's over. His Marines acted like Marines, but they lost one. Big.

J.B. says to me, "Well, Ernie, let's go see the Old Man." We walk out in the open, striding. Oblivious to possible incoming. In the dark, together and alone.

Regimental CO is where he always seems to be. In his bunker. It is the old French bunker. Khe Sanh has a lot of tradition. As superstitious as this guy is, I can just imagine the fucking tripping out he does on that.

J.B. runs down the facts for the CO. . . . Most of one platoon is left out there, status unknown. Relatives of the missing will be told in twenty-four hours. In twenty-four hours the world will know—there are news photographers at the trenchline.

J.B. asks to go out to get his men. Regimental CO tells J.B. that the battalion is needed to defend the airstrip. He is right.[5]

Cpl GILBERT WALL
81mm Mortar Platoon, 1/26 _____

When I got back to the command post, Captain Pipes said that he wanted me to go back on patrol to get our wounded and dead people back to the base. I waited about an hour for them to clear the patrol, but the regimental commander canceled it.

Capt JIM LESLIE
26th Marines Assistant Communicator _____

Later that day, I went over to Captain Pipes's bunker to see how I could help. Pipes was sitting on an ammo box with fresh wrapping on his wounds, his head in both of his hands, tears running down his sleeves. He said, "Why couldn't they wait till the fog lifted? My men. I've lost most of my men."

Colonel Lownds came in, put his arms around Ken, and said, "It's not your fault, son. You did all you could do. There were just too many NVA out there. I didn't realize how many there were, or how close."

I've wondered in retrospect if the NVA might have been monitoring all of our radio conversation and knew exactly when and where and what the Marines were doing every minute while we were there.

2ndLt SKIP WELLS
Charlie Company, 1/26 _____

When I heard about the Bravo patrol, I felt betrayed. It was my first experience of being expendable. The only difference between Jacques's patrol and mine was that he went first.

1stLt JOHN KAHENY
1/26 Combat Operations Center _____

First Lieutenant Walt Chapman, the Commandant's son, who was serving as the Delta Company exec, later told me that orders to leave the bodies out there came from as high as the White House.

Cpl GILBERT WALL
81mm Mortar Platoon, 1/26 _____

The next day, Lieutenant Spencer, the battalion intelligence officer, talked to me. They wanted to know if I knew for sure who got killed. My answer was, "I saw many Marines get killed, but I don't know their names." Lieutenant Colonel Wilkinson asked me, "What happened out there?

Did we have a leadership breakdown?'' I answered, "I don't think so.''

I don't think there is a unit in the world that could have walked into that ambush and done better. We fought good and hard, but we just ran out of men.

Of the forty-three Marines who made up the Jacques patrol, and several dozen in Lieutenant Weise's 1st Platoon who were subjected to intense small-arms and mortar fire, the official tally lists forty-seven casualties: 1 KIA (Lieutenant Jacques), 13 WIA (medevacked), 8 WIA (minor), and 25 MIA.

☐

SIEGEWORKS

26th Marines Command Chronology _____

On February 25, the first sighting of NVA trench systems being dug in toward KSCB was made. As weather cleared, aerial observers were able to pinpoint several more trenches extending to within 100, 50, and 30 meters of the combat base perimeter. The trench systems came generally from the south and southeast. Immediate steps were taken to destroy them with supporting arms.

Capt KEN PIPES
Bravo Company, 1/26 _____

A Bravo Company patrol on February 23 had turned up no evidence of the NVA presence on precisely the same ground as Don Jacque's patrol traversed on February 25, but Don's patrol uncovered numerous trenches, from which the ambush was sprung. Some of the trenches crossed the access road and were about a hundred yards from my lines and those of the 37th ARVN Rangers.

Capt HARRY BAIG
26th Marines Target Information Officer _____

Intelligence conceived that the NVA would conduct a formal
siege in the best traditions of the eighteenth century. They
had learned these tactics at Dienbienphu. At Con Thien,
they had learned something else; namely, that we never
conducted B-52 strikes at ranges less than 3,000 meters,
rarely made [radar-controlled bombing] runs at less than
2,000 meters, and hardly ever fired unobserved, unadjusted
artillery missions less than 1,000 meters from friendly
positions. We knew these things, too. It was obvious,
therefore, that General Giap would attempt to tuck himself
as closely about us as possible for safety's sake (and to
facilitate his construction program). A siege campaign
involves three distinct phases: arrival on the scene and
investment of the fortress; construction of siegeworks and
preparation of supporting facilities; "T-ing" the sapheads
and the final assault.

The Intelligence Section, through intelligence channels,
used every discovery system to develop a picture of enemy
activities. (Ground and aerial observers, aerial photography,
infrared imagery, target lists of higher headquarters, crater
analysis, and shell/flash reports, Spotlight reports [from
Thailand], and signal-intelligence and accurate agent reports—
all these were used to give us an understanding of the
enemy situation.) When compared against the target map
and reasoned against known enemy doctrine in like cases,
the Khe Sanh intelligence community was able to estimate
to a high degree of accuracy the intentions of the enemy on
a day-to-day basis. Colonel Lownds's intimate knowledge of
the terrain around Khe Sanh put a final fillip to the dish that
was served to him daily. Except for the attack on Hill 861A,
the enemy never surprised us—and he should not have done
so then.[6]

Chapter 7

Lt RAY STUBBE
1/26 Battalion Chaplain _____

[DIARY ENTRY] Walked along the Charlie Company lines. A sniper was firing at me while I was in the trenches. Then the soft sound of the "bass drum" began again—rockets were being fired—and I fell into the trench as shrapnel was flying all over the place above the trench where I was, making odd zinging sounds. Eight pallets of land mines at the Shore Party [dump] near me had taken a direct hit and exploded with such force that the shitter at the 1/26 Battalion Air Station was almost demolished by the blast. I felt the fear! I trembled uncontrollably, close to the earth—something I hadn't experienced up to this point.

There were 1,200 enemy rounds today.

Cpl DENNIS MANNION
Charlie Battery, 1/13 (Hill 861) _____

A guy in one of the Kilo Company rifle platoons, LCpl William Huff, made corporal and had to go to Okinawa for

Noncommissioned Officers' School. He left the hill and went into Khe Sanh. As luck would have it, Huff got hit by a rocket while he was running off the chopper that took him down to the combat base.

FEBRUARY 26

Lt RAY STUBBE
1/26 Battalion Chaplain ⎯⎯⎯⎯⎯⎯⎯⎯⎯⎯⎯

[DIARY ENTRY] Returned to Charlie-Med. There were two patients from Echo Company, 2/26, on Hill 861A. One had a head wound, the other will lose his right arm and right leg and possibly will be blind. It was a very ghastly sight— black, charred flesh hanging down from a ripped-open area of the leg, to the bone. The hand was off; the arm was a stump. One corpsman walked to where I was: "I don't want to look at that, but I have to," he said resignedly, and walked back to aid the patient. Bloody clothes, poncho, and bamboo poles that had served as a stretcher were all over the deck.

Walked over to Graves Registration and said prayers over the bodies of Pfc Billy Dale Livingston, from Combined Action Company Oscar, who died while getting out of his bunker to watch rockets being fired from a Huey; he was killed by the shrapnel. And Pvt Ransom Lee Stuck, a man who had seen me before. He was due to be "out" this month, but, owing to "bad time," had to continue to serve here. He had two scholarships.

☆

Capt BILL DABNEY
India Company, 3/26 (Hill 881S) ⎯⎯⎯⎯⎯⎯⎯⎯⎯

For the first two or three weeks, as they fired artillery at us, we didn't get any aerial observation out to the west because they didn't seem to believe us at Khe Sanh. Finally we asked for, and up on a helicopter came, pedestal-mounted binoculars. That gave us significantly improved capability for scoping because, first, it was solidly, rigidly mounted, and second, it was a 20-power system with a good, long-range focus capability—the kind you find on a ship's bridge.

We had on the hill a lance corporal by the name of Molikau Niuatoa, an American Samoan who had come to my attention because he fired, with the M-16, a qualifying score of 241 in boot camp. That's a pretty hellacious score for a brand-new recruit. And if it told us nothing else, it told us he had pretty good eyes. He was also a bull of a man, and an extremely patient fellow. He had the patience of Job, so we assigned him to look to the west through those 20-power binoculars and see if he could figure out where the devil the artillery was coming from. "Do it any way you can!" So, the way he came up with doing it was to pick a spot that looked like it had possibilities of being an artillery position and freeze his eyes on the spot and watch it until the artillery fired. If he did not detect anything in that little area he was looking at when the artillery fired, he'd reject that and move the glass a little bit and watch someplace else until the artillery fired again. And he kept, by that sort of a process of elimination, trying to figure out where the damned stuff was.

That sounds fairly simple, but you're talking about a guy standing with his eyes glued to a naval telescope for ten to fourteen hours a day, depending on what kind of visibility we had, and watching that one spot for that length of time, looking out twelve to fifteen kilometers. Sometimes, for a whole day, the artillery wouldn't fire and he'd just stand there. You had to remember to go up there and give him chow or give him a break so he could take a leak, whatever, because he was just that kind of Marine; he'd just stand there and freeze on that damned thing and watch a spot until something happened or until he rejected it.

On February 26, I got word—I was off in the other end of the trench someplace—that Niuatoa thought he had found something, some artillery had just gone by. I walked over to him and asked him, "What have you got?" And he said, "I think maybe the two things are related." He said, "Every time I'm looking out there and I see a little kind of pinpoint of light and then, fifteen, twenty seconds later, I hear the pop. A few seconds later after that I hear this sound like a squirrel running through dry leaves as the round goes by." And he said, "It only happens when I see the flash and hear the pop, so there must be some relation between the two." I said, "Well, you got a good sight?" And he said, "Yes, sir." I said, "Well, don't lose it, just hang in there." I got on the radio and called down to Khe Sanh and told them we thought we'd found the artillery piece.

They sent up a fellow named O'Toole, who was at the time the artillery observer—the back seat of a spotter plane. "Southern Oscar" was his radio call sign. "Southern" was the call sign for the artillery regiment, "Oscar" was the first initial of the last name of the aerial observer. We had had, throughout the Khe Sanh siege, two of them, a fellow named Happy and a fellow named O'Toole. At any rate, O'Toole came buzzing up there with his pilot in the spotter plane, asking us if we could give him some idea where the stuff was. We gave him the general azimuth and suggested to him that we fire at mid-range, and at max range, one round each from the [two Charlie Battery] 105s we had on the hill, with white phosphorus, so he could get a line, at least for orientation. It was obvious that the 105mm phosphorus round wasn't going to reach this point Niuatoa was looking at. We did so. He found the first 105 round but couldn't find the second round. And there was a lot of danger for the gun crews in standing on that damned hill for any length of time, in the artillery revetments firing the damned stuff casually, because we tended to get 120mm mortars in every time we did that sort of thing. You're liable to lose a gun crew. We'd lost a couple. So we secured that because the aerial observer couldn't find the rounds.

"Look," O'Toole finally said, "somebody believes that we found something, and I've got four flights of A-4s over me. They're going to go bingo fuel in a little while, so we've got to get on with it." And he said, "How about I just take a flight of A-4s and pickle a stick of bombs on the highest ridgeline?"—more or less where we'd been talking to him about. We could see the bombs hit, but we hadn't been able to see his marking rockets or anything. Too far out. Hell, we couldn't even see the airplane! We're talking fifteen kilometers or so out west from us, in Laos. And I'll never forget the first adjustment Niuatoa give me—he was still on the glasses—he said, "Left one kilometer, add two ridgelines!" Major adjustment, but that's the kind of frame of reference we were working with. So we passed that on to O'Toole, he dropped a second string of bombs—more or less the same thing. Niuatoa could see them and he said, "Okay," he said, "drop about halfway down the ridgeline and come left 500 meters." Another fairly major adjustment. We pickled the third string of bombs, and Niuatoa is saying to me in his broken English, "Right below where that last string of bombs dropped, there is a vee of trees, it looks like it is running up a gully." He said, "If they find that vee out there—it is on the east face of the same ridge the bombs just hit—follow it down until the point of the vee. We may have something because that's where I've been seeing this stuff." Well, they did that as best they could, and, apparently, successfully. I couldn't see a damned thing—8-power binoculars wouldn't help a bit. Niuatoa said, "Yes, you got them right where I want them." And about five seconds after that, Southern Oscar was on the phone saying, "Hey, we got something out here!" I asked, "What have you got?" After the last bomb string dropped, a big square hole had opened in the deck. It was a big bamboo mat that had fallen off to the side from this string of bombs when the overpressure blew stuff around. And sticking out of this hole was a muzzle of what he thought was a 130mm gun. Apparently what they were doing was rolling the gun out, firing a round or two, and then rolling it back in, putting this cover back on top and being relatively impervious to aerial observation, which was the only kind of observation we could get at that distance. This is out in Laos; this is probably seven or eight kilometers beyond the Vietnamese border.

Over the course of the next few days, not under our control, O'Toole and the other aerial observers worked their way forward and back along the Khe Sanh gun-target line from that gun and found four or five more, as best they could tell. The way O'Toole described it led me to believe that because there were so many B-52 strikes and that sort

of thing, the North Vietnamese had probably emplaced
those guns not in a battery position, but in single-gun
positions on the gun-target line, so that in order to hit Khe
Sanh they only had to adjust for range, not for deflection.
And once they cranked in that range adjustment for each gun,
which adjustment would remain more or less constant since
Khe Sanh wasn't going to move, they could fire in battery fire,
even when the guns were not emplaced in a battery position. It
sounded like they had emplaced the guns at about 500-meter
intervals, with the rear guns probably pretty close to max
range, which is 27,000 meters for that 130mm field gun—and
then forward from there. I had suspected they emplaced them
that way, because although we'd always hear only one tube
pop, or several pops almost simultaneously, the sounds, as the
rounds came over the hill, were always separated, as if the
guns were firing together, but from different ranges. As O'Toole
described it, they'd probably gotten four or five. That was not
the only artillery out there.

It could have not been done without Niuatoa and his incredible patience. He'd been standing there on the skyline for a
couple of weeks, twelve to fourteen hours a day, under constant
mortar fire, with a few sniper rounds thrown in. He was
fearless. A round—120mm—would land nearby, and he wouldn't
even flinch. Oblivious to danger may be a better description.[1]

FEBRUARY 27

Lt RAY STUBBE
1/26 Battalion Chaplain _____

[DIARY ENTRY] At the morning briefing, the adjutant announced that 1/26 had suffered the following casualties: 23
KIA, 47 WIA serious, 27 MIA, 247 WIA non-serious, 92
evacuated. Total casualties: 320.

☆

LCpl MIKE GUESS
Charlie Company, 1/9 _____

I was just standing there in the trenchline when a mortar

round came in. By then, I was so accustomed to them that I didn't duck as low as I should have. I took three pieces of shrapnel in the back of the head, right between the edge of my helmet and the collar of my flak jacket. There was blood all over the flak jacket, but the wounds weren't serious. I went down to Dong Ha to have them fixed up. They put a few stitches in and kept me overnight.

Next morning, flying back on a chopper, I realized that, of all the guys going to Khe Sanh, only me and one or two others had been there before. Everybody else was new. There had to be twenty or twenty-five brand-new guys. I had been sitting up on our trenchline for weeks, watching the airfield get hit constantly—all day—so I knew that we were going to get rounds as soon as the chopper came in. So, there I was, the eighteen-year-old kid, giving everybody orders. All I said was, "When this chopper lands and that back door drops, just pick up your ass and get *moving*! Run to the sides. Just get going, 'cause the rounds are going to come in."

I guess by then the battle for Khe Sanh had had a lot of publicity back in the United States. Some of the guys had been hearing about it, and they were—wow!—*happy* to be going there. That surprised me. Sure as heck, when the back door of the chopper went down, these guys *trotted* out there and just looked around like, "Hey, this is it; we're at Khe Sanh." I was in the middle of the pack, but I went storming out, knocking these guys out of the way. I just kept cruising. Sure as shit, *ten* of these new guys never even got off the chopper pad. They got killed right there.

FEBRUARY 28

Lt RAY STUBBE
1/26 Battalion Chaplain _____

[DIARY ENTRY] Transferred from Khe Sanh. Landed at Quang Tri. I had quite a growth of beard and my clothing was absolutely scroungy—mud, blood, sweat. I had not been out of my clothing in weeks. A Marine took a picture of me as some sort of odd figure from another world. Several enlisted men invited me in for a beer as I walked along the road. One pilot looked up at me and said, "It must have been Khe Sanh."

Although Chaplain Stubbe was officially transferred from 1/26 to the 3rd Marine Division chaplain's office, he continued to make his way back to Khe Sanh for flying visits as he roved through the division's area of responsibility.

☆

LCpl PHIL MINEER
Bravo Battery, 1/13 _____

While accompanying Lieutenant McGrath to pick up the battery payroll at Danang in late February, I flew up to the 1/13 battalion rear area at Dong Ha. While I was there, I ran into an old buddy.

Cpl Ronnie Dempsey was one of the original Bravo Battery Marines. He had shipped out of the States with the battery when it first went overseas. He was one of a few original members of the unit who had extended for another tour when everyone else finished their time and went home. That got him a thirty-day extra leave that he could take anytime he wanted during the second tour. He went home right before he went up to Khe Sanh—thirty days, plus ten days for travel time. I happened to be at Dong Ha when he got back, so we hung out together. He wanted to get back to the battery, but I told him that no one was pushing him, that he ought to hang back in the rear until someone asked for him. But he wanted to go, so I drove him to the chopper pad and he flew out. Five or six hours later, somebody came to the battery area and told me that the chopper had taken ground fire getting to Khe Sanh and that Dempsey had taken a .51-caliber round under the chin that went through the top of his head. I claimed his body at Graves Registration that night.

FEBRUARY 29
ASSAULT

Capt HARRY BAIG
26th Marines Target Information Officer _____

Sensors clearly foretold the attack on Khe Sanh Combat
Base during the night of February 29–March 1, and gave us
time to divert two Arclights, one of which struck the best
part of two battalions moving up to support and reinforce
the assault battalion.

Defensive fire plans were not used to prevent an enemy
assault force from closing onto the perimeter wire. They
were designed to prevent him from escaping and being
reinforced. Their purpose was to isolate the battlefield and
to defeat the enemy in detail by fragmenting his forces and
separating his elements. The fires took the following form:
A three-sided box, open at the friendly side, was emplaced
about the location or suspected location of the assault unit.
Three batteries executed this mission. A fourth battery then
closed the remaining open side of the box and rolled
forward into the box in the manner of a piston within its
cylinder. Having reached the far side of the box, it proceeded
to roll back. And so on. The enemy force inside the box
could not escape out of it and could not avoid the roller or
piston effect of the rolling barrage. The use of firecracker,
[CORFRAM] ammunition vastly magnified the effect of this
battery. This box was known as the "primary box." At the
same time this was going on, the Fire Support Coordination
Center put into effect a "secondary box." The latter was
fired outside the former. The 175mm guns of the U.S. Army
delivered fire missions in long lines about 500 meters away
from the primary box, each gun zoning and shifting when
required. Generally, the guns took two sides of the secondary box. On order, their fires rolled in toward the center and
out again. The third side of the secondary box was closed
by aircraft under the control of AN/TPQ-10 radar. Where
possible, and only when we were convinced that an attack
was imminent, an Arclight strike, diverted three hours

earlier, would deposit its bombs across or along the main avenue of approach into the battle area.

The Fire Support Coordination Center responded to the enemy's assault by employing the pattern of [the] defensive fire [plan] described above. Primary box with a modified rolling barrage (piston effect) within it; secondary box, using 175mm guns and [radar-guided] aircraft; and two Arclights, diverted three hours before.[2]

Cpl WILLIAM ROBERTSON
Logistics Support Unit _____

The NVA charged the line, coming right up on the end near the ammo dump, where 105mm battery was. They were coming right up a bow in the land. I guess there were 300 or 400 of them. They were charging the line across a broad, open field. They were banging the devil out of us with mortars, right there at the artillery battery and along the edge of the ammo dump. They were going for the artillery battery more than they were going for us. There was very heavy overcast; I guess the ceiling was maybe 100 feet at the most. They charged the line three times, but the closest they got was about 100 feet from the perimeter wire. The artillery battery was unable to fire at them; the gunners had to get 81mm mortars and 105s from the other end of the perimeter to get to them because they had revetments built all around the 105s so they could shoot and not have to worry about getting hit by anything. The revetments prevented the battery near us from lowering their barrels enough to shoot directly at the NVA who were attacking. We were cutting them down pretty good with M-16s—I had an M-14—and machine guns. I saw a mess of them fall, but it looked like, each time they charged, there was just as many of them as there had been the first time. I saw them fall, but the grass was high enough that, once they fell, I couldn't see them again. I don't know if they crawled out of there, or what. Finally, jets were called in. They came in and first strafed the area—which they couldn't see—and then they dropped some bombs. One of the bombs fell into one of our bunkers and killed two ARVN Rangers. The jets didn't drop any more bombs, but the NVA never charged us again up through that area. At the last minute, they just turned back. I heard later that the 105s on the other side of the base were dropping their rounds on the other side of the NVA who were doing the charging. Instead of taking care of the ones doing the charges, they were preventing the ones coming up to reinforce from getting through. That was probably the reason they backed off.

Capt HARRY BAIG
26th Marines Target Information Officer _____

This attack reinforced our belief concerning the enemy's mental rigidity and inflexibility of mind.[3]

LtCol JIM WILKINSON
1/26 Commanding Officer _____

I visited the 37th ARVN Ranger Battalion command post on the morning of March 1. The Rangers were examining equipment and material taken from dead NVA or left behind by retreating NVA. Included were a large number of enemy devices to be used to breach the wire of KSCB. These crude but workable devices were constructed of bamboo strips laced around blocks of TNT. The enemy planned to use these as bangalore torpedoes, but they never had the opportunity.[4]

LATE FEBRUARY

Capt HARRY BAIG
26th Marines Target Information Officer _____

In late February, Maj Robert Coolidge and Maj Jerry Hudson [intelligence officers] discovered the exact locations ... of twelve artillery positions and two major ammunitions dumps (not to be confused with battery dumps or ready-service dumps). These were concentrated in two general areas to the south. Two Arclight strikes, already airborne, were diverted to these two target areas. After the bombers had departed,

the ground erupted for some forty minutes on account of the
secondary explosions, observable from KSCB.[5]

☆

Maj ALEX LEE
Seismic Sensor Consultant _____

One young Marine was a cook pressed into service in a line
company, but he had such rotten vision that he could do no
good in a fighting hole. I found him cooking in a cul-de-sac in
the trenchline. He was using cans found in the blown-up
dumps, and he would serve anyone who stopped by. He had
rules: wash your own tin plate, no more than four guys at one
time, and officers *last* in the chow line. He seemed to work
twenty-four hours a day. When I suggested to his battalion CO
that he be decorated for such far-reaching personal effect, I
was told that I was stupid, that he was just trying to get out of
line duty. Since I ate every meal there for several days, and
since the activity took place in the front-line communications
trench, I hardly think the Marine was a slacker.

I cannot be so thoroughly complimentary of my brother
officers. Many were "bunker rats," and others failed to
enforce sanitation—thereby creating the presence of more
real rats in the underground command posts. Sadly, some
senior officers were most guilty, throwing half-filled cans on
the deck and leaving partially eaten food in the sleeping area
of the CP bunker.

☆

LCpl TIM SNELL
Hotel Company, 2/26 _____

I was the company driver. One day I received word that the
supplies were ready for pickup at the supply bunker. I was
driving a truck, due to the amount of supplies I was required
to pick up. I arrived at the supply bunker and loaded the
truck without incident. While driving to the helo pad, I was
thinking about how quiet it was, and how I had not heard or
seen any incoming yet. The chopper was just coming into

view as I was approaching the pad. I pulled up to it so that we didn't have to carry the supplies very far to load them. As we started unloading the truck, we noticed a plane coming in to drop supplies. Just as the plane was coming in, the NVA started sending in mortar and artillery rounds to try to take it out. The first rounds weren't close enough to make us run for the nearest trench, but we kept an eye on what was going on.

We were about half unloaded when, all at once, there was a tremendous explosion right behind the truck. There were two Marines back there, an enlisted man and a lieutenant. I was standing by the truck door, on the driver's side, when the round hit. It threw me over the door. I woke up on the ground and just started running for the nearest trench. Things were happening really fast, and I didn't see the two men behind the truck. As the rounds kept coming in, I looked out to see the condition of the truck. As I started to look, we heard some yelling; someone wanted to know who the driver of the truck was. I yelled that I was, and the lieutenant yelled that he had a wounded man and wanted me to drive him and the wounded man to the battalion aid station for medical assistance.

I ran to the truck and, when I got to the back of it, where the officer was, I could see the wound in the back of the enlisted man's head. At first the wound did not look serious. The officer and I picked the man up by his shoulders and feet. I was at the head, and this is when I got a good look at the wound. The man was bleeding quite freely. With my time in-country, I had seen plenty of wounds, and I knew he was in serious trouble. The wound appeared to be at least the size of a half-dollar, and it was at the base of the skull.

The officer jumped in the back of the truck and said he would hold the man's head in his lap and help me get him into the battalion aid station when we got there. I jumped into the front seat and headed straight for the aid station. All I could do was get as low as I could be in the truck and pray.

We started across the runway, and the rounds started to get even closer. Some rounds hit close enough to kick up the dirt in front of us. Having been around awhile, I knew they were just getting the range so they could drop one right in my lap. That's when I decided to duck a little lower and begin to zigzag across the airstrip. We drove from the east side to the west side of the strip without getting ourselves or the vehicle hit.

Upon arriving at the aid station, the lieutenant and I jumped out and grabbed the wounded Marine. I think that we both knew by then that the man didn't have much of a chance, but we still had to try. When we carried him to the operating table, we could see that his eyes were rolled back and there were no apparent signs of breathing. We both expected this, but it still didn't make it easier to lose another Marine.

☆

LCpl ARMANDO GONZALES
Bravo Company, 1/9 ⎯⎯⎯⎯⎯⎯⎯⎯⎯⎯⎯⎯⎯⎯⎯⎯⎯

The NVA were very good at giving us just enough rope, enough confidence, to hang ourselves. While water was rationed, we sometimes went out to collect some at a little stream that ran between the Rock Quarry and the combat base. One day, as my squad was going out, one of the pointmen had set off a booby trap. As everyone dived for cover, we set off a chain reaction of more booby traps. Several Marines were killed or wounded, and it took the help of another squad from our platoon to get everyone back inside our wire.

☆

Pfc LIONEL TRUFANT
106mm Platoon, 3/26 ⎯⎯⎯⎯⎯⎯⎯⎯⎯⎯⎯⎯⎯⎯⎯⎯

Some nights, when I was alone on watch, it was so foggy that I thought I was the only person on Earth. I couldn't hear anything and could barely see anything in the fog. I had to be alert for the enemy—we had all seen movies where the sentry got his throat slit at night—and also for the officer or the staff noncommissioned officer who checked the lines at night. Night watch gave me lots of time to think—of things like Dienbienphu, of home, of what the hell was going to happen at Khe Sanh, about what else the NVA might throw at us.

Cpl ALLAN STAHL
Logistics Support Unit _____

I was standing sentry duty one night when the whole
ridgeline outside the base lit up like when everybody in a
football stadium lights a lighter. The whole hillside was
speckled with lights, hundreds of them. We assumed they
must be coming to get us. It went like that for three nights
in a row, but nothing happened.

☆

GySgt MAX FRIEDLANDER
17th Interrogation-Translation Team _____

One day, I stood up on top of my bunker and looked around
at the countryside, which had been totally magnificent,
beautiful country. When I noticed what was left of that
beautiful countryside, it was a real jolt. I could see the
devastation taking place on an hourly basis. Bombs from
our aircraft, the strafing, the napalm, the artillery—it seemed
like there were constant explosions going on. It was hard to
believe so much devastation could take place in any twenty-
four-hour period in that one relatively small area. The smell
of cordite was always there.

As time went on, as the North Vietnamese built their
trenches closer to our lines, our aircraft kept getting closer
and closer to the perimeter. The accuracy of the fighters and
bombers was beyond belief. On those few occasions when
there were no bombs or artillery shells going off, one could
stand in the open anywhere in the combat base and just get
the feeling of death in the air. The silence was eerie, as if a
material thing was present.

LCpl RAY NICOL
Bravo Battery, 1/13 _____

After the napalm and bombs burned off the elephant grass
and cover outside the wire, we could see that trenches were
being dug up to within 50 meters of the wire in some
places. Napalm was dropped unignited and left to run into
the trenches. Then the fighters came in and set the napalm

off with rockets. After the grass burned off, we could see rats feeding on the enemy dead. Whenever the wind came up from that direction, it was difficult to eat aboveground.

Cpl DENNIS SMITH
Bravo Company, 1/26 _____

One day toward the end of February lots of rockets were coming in. James Jesse, Virgil Crunk, Jerry Dorn, and I had taken refuge in my hooch when Dorn said he had to take a dump. I told him, "Not in my house. I don't care if all the incoming in the world is hammering us; nobody takes a shit in my house."

Dorn, who was always a gentleman—he should have been an officer—says, "I'll wait until the next lull and then I'm taking off."

I picked up my watch and told him, "I'll time you." The nearest shitter was forty or fifty yards away.

We waited until it got quiet. Dorn took off. He was back through the hatch fourteen seconds later. "I did it," he said as soon as he was inside.

We all said, "Bullshit! No way!"

"I did it."

We had to ask him how.

He said he already had the shitpaper in his left hand and he unbuckled his belt as he ran. He hit the door full speed, dropped his drawers, hit the seat, let fly with everything he had, wiped on the upstroke, and was out the door running again.

Cpl BERT MULLINS
Bravo Company, 1/9 _____

Radio operators invented simplified codes for everything we could—certain type units or certain numbers, for example. One day, one of our radio operators got confused. He was trying to tell us by means of code that he had seen one NVA, but he used the code to indicate that he had seen a *platoon* of NVA. Before we could get the matter straight-ened out, we had an air strike coming in. The powers that be decided that we were not going to explain what happened or call off the air strike. So we let the strike come in.

The A-4s dropped their bombs where that one NVA had been, and shrapnel from one of the bombs traveled all the way over the top of the hill. I was crouching in a trenchline next to one of our bunkers. That chunk of shrapnel, which was as big as the palm of my hand and a half-inch thick, embedded itself in the wall of the trench not six inches from my head.

☆

Capt KEN PIPES
Bravo Company, 1/26 _____

The big stuff is what bothers most people the most when it's going on. After a while, you get immune to the smaller stuff when you're also getting hit with the real heavy artillery and rockets.

The NVA had a 57mm recoilless rifle out in front of the ARVN Ranger position that sniped at anything that moved. Whenever I went back to battalion briefings, I usually accompanied Capt Walt Gunn, the Army adviser to the ARVN Rangers. Realizing that the 57 would snipe at us, we often ran short sprints in the open outside the trenchline— just for something unusual to do. We always made it back into the trench before they fired. We'd laugh, go down the trenchline a little farther, and do it again.

LtCol JIM WILKINSON
1/26 Commanding Officer _____

The NVA took advantage of periods of limited visibility to dig the trenches closer to KSCB. Marines of 1/26 used periods of good visibility to register M-79 rounds on the close-in NVA trenches. At night, during periods of invisibil-ity, M-79s would fire a version of H&I fires into the

trenches. This was an effective method of countering the
trenching activity close to the perimeter.[6]

☆

Pfc MIKE DeLANEY
Echo Company, 2/26 (Hill 861A) _____

We hooked a transistor radio up to a long piece of electrical
wire wrapped around some old radio batteries. It was a good
enough antenna to bring in Hanoi Hannah. One day she
dedicated a song to Echo Company, 2/26, at Khe Sanh. It
was Martha and the Vandellas singing, "No Place to Run,
No Place to Hide." Talk about giving goosebumps! We sat
around looking at each other like, "I don't believe this!"

Chapter 8

March 2

HM3 BILL GESSNER
Delta Company, 1/9 ⎯⎯⎯⎯⎯⎯⎯⎯⎯⎯⎯⎯⎯⎯⎯⎯

We had harassing mortar fire, but no ground attacks as we dug, emplaced wire, and emplaced a minefield. We ran patrols out toward Khe Sanh Village. We ran two wire-sweeping patrols every day. We put out a squad-size ambush every night. Then a platoon from the 26th Marines got its ass handed to them and our patrolling was reduced to sweeping the wire twice a day. The main threat to us was the indirect fire and a guy who was sniping at us with a .51-caliber machine gun. He had our latrine zeroed in, and it was a bad idea to take a crap during daylight.

The enemy dug trenches toward our lines. We could hear them at night, but we never really did much to stop them. Mortars weren't fired because they might learn where the tubes were. Claymores were stolen. Ambushes were not permitted. So they dug. One morning the fog lifted at dawn and we caught four or five NVA trying to get away. M-79 grenadiers cornered them on a knoll, and we got permission to get them. We later found three bodies and a blood trail.

As the patrol returned, they were fired at by an NVA recoilless rifle as the lead fire team was passing through our wire and mines. The lead men were able to get to our lines, but everyone else was trapped in the lane or outside the wire. The recoilless rifle fired four or five times, then HN Tim Wethington and I went out to bandage the wounded men.

The recoilless rifle fired a few more times, hitting in the lane about twenty meters away and scaring the hell out of us. We scrambled about looking for cover and sat out the attack. During a lull, the lightly wounded men helped carry the seriously wounded men up the ridge and into the company perimeter. After we gained the safety of the trenchline, the recoilless rifle fired again. Tactical air was requested to knock out the recoilless rifle, but it stopped shooting while the air cover was around.

When the airplanes left, Tim Wethington was standing in the 1st Platoon trenchline. The recoilless rifle fired and the round hit him in the chest. The man was literally blown to pieces.

MARCH 6

Sgt FRANK JONES
26th Marines Scout-Sniper Platoon _____

I flew down to Danang to drop off a wounded buddy's personal gear so he would have it with him when he went back to the States. I caught a flight out under some mortar fire, but I got to Danang okay and left the gear with my buddy. But I couldn't get back to Khe Sanh. Newspeople who were trying to get in there kept asking why I was trying so hard to get back. I told them that my platoon was up there, that's what I had been trained to do, not stay down there. A *Time* magazine writer took it all down and wrote an article about the crazy Marine who wanted to get back into the siege. I finally got a seat back on an airplane. The next airplane after mine got hit and everybody aboard it got burned up.

Maj TOM COOK
26th Marines Assistant Logistics Officer _____

While the C-123 was on its final approach, a single-engine Air America plane swooped in and landed right in front of him. The C-123 aborted his landing and went back around. By the time he set up his second approach, the NVA knew which way he was coming and where he was going. They had him zeroed in and shot him down.

There were no survivors. The official death count was 43 Marines, four Air Force, and one Navy killed. The lone sailor was a corpsman from Lima Company, 26th Marines, who was coming back from R&R leave. Robert Ellison, a Newsweek *photographer, on his second trip to Khe Sanh, was not in the official tally.*

MARCH 7
THE BRU

26th Marines After Action Report _____

During early March, NVA propaganda teams entered [near-by Bru-occupied] villages, advising the Bru to relocate to southern Huong Hoa District, where they would be cared for. They were told the major offensive against KSCB was about to begin and that U.S. forces would strike the villages in retaliation. Many groups started south. However, the first groups found that there was no food available there, so the migration to KSCB and across country to Cam Lo began.

The Bru began arriving at the base on March 7 and continued to filter in through the remainder of the month. As many as 661 were evacuated in one day, with as high as 440 being kept overnight in the FOB-3 compound. The total evacuated through KSCB during the month was

1,428. Countless others migrated across country to eastern Quang Tri.

LCpl PHIL MINEER
Bravo Battery, 1/13 _____

On March 7, hundreds and hundreds of refugees started coming into the base. For a while, it was what the Marine Corps calls "asshole to bellybutton"—really tight living conditions on the base. But, slowly, they got them all flown out.

26th Marines After Action Report _____

> Many Bru attempted to migrate to Cam Lo (in eastern Quang Tri Province); however, they were intercepted by the NVA and forced to resettle in the villages of Lang Con, Lang Bu, and Lang Vei. Some migrated into Laos. These areas were designated "no fire areas" for friendly forces.

BOB BREWER
Quang Tri Province Senior Adviser _____

The Bru, about 10,000 strong, were the montagnard people of Huong Hoa District, of which the Khe Sanh Combat Base was a small outpost. The Bru were a noble, peaceful, hard-working people. Nobody understood them better than the missionary John Miller and his family. John spent six years with them. His kids were born there. He and his wife learned the Bru language and transliterated it into the Vietnamese script, then they translated the whole Bible into Bru. By the time I ordered John Miller and his family out of Huong Hoa in mid-January 1968, Bru children were reading their own language in the perfectly logical Vietnamese script.

I said these people were peaceful. They were, more so in my opinion than any of the other montagnard tribesmen of Indochina. But they had a messiah who led fantastic patrols through and around the NVA positions. He provided intelligence of the most valuable kind. He was adored by all the

Bru people, and as long as he lived, they would go anywhere and do anything if he said it was okay. Needless to say, he fell during the siege, and Huong Hoa began to unravel.

After the Huong Hoa District Headquarters was abandoned on January 22, all 10,000 Bru were brought to the lowlands of Quang Tri Province. The Communists did nothing to impede the exodus. We brought the Bru down to our major refugee community near Cam Lo District Headquarters. Soon it became apparent that the Bru tribesmen were withering away. Sickness and disease and a strange ennui were claiming them. John Clary, the chief USAID adviser in the district, said that it was the low altitude and lack of flowing water. So we found a new, wild, high country just southeast of Camp Carroll. The second move was made, and to this day I can still see the Bru children splashing and laughing in the free-flowing streams where we resettled them.

26th Marines After Action Report _____

> The Bru provided valuable information on [enemy] troop dispositions and attitudes. Numerous secondary explosions [resulted from] strikes against targets plotted from their information. Those who arrived early in the month were of the impression that attack was imminent while those who arrived later indicated the NVA propaganda theme had changed to one of Ho Chi Minh would be unhappy if they [the NVA] wasted their time on only 6,000 Marines at Khe Sanh. Interesting along this line is the fact that the same general theme was echoed by Radio Hanoi's English-language announcer, Hanoi Hannah, a few days later.

MARCH 8

Cpl GILBERT WALL
81mm Mortar Platoon, 1/26 _____

This was the second day that I tried to get a plane out of Khe Sanh. In the morning, we went to the headquarters to get rifles and other weapons to carry out of Khe Sanh, which was almost guaranteed a trip on the plane.

After waiting all morning, a Marine and I got fifteen .45-caliber pistols in an artillery ammo box to take out. When we got to the area by the airstrip, the Marine who took the names of the people getting on the plane told us that whoever carried a dead body to the plane would get to go first. I volunteered to take one. We put our seabags and the box with the fifteen .45s in it alongside the dead body on a stretcher. It was almost certain that we could get to the plane—but out of Khe Sanh? Who knew?

The plane taxied down the runway, made a turn, and started dropping its load without ever stopping. When it was through unloading, they told us to go, so we started running after the moving plane. The load was so heavy that the stretcher looked like it would break any moment. We tried to keep everything on it as we were running. Twelve running Marines along with six dead bodies we were carrying were getting closer when they let all the other waiting Marines start running for the plane. In no time, they passed us and jumped on the plane. They were all standing along with the plane crew, shouting, "Run faster, run faster!" and screaming that the incoming was starting up.

I was in the back of our stretcher, trying to keep it balanced and move faster at the same time. I was scared even though I didn't see or hear any incoming.

Finally we got there and started climbing on the plane before it made for the runway. The plane moved down the runway and took off. I could hear the incoming.

The dead bodies were on the floor, so we just laid on them. I could feel the softness of the dead body and feel the fear of death itself. Nobody moved or made any noise. Everybody was terrified. I could smell the rubber of the body bag.

It was easy to guess what was going on outside the plane. I had spent many days watching the NVA shooting at the planes; I knew where the .51-cals were coming from and when they would be shooting at us from the north side or the southeast side of the base. I had seen a big plane, a chopper, or a fighter-bomber getting shot out of the air so many times that I could picture the heavy fire they were putting on us very clearly.

The plane went straight up and everybody remained very quiet. It wasn't until we went higher and farther from Khe Sanh that one of the crew members said, "All clear." After a second of doubt, we all started hugging, shouting, and congratulating each other. Some of the Marines applauded, but some got their anger and frustration out by shouting, "Fuck you, Khe Sanh." Some got emotional and started crying. We were all happy. We knew we had made it.

Pvt JONATHAN SPICER
Charlie-Med _____

[NAVY-CROSS CITATION] For extraordinary heroism while serving with Company C, Third Medical Battalion, Third Marine Division, in the Republic of Vietnam on 8 March 1968. During an intense enemy rocket, mortar, and artillery attack against the Khe Sanh Combat Base, Private Spicer unhesitatingly volunteered to serve as a stretcher bearer and assisted in embarking the numerous casualties aboard transport helicopters for evacuation. Completely disregarding his own safety, he continued to expedite the loading of the wounded aboard the aircraft, despite the increasing intensity of the attack, and was the last man to seek shelter in a bunker at the edge of the airstrip. Observing a mortar round exploding near an evacuation helicopter loaded with casualties, he unhesitatingly left his position of relative safety to assist the wounded who were unable to move from their exposed position. Moments later, another round exploded within a few feet of Private Spicer, seriously wounding him, as he shielded a Marine from the blast with his own body. Unable to walk, he warned his comrades to remain in their protective positions while he attempted to crawl from the hazardous area to safety by himself. His selfless actions undoubtedly prevented serious injury or possible death to his fellow Marines and were an inspiration to all who observed him. By his dauntless courage, unfaltering determination, and selfless devotion to duty at great risk, Private Spicer upheld the highest traditions of the Marine Corps and the United States Naval Service.

EARLY MARCH
OUTGOING

LCpl RAY NICOL
Bravo Battery, 1/13 _____

The fog in the morning was so thick we couldn't see ten meters. A recoilless rifle started firing at us from the ridgeline to our south. It would fire two or three rounds starting at daybreak, when the fog was really thick. All we could see when it fired was a big orange flash in the fog, but we couldn't tell where the round was going to hit. Then it was too late. It hit our common bunker one morning, and I spent an hour helping dig everyone out. Fortunately, no one was hurt. We just couldn't spot the recoilless rifle because it never fired after the fog lifted.

Maj TOM COOK
26th Marines Assistant Logistics Officer _____

Almost every morning, at approximately 0700, we had a wake-up call from a recoilless rifle. Every morning, from one position or another, the NVA would hit us with that single recoilless rifle round, right in downtown Khe Sanh, which comprised the Combat Operations Center and all the staff bunkers. We never knew where it might hit. There was a small aperture in the bunker that housed our generator. I'll be darned if he didn't put a round right through that aperture. He never knew what he hit, of course, but he destroyed our generator. Quite a shock.

1stLt FRED McGRATH
Bravo Battery, 1/13 _____

We had been taking some sporadic incoming from what appeared to be a 57mm recoilless rifle. The man was a poor shot. One day the NVA gunners became bolder than usual. They placed the gun in an unprotected position and began to fire at our position. Not having a similar weapon to engage him, one of the battery officers, adept at computation, took a Graphic Firing Table and went to a howitzer that had a direct line-of-sight to the enemy position. After three attempts, the gun crew scored a direct hit on the 57mm recoilless rifle. The crew felt it had earned the bragging rights as "Best Dingers" in the battery. They got no argument.

LCpl RAY NICOL
Bravo Battery, 1/13 _____

We also blew up the Frenchman's plantation house, south of our position, using the only concrete-piercing round I ever saw used in Vietnam. The house was being used by the NVA as a headquarters and for cover for their snipers.

1stLt FRED McGRATH
Bravo Battery, 1/13 _____

Not all the rounds we fired hit the intended target. In fact, one round we fired never hit anything, literally. When you prepare a round for firing a 105mm howitzer, you have a projectile with fuse, powder bags, and a canister. The number of powder bags used is determined by the charge required. We had a fire mission going that had a fairly high quadrant (elevation), so the tube was facing skyward. The powderman was new, this being the first unit he was in. The charge called was four. That meant bags one, two, three, and four. I guess he was a little nervous. He only put in the number-four bag! The round never left the tube, although the propellant ignited. The projectile lodged about eight inches from the muzzle. Since there was a VT fuse on the round, we could not dislodge it by using a bell rammer. Too dangerous. We had no choice but to call EOD. They took the tube off the howitzer and blew the whole tube up!

Again, the priority of Khe Sanh worked. The howitzer had a
new tube two days later.

INCOMING

Cpl ALLAN STAHL
Logistics Support Unit _____

The NVA was always shooting at our supply and ammo
dumps, and they always eventually hit something and started
a fire. We were the guys who always got to put the fires out.
They were our dumps. We didn't have any fire hoses, of
course, so we had to shovel dirt on the fires to put them out.
We had to let certain things burn because there was no way
to put them out, or, in the case of ammo, it was too
dangerous to fight the fires.

One time, after we had already put a few big fires out, we
got down to ASP-1 and started giggling and acting silly. It
wasn't a very serious fire, so eventually, we started pissing
on burning boxes to put the fires out. I was standing there
taking a piss when something went *bloomp*. It didn't hit me
hard, but it did hit me, and I got all scratched up. It was a
very sobering experience. That ended the joke. I picked up
my radio and went on home. The party was over.

Another time, they hit the CS gas. We had a new kid, and
he and I were sent to the ammo dump. We ran right into the
cloud of CS. I was breathing deeply from running, and it
got me. It really hurt. I panicked. I had my gas mask with
me, but I really panicked. It hurt! I tried to run, but I
couldn't get away from it. Finally I got hold of myself and
got my gas mask on. As I got my breath back, it dawned on
me that I had lost track of the new kid. I thought, if *I*
panicked, there was no telling what the new kid had done. I
found him lying in a ditch. He had done it by the book. He
smelled the gas, put his gas mask on, cleared it, and lay
down. His eyes were as big as silver dollars behind the
gas-mask lenses, but he was okay. The only thing wrong
with him was that he had just seen the old pro go nuts.

We had a night fire at ASP-1. I grabbed my radio and

Private First Class Rodriguez followed me out of the bunker. We were running down the road when all hell started breaking loose and all kinds of stuff started falling around us. There was a ditch, but it offered no protection at all. We were in the ditch, listening to our home base call us on the radio, trying to find out where we were and how we were doing. I tried to call back, but they kept asking the same questions, so I knew they couldn't hear me. All that shit was still falling out of the sky as Rodriguez and I were lying in the ditch facing one another. Suddenly, a 60mm mortar round goes *thud* right between our faces. It was smoking! We vacated the ditch and headed back home. On the way, we passed another radio team they had sent out to find us. I was ashamed to be heading home past them, but I had had enough for one night. As the other radioman passed, he said, "I know you fuckers did something with your radio, and I'm going to find out what." I appreciated his emotion; I'd have felt the same way, but I was unnerved. Next morning, he stripped my radio down and found a damaged crystal.

LCpl ARMANDO GONZALES
Bravo Company, 1/9 _____

We got some sort of incoming every day—maybe only a round or two of heavy artillery or a few recoilless-rifle or mortar rounds, but something every day.

One day, as my fire team and two or three other guys sat around in my bunker—I was reading a book, a few of the guys were playing cards, the others were writing letters—we started getting hit by incoming. Suddenly there was a big *THUMP* and the whole bunker shook. We ran out to see what was what. We found a dud 82mm mortar round with its fins sticking right out of the roof of the bunker. It was a direct hit.

The nearest toilet to my bunker was an ammo box set over a hole in the ground and surrounded by a five-foot-high triple wall of sandbags. I was out there sitting on it one day when the other side of the Rock Quarry started taking

incoming. I tried to finish up as fast as I could, but one of
the first rounds to land on our side of the hill landed right
behind me. It blew away the first sandbag wall, shredded
the second layer, and moved the inner layer toward me.
When I felt a big thump on my back, I upped and ran into
the trenchline with my pants halfway up. As soon as the
incoming lightened up and we all got up, one of the fellows
milling around in behind me said, "Oh my God! Gonzales,
take off your flak jacket! Look!" I took it off and found a
big chunk of shrapnel, about the half size of my fist, lodged
in the back of my flak jacket.

   Another time, I was standing around staring out of the
trenchline toward the Laotian border when, for no reason at
all, I moved a few feet around a sharp corner. Seconds later,
a round landed right in the trenchline. It killed a few
Marines and blew out the corner in which I had been
standing moments earlier.

□

Cpl DENNIS SMITH
Bravo Company, 1/26 _____

This thing about women waiting back in The World was
serious business. Showing your pictures—wives, girlfriends,
kids—was a sort of sacred ritual. One soul brother from
some bad-news Philly neighborhood was showing me an
R-rated picture of his lady. I didn't want to comment on her
looks, so I asked, "Who took the picture?" He got a funny
look on his face.

☆

Pfc LIONEL TRUFANT
106mm Platoon, 3/26 _____

I remembered seeing the documentaries on Dienbienphu on
television when I was a kid, so it naturally occurred to me
that we were in a situation similar to the one the French had
been in. Every day, in my mind, when the incoming got hot
or when they probed our lines, I just *knew* it was going to

be another Dienbienphu. It was always in the back of my mind. We all envisioned that if they did hit us, they would send tanks down, probably at night. We heard they had rangefinders with which they could lock in on us when we fired a round, so we envisioned that our 106 would be useless after we got off only a very few rounds. Since the secondary line was in back of us, we wouldn't have anywhere to go if we did get hit. Getting back depended on our being able to talk to the people behind us on the land line we had to the rear, but the incoming often broke the communications wire. About all we figured we could do if we were attacked was fire as many rounds as possible, stick a thermite grenade in the breech, stick another thermite grenade in the ammunition, head for the trenches, and hope for the best.

LCpl PHIL MINEER
Bravo Battery, 1/13 ⎯⎯⎯⎯⎯⎯⎯⎯⎯⎯⎯⎯⎯⎯

So many guys were getting wounded or blown up at Khe Sanh, and it got so hard to find replacements, that they cut a deal with the guys in the brig at Danang. They offered to commute their sentences if they did the rest of their time at Khe Sanh. Real encouraging.

☆

BOB BREWER
Quang Tri Province Senior Adviser ⎯⎯⎯⎯⎯⎯⎯⎯⎯

The "military mind" tended to give low priority to the local people and their social, economic, and political needs. The brass tried, but most of the time their efforts fell just a tad short of the mark. For example, KSCB in late February or early March had information that an important NVA headquarters was operating in a village not far from the abandoned Huong Hoa District Headquarters town of Khe Sanh. Somehow this village had not been utterly destroyed yet, and some elderly civilians were still living there. I was asked my opinion as to what should be done. I suggested that a surgical combat-team heliborne operations be sent in under cover of CS or CN gas to capture as much of the NVA brass and documents as possible *and* remove any civilians who wanted out. KSCB used gas, all right. They used time-delay-fused gas rounds to force everybody out into the open, then followed with high-explosive rounds to obliterate them.

☆

LCpl KEVIN MACAULEY
Bravo Company, 3rd Recon Battalion _____

We steadily improved our bunkers and company area. We dug a trenchline between all the bunkers so that we were below the ground most of the time we were in the company area. Our captain decided we might have to use the trenches to fight from, so he ordered us to dig roll-outs on the trench floor. We cut into the wall of the trench at the floor line and dug a hollow out of the wall that we could roll into if the NVA grenaded the trench. We now had positions two and a half feet to four feet below the trench floor for added protection from shrapnel from grenades, mortars, or rockets. However, our captain stated that they weren't deep enough; he wanted them so deep that we could stand in them and have the floor of the trench at chest level. The trench became six feet deep and the roll-outs were five feet deeper than that. Anyone sitting on the floor of a roll-out was now ten feet below ground level. What we were going to do from this position to fight the NVA was beyond the comprehension of many of us in Recon.

As the weather began to clear up for longer periods each day, the sun beat down on the base and baked the ground cement-hard. The constant shelling and rumbling of the trucks, jeeps, tanks, and other vehicles caused cracks to appear along the lip of our trench. One day, two Marines from my platoon were sitting in their roll-out, scooping the dirt that had fallen into the floor. I was about twenty feet away from them when I heard a muffled *thump*. I didn't know what it was. The captain happened to be walking by when a young corporal from Hawaii started yelling at him—yelling that it was his fault they were dead. I still didn't realize what was going on, but then it dawned on me. The earth was so dried out that about ten feet of the trench wall had collapsed down on the roll-out. Two Marines were buried under all that dirt and no one was doing anything.

I jumped into the middle of the pile of dirt and started digging for all I was worth. Someone handed me an entrenching tool, and I used that. Our company exec chased everyone from the immediate area, fearing further cave-ins. Pfc Daigle helped me with the digging; as I grew winded, he took over. As he tired, I went back to work. We estimated where the two marines were and used the entrenching tool in the area between them. As the minutes passed away, I began to wonder whether our efforts were going to be futile. After what seemed like an eternity—ten or twelve minutes—I uncovered one Marine's head. It was bent forward and his face was in a little pocket formed between his updrawn knees. As I pulled his head free, he began to cough and cry. He was alive! He strangled and screamed until we freed his arms. We soon found the other Marine, but he was unconscious. His face was looking upward as the dirt fell on him, and his mouth was full of the red dirt. The corpsmen started working on him even before we freed him. Someone started to force air into the second Marine's lungs. He did not respond, and he was still unconscious when they carried him to Charlie-Med. I still don't know whether he lived or died. The first Marine, Pfc Ed Stevens, was also carried to Charlie-Med for medical attention. He seemed to be in shock.

I slumped down in the trench; I was exhausted, both physically and emotionally. Guys from the company kept coming over, congratulating me for the job I had done. I felt drained. Later, that evening, I experienced my most rewarding moment in Vietnam. As I sat in my bunker, Stevens came back in, sat down next to me, and threw his arms around me. I held him as we both cried for a while. My tears were tears of joy as I realized I had saved another human being's life. His tears were tears of thanks. I told him I was only doing my job and that I was sure he would have done the same for me. He left the bunker. I don't remember seeing him anymore. I think he was medevacked from Khe Sanh soon after the incident. Being buried alive for as long as he was would have affected me, too. I went to sleep that night with the glow of self-satisfaction about me. I had made a difference.

1stLt FRED McGRATH
Bravo Battery, 1/13 _____

Mail service was sporadic. But when it did arrive, you could almost feel the difference—and certainly taste the difference. The men would receive some of the oddest food-stuffs, like goose-liver paté! It made for a good laugh, but its rib-sticking properties were suspect! Jelly beans and peanut butter were my gifts from The World. As far as I can recall, no Marine in Bravo Battery received a Dear John letter, which, given the circumstances, could have had a disastrous effect. News from The World was always welcome. The *Pacific Stars and Stripes* was a particular favorite. Each copy was completely dog-eared by the time the next one arrived. And, although we began to think women really did fold in the middle, *Playboy* magazine was a cheered event.

☆

I SCREAM, YOU SCREAM...

LCpl PHIL MINEER
Bravo Battery, 1/13 _____

For about a twenty-day period we were cut down to a quart of water. We had a water trailer, but it kept getting shrapnel through the side, so we kept losing all our water. We also got one box of C-rations per day during that time. There wasn't even enough for the rats to eat.

Cpl ALLAN STAHL
Logistics Support Unit _____

They dropped in a pallet load of ice cream one day, and one of our forklift operators drove it back to the supply dump.

What a terrible thing to do to us! We couldn't figure out how to disperse it without risking someone's life. We couldn't call all the troops in, and we couldn't get it out to them. It was getting dark. What an absurdity!

So, in walks the major in charge of the Air Force radar units. He knew there was ice cream on the base, and he told our skipper, also a major, that he wanted it for his troops. Our CO was sweating bullets over the dilemma the ice cream caused; he was genuinely trying to get the ice cream to the troops. He didn't need this Air Force guy, who, incidentally, rotated through the combat base with all the other Air Force guys for only a week at a time. The CO said, "I'll get you your ice cream when everybody else gets theirs. But you get fed last. I feed Marines first." The Air Force guy proceeded to get on the CO: "I want my ice cream!" They were nose to nose, arguing like two little kids. The Air Force major said his people were sharing the same risks as the Marines, and our major said that the Marines had been there for two months without rotating out like the Air Force guys.

LCpl CHARLIE THORNTON
Lima Company, 3/26 ⎯⎯⎯⎯⎯⎯⎯⎯⎯⎯⎯⎯

We were rationing water when we learned that a resupply aircraft had dropped hundreds of gallons of ice cream at the airstrip. What a laugh. We are rationing water and the Marine Corps sends in ice cream! We never saw any evidence of ice cream. It probably melted on the runway.

Cpl ALLAN STAHL
Logistics Support Unit ⎯⎯⎯⎯⎯⎯⎯⎯⎯⎯⎯⎯

The ice cream melted on the pallets. There was no way to distribute it.

☐

Sgt MIKE STAHL
4.2-inch Mortar Battery, 1/13 (Hill 861) ⎯⎯⎯⎯⎯

Sometime in early March, we began hearing the engine noises of one armored vehicle of some sort as it moved around the base of the hill at night. The noises went on for a while. We had been able to see Lang Vei the night it was overrun, and we had seen the PT-76s firing that night. We knew what the PT-76s could do.

There had been Ontos on Hill 861 at various times before the siege, and there was a nice little tank trail from the bottom to the top of the hill. We had nothing with which to block the trail against an attack by a tank.

Finally, after about three days, I decided to go down and take a look. I had thoughts of getting a Medal of Honor. I thought I'd go down there, knock off that one tank, and come back. How hard could it be? I didn't know enough to realize that whereever there's a tank there's infantry, too.

I took a LAAW and extended it before I left the perimeter. I also had a .45-caliber pistol. I left early in the morning, after daylight, and descended through thick jungle paralleling the tank trail to the bottom of the hill. I got down to a point where I could see it, but all I could see through the bushes was where the turret met the hull. That's what I aimed for.

As I started to aim in on it, I began to hear voices. Vietnamese voices. They were to my left, they were to my right, they were behind me. Somehow I had gotten into their position. I figured I was screwed, that I might as well take my shot. The pucker factor was maximum, or I'm sure I wouldn't have missed. But, sure as hell, I squeezed off the LAAW and missed by a mile.

Immediately, AKs started to pop and I heard the *whir* of the motors as the PT-76's main gun was brought to bear on my position. I stood up and ran like a bat out of hell, straight up the hill, straight up the tank trail to the top. They were popping rounds in from everywhere, but they never hit me.

Chapter 9

MARCH 10
MEDEVAC

LCpl CHARLIE THORNTON
Lima Company, 3/26 _____

On March 10, during a routine incoming barrage, an artillery round hit the treeline just above my bunker and exploded in the air. The blast knocked me ten feet across the bunker floor into a dirt wall at the other end. I awoke dazed, my ears ringing, and I felt as if a mule had kicked me in the chest. As I began to check myself for injuries, I found shrapnel wounds in my right leg and left hand. While examining myself further, I had a sensation of something warm running down my shirt. In the dim light of the bunker I could see that the left side of my shirt was soaked in blood that was running into my trousers. There was a hole in my chest the size of a half-dollar. Shrapnel had entered the left side of my chest at a downward angle, exited under my armpit, and creased my bicep. After being stabilized by a corpsman, I was taken to the airstrip for evacuation.

Pfc LIONEL TRUFANT
106mm Platoon, 3/26 _____

I hated it when I was sent down to be part of the medevac
detail at Charlie-Med. Number one, Charlie-Med was near
the airstrip, which was hit the most with the heaviest
incoming. Number two, I saw suffering every day at Khe
Sanh—we were always seeing someone getting it or who
had been hit—but Charlie-Med had worse suffering than
anywhere.

We sat there, waiting in trenches and behind bunkers.
When the helicopters came in, we had to run out and put the
stretchers aboard. It was timed to the second. The helicopters had to judge when to come in because they were going
to draw incoming, and we had to judge when to bring the
wounded out to put them on the helicopters. When the
signal was given, two guys would grab hold of each
stretcher, haul ass, and stick them on the helicopters.

LCpl CHARLIE THORNTON
Lima Company, 3/29 _____

The evacuation process at Khe Sanh may have been one of
the worst fates that a Marine could encounter. Helicopters
would land on the runway to pick up the dead and wounded.
Each time they landed, the NVA gunners would pound the
airstrip with incoming rounds. Charlie-Med had a deep
bunker next to the airstrip where the wounded would be
placed on stretchers to be taken to the helicopters as they
arrived. As I lay there in the bunker on the stretcher, I heard
the incoming rounds begin to impact the airstrip, so I knew
the helicopters were approaching. It was a truly helpless
feeling as two Marines picked up the stretcher and began
running toward the helicopters. I could see the impact of the
rounds "walking" down the runway as the NVA gunners
zeroed in on the helicopters. The helicopters used to evacuate the wounded were mostly H-34s, which were widely
used in Korea for medevacs. Once we were loaded into the
helicopter, it seemed like an eternity before we left the
ground. The helicopter had so many wounded Marines

aboard that it actually had to get a running start to get off the ground.

I can remember vividly looking out the helicopter door as we circled Khe Sanh and seeing the trenchlines and bomb-scarred terrain become smaller as the helicopter flew higher. I thanked God for allowing me to be wounded in order to escape that hellhole.

Maj TOM COOK
26th Marines Assistant Logistics Officer _____

Once I saw several Marines loading stretchers on a CH-46 when mortar rounds started coming in. The helicopter took off while two Marines who weren't flying out were still on the rear ramp, standing on the cargo rollers. All of a sudden, here come these two bodies, off the ramp from about fifty feet in the air. One, who was due to be rotated the next day, wound up with a broken leg, and both were shaken up, but they both survived.

Another time, a CH-46 which was coming in hovered and fooled around back and forth—obviously he wanted to land but didn't know where to set down. But the NVA knew exactly where he would land if he ever figured it out, and they were ready for him. Finally, after about ten minutes, he settled down onto the pad. He was down only fifteen seconds when a recoilless rifle round hit right in the center of the aircraft. The pilot immediately took off. He got 600 or 700 feet down the runway and then crashed.

☐

MARCH 11

LCpl MIKE GUESS
Charlie Company, 1/9 _____

After I got back from my one-day medevac to Dong Ha, I went back to my unit and started right in re-digging my new bunker in the exact spot that the round that had gotten me had hit. I was sure it was like lightning, that two rounds wouldn't hit in the same place. This was the Taj Mahal of bunkers. It was off the trenchline, then into the trenchline, then down about four feet, then in again. If the NVA wanted to get me, they'd have to come in there and get me. I was ready for them as much as I could be.

As I was digging my new bunker, I noticed some replacements moving up the hill toward Bravo Company. There he was—Danny Meysembourg, a guy who lived in my neighborhood back in Madison, Wisconsin. I couldn't believe it! It was like I was dreaming, like a mirage. After that, I walked up the trenchline every chance I got to visit Danny. We shared our letters from home or just talked. One day we got just about a direct hit on his bunker that buried us. After other Marines dug us out, we found that all we had gotten was a little shaken up; nothing hurt except our pride.

I should have qualified for my second Purple Heart, but the CO wouldn't give it to me because I wasn't supposed to be up at Bravo Company when I had my bell rung. I was disappointed because it took three Purple Hearts to get out of country. I didn't want to get killed and I originally didn't want any Purple Hearts, but after I got the first one, I started thinking about getting the other two I needed. I wanted to get out of there.

Danny Meysembourg lasted fourteen or fifteen days. On March 11, a direct hit got Danny. He didn't even know what hit him.

March 15

HM3 BILL GESSNER
Delta Company, 1/9 ——————————————————————

15 March

Dear Family:
How are you all on this overcast day? I am pretty good. A little head cold, that's all.

Three water buffalo presented themselves near our wire today. Since they could have set off mines, we got permission to shoot them. Three of us went

after them. I had the one on the right who refused
to show me anything but his south end. The others
had good shoulder shots. Sergeant Grubbs opened
up on his and dropped him where he stood. The
other guy, Staff Sergeant Duden, got a body hit.
Me—I think I hit his tail.

Needless to say, I was upset that mine got away
clean, but it was a diversion from the daily routine
anyway. We got credit for one "KIA" and two "WIAs."
The 3rd Platoon didn't get a significant wound two
days ago when they spotted one, and the whole
platoon opened up on him, too. So I don't feel too
bad. What a title for a book—"Water Buffalo Hunting in Vietnam—A Dual Danger."

All has been quiet here for some time. Well, at
least no one wounded seriously. My house took a
direct hit yesterday. Thank God I built it strong.
The only things I sweat are delayed fuses. So far,
the gooks have shot only two in our area of the
hill. So I guess they save them for Khe Sanh itself.

Well, I must close. Much love to you all.

P.S. I have a gray-black Vandyke at the present.

Pfc LIONEL TRUFANT
106mm Platoon, 3/26 _____

One day, two water buffalo came in toward our line. We
didn't know what the hell they were, but they gave us the
opportunity to get some frustration off. We opened fire on
them. I'm sure we didn't kill them outright, but an M-79
round hit one on the butt.

MARCH 18
PAYBACK

LCpl PHIL MINEER
Bravo Battery, 1/13 _____

All the movies I watched as a kid—the John Wayne movies—
all that bullshit went out the window at Khe Sanh. Nineteen-

year-olds are supermen, immortal? Most of us were sure we were going to get blown the hell away. Every day we saw somebody getting hit—a guy losing an arm, a leg, getting blown all to shit.

When I was in Khe Sanh, I wore what everybody called a diaper—lower-body armor. I always kept my flak jacket buttoned, and I always wore my helmet. Stuff was always going through the air. You never knew.

Cpl Lou Goi was older. He was twenty-two, and going bald. His hole was right across from mine. We always used to get in Lou's shit about buttoning up his flak jacket. One day he got tired of being in his hole—being *driven* in that damn hole—and he went outside. He was going to eat his chow sitting on the side of the parapet. One of the guys said something about his flak jacket, and Lou said, "Fuck it."

By that time, the NVA had been trenching in. They had trenches right out in front of the wire, maybe eight hundred or a thousand meters. We could see them with the naked eye when they came up to relieve themselves. They had a 57mm recoilless rifle on sticks. A couple guys would lift it up, lay it on ground level, and take a shot into the combat base. A round from the recoilless rifle hit to Lou's left. The full effect got him in the chest and the head.

1stLt PAUL ELKAN
Bravo Battery, 1/13 _____

I heard this call for a corpsman over the phone from Gun-4. It was my practice to go out to wherever anybody was wounded and try to help. Two people were wounded out there. One of them had a chunk of shrapnel near his heart; we got him to the aid station. I couldn't tell who the other one was. The entire top of his body had been blown off from the left shoulder to the right side. There was no chest and no head. I had the troops cover him with a blanket and get him out of there; I didn't want people getting too shook up, looking at what was left of the body. As I was walking back to the executive officer's pit, I asked somebody who the dead man was. "He was Corporal Goi, sir."

I got back to the exec pit and broke down. That was the

only one that got right next to me. I had known Louis Goi a long time. I got him a job and tried to keep him in the battalion fire-direction center so he wouldn't get hurt. I promoted him to corporal just a few days before he got killed. I never let anyone get close to me after that. It was too hard.

LCpl PHIL MINEER
Bravo Battery, 1/13 _____

That day, after Lou was killed, I was in the exec pit with the skipper, Capt James Uecker, talking to Regiment, telling them that this mission or that mission was shot, and also recording everything that was going on. As we were firing, the NVA got lucky with a recoilless rifle round. It came in the entrance to the exec pit. I got a little concussion when I was knocked back against the wall. I seriously thought the skipper got it. The exec, Lieutenant Elkan, was sleeping in the back of the pit, but he sure woke up when the round came in! It threw up a bunch of red dirt that all fell on the lieutenant. When he got up, he looked like a red Stepin Fetchit.

By the time I left the exec pit after firing the Mini-Arclight, I was pissed. I hooked up with a kid named Smith, who was a forward observer with 2/26. I said, "We gotta get them bastards. They got Lou." Smith had field glasses, so we stood out there for hours, waiting for someone to come up out of the NVA trench. Meantime, we were hooked up with my gun, Gun-3. We leveled the tube for direct fire and I calculated for an airburst with a VT fuse. The only problem was that the fuse was armed by means of centrifugal force only after it had flown a certain distance. Eight hundred meters was a little short, so I had to cheat a little. As result, the first fuse started smoking and we had to get it off the gun real quick and throw it. But we finally worked it out. After a long wait, a lot of NVA got brave and came up. We took the shot, and it went off about twenty-five feet over their heads. That was the first time I realized I was a little sick. When I saw those body parts going through the air, I was glad. I was really glad. That one was for Lou Goi.

MID-MARCH

Cpl ALLAN STAHL
Logistics Support Unit _____

Everybody had bad days or pet bitches, but I never saw any
bad morale. I never saw a minute of bad morale. Certainly,
there were none of the morale problems depicted in the
newspapers. My attitude—the attitude of the average Marine
there—was that this was our moment in history. There was
no doubt that they were coming through the wire. That was
accepted fact. But there was no doubt that we were going to
deal with them. There was no lack of confidence. Each
individual had to live with the fact that he was going to be one
of the survivors, but that there weren't going to be very many.
We all looked at ourselves as future survivors of Khe Sanh.

☆

Pfc LIONEL TRUFANT
106mm Platoon, 3/26 _____

We heard a rumor that the NVA were going to attack us in
biplanes. We didn't know what to expect.

Cpl ALLAN STAHL
Logistics Support Unit _____

My CO called me in late one day and said, "Stahl, do you
know anybody over at Regimental Communications?" I told
him that I knew a fellow communicator over there, so he
said, "Get your ass over there. I just spoke with someone
who told me there are MiGs heading south toward us. Find
out if it's true." The skipper was really nervous, so I
hightailed it over to the regimental communications center.
It was pandemonium there, sheer panic. There was obviously something going on. I found my friend and asked what
was going on. "They picked up planes on the radar.
They're coming in from the west. They're over Laos and
headed this way, and the Navy can't get them."

I had seen the effects of bombing every day I had been at

Khe Sanh. I knew what an air strike could do. This was serious. I ran out of the comm center to report. The whole base went on Red Alert and everybody went underground.

Thirty minutes later we started asking ourselves, "Where are the MiGs? There were certainly no airplanes above us. Soon, word came out that there were no MiGs. The Red Alert was relaxed, and that was the end of that. But we had to know what had caused the flap, so the skipper sent me back to the comm center to find out. The enlisted pipeline gave as absolute gospel that a bunch of planters from Cambodia were flying up in biplanes to get a firsthand look at the war. They were intercepted by the Navy and turned back. Unbelievable! I have no idea if that's what really happened.

☆

LCpl ARMANDO GONZALES
Bravo Company, 1/9 _____

We had a thing we called "doing the job." It meant intentionally acquiring a wound, usually a self-inflicted wound. One day, during incoming, one of the fellows raised his hand above the trench, hoping to get it nicked. The shrapnel took off the whole hand. He got more than he bargained for, but he got out of Khe Sanh alive.

☆

Capt JIM LESLIE
26th Marines Assistant Communicator _____

In mid-March, water was at an all-time low. By then, it was used only for drinking, for coffee, or for brushing teeth. It was not for washing one's face, showering, or washing clothes. This was not a big problem, as most Marines by this time had reverted to their basic animal needs—living in a hole, eating one C-ration a day, and existing from one day to the next. The mind was in neutral gear, no longer creative, intuitive, or willing to learn. The mind was just idling. The "real world" was a million miles away, something we would probably never see again.

First Lieutenant Jack Blyze and I were ambling up the road inside the perimeter along the airstrip. I don't recall where we were going. As we approached the old Staff-and-Officers' Club, Jack remarked about how the club used to be a nice place to go after work, before the offensive began.

"Let's go check it out," he said. I recall orders being passed that no one was to go near the old club, as it had been targeted by the NVA gunners. Each day it was the first place to receive incoming artillery in hopes of catching some of the leaders there as they had done in early January. No one went near the club, partly because it was off limits and partly because of the beating it took daily from the NVA artillery, rockets, and mortars. At about 1400, we decided that the NVA artillerymen were probably asleep, so we proceeded over to the club.

The club was mostly underground, with only the roof aboveground. The tin roof had a few sandbags on top to keep the tin from blowing off during windstorms. It also had large, gaping holes from many rounds of artillery and mortar shrapnel.

We walked down eight steps to the plywood door, which was secured with a hasp and lock. Jack solved that problems with a strong kick with the sole of his boot. The door swung open. It was surprisingly light inside because of the holes in the roof. The red plastic bar tables and chairs were upside down, scattered over the floor. It was apparent that no one had been inside the club for months. We righted a table and two chairs as we surveyed the situation.

We found the greatest treat of all lying behind the bar—a full rack of red pistachio nuts. This was a find too good to be true! Salty nuts, untouched by the mice or rats. I brought the whole rack of nuts over to our table and we sat down, took out our canteens of precious water, and set them on the table. What a find we had!

We began to eat the nuts and drink our canteens of water just like we were in a real bar with beer. Just having something a little more than the next Marine made us feel superior. We talked about unimportant things as we broke open the red-shelled pistachio nuts and sipped on our canteens of lukewarm water.

"I wonder what's behind the door," Jack said. Simultaneously, we both got up and walked over to the plywood door in the corner. Without command, the sole of each of our boots struck the door at the same time. The door swung inward and—would you believe!—we found a room full of Budweiser beer. Cans and cans of beer! The room must have been ten feet square, and it was *full* of beer. Cases of beer! More than we could ever drink. We each grabbed a case, carried it over to our table, and popped a top. We were in heaven. We toasted the Marines, our boss—Maj John Shepard—the Commandant, President Johnson, and the war protesters. We each drank a can, then a second, then a third. Then we slowed down. We propped our feet up on a couple of extra chairs, broke open pistachio nuts, and drank beer. We were in seventh heaven.

Two hours and almost two cases of beer later, a shadow swept across the hatch. Then the shadow returned. We heard footsteps coming down the steps. Our boss, Major Shepard, had tracked us down. He stood in the doorway, hands on his hips, and shouted, "What in the hell are you two doing? I've been looking everywhere for you. I thought you were in trouble, and here you are drinking beer." Then, after a slight pause, "Hey, where'd you find that beer?"

We told our story as we cracked open a beer for the major. By a few beers and a few bags of nuts later, Major Shepard was one of the boys. He helped us to demolish the rest of the second case of beer.

"We must make this beer available to the rest of the Marines," Major Shepard said at length. So we stumbled back to our bunker two hours later and announced our find over the radio to our friends in other companies. At dusk, we loaded cases of beer on jeep trailers and passed the treasure out to lines of open-armed Marines who lined up to get their rations of gold. Of course, we took several cases back to our bunker for storage. We had a great day; we had found a fortune and shared our wealth with our friends.

SSgt HARVE SAAL, USA
FOB-3 _____

One day, just after the end of a barrage, a newly arrived
Special Forces radio operator was told to run a new field-
phone wire system from the main bunker to the front gate.
The "newbee" was gone for what seemed to be a long
time, so someone went looking for him. The young radioman was found sitting down in the bunker at the front gate.
He was completely out of breath; he looked like he had just
finished running a marathon. When asked if he had run the
field-phone line to the bunker, the young man said he had.
They guy who found him picked up the field phone and
tried to call the main bunker, but there was no answer.
Asked why the field phone wasn't working yet, the radioman pointed down to the *full* roll of wire on which he was
seated. "You mean I ran this heavy roll of wire all the way
out here and now it don't work?"

☆

1stLt FRED McGRATH
Bravo Battery, 1/13 _____

Life at Khe Sanh was somewhat different from other areas
in I Corps. You developed a bunker mentality at Khe Sanh.
When I was at Phu Bai or Dong Ha, we had sandbagged
holes to jump in, but we slept and moved aboveground. Not
so at Khe Sanh.

The situation at Khe Sanh tended to isolate one unit from
another. I cannot remember having any contact with any
other unit, except by radio or telephone. It was as if we had
our own little war going on, and, although we knew the
26th Marines were out there, we were alone. At night, we
would receive H&I fires from a U.S. Army 175mm gun unit
at the Rock Pile. They would shoot at prearranged targets
just outside our perimeter. Fortunately, they were good
shots. But radio and wire were our only physical contact

with the rest of the base. It is easy, now, to understand why that had to be. But there were times when we wondered if the grunts really were up in those hills.

☆

1stLt NICK ROMANETZ
Charlie Company, 1/26 _____

Some of the reasons Charlie Company didn't do much real patrolling was because of the terrain in our sector and the fact that Lang Vei had been overrun, because we knew there were snipers out, and most of all because there was the threat of a large-scale attack. And, of course, the loss of the Jacques platoon had an impact. However, somewhere into March, we were finally allowed to do some patrolling. I got the green light to take my platoon out to the Finger, about 800 meters in front of us. I was very cautious and concerned that we might get ambushed or come upon something like snipers in spiderholes who would shoot us after we walked by. Since the elephant grass was still pretty high in front of our position, we would have to stick pretty much to the trails. I took the platoon out and conducted a sweep from the left flank through the whole sector north of the combat base, where 1/26 had responsibility.

The battalion intelligence officer sent out an intelligence scout with us, to help us look for information or signs of enemy activity. When we came to a fork in the trail, I split the platoon and sent half up one trail and led the other half up the other trail. I wanted to at least stay in radio contact with the other half of the platoon. My gang stayed out for about another hour, sweeping along the Finger. We never found any enemy, and we could never make any radio contact with the other guys. They later swore they were up on the net, but the best I can figure, the sergeant I put in charge of the reinforced squad got a little uptight, shut his radio off, and headed right back into the combat base, as soon as we split up. The thing that really bugged me was that the intelligence scout went back and reported that we didn't find anything because we got lost.

Maj TOM COOK
26th Marines Assistant Logistic Officer _____

I don't know whose idea it was—it might have been mine—
but at one time it was suggested that when the rear-area
supply people didn't have a full aircraft they might put some
fresh fruit aboard for us. Everybody thought that was a great
idea, and the first morning we got a pallet of apples we
thought it was great. We brought the pallet back and
allocated apples out through the organization, trying to
make sure nobody got cheated. From then on, we kept
getting apples. Sometimes we got four of five pallets of
them in one day. It just went on and on until we had pallets
of apples sitting all over the combat base. But the people
had had their fill of apples, so they just sat there—all over
the place—rotting. Finally, during one of my nightly calls to
Dong Ha, I asked them what the hell was going on: "I need
artillery ammo in case we get attacked. What do you want
us to do, throw apples at them?"

☆

Cpl ALLAN STAHL
Logistics Support Unit _____

One day a guy we called Corporal Red herded a Marine
grunt into our command post and told the major he had
found a guy stealing food from one of our supply dumps.
The major never batted an eye and said, "Corporal, I told you
to just shoot the next son of a bitch you caught stealing food."

Of course, the major never actually had said that, but Red
picked right up on it. "Yes, sir, you did. But I thought
maybe you'd want to do it."

"No," the major picked up, "I don't *want* to do it. But I
think we have to set an example around here."

The captive was shaking in his shoes when the major
spoke directly to him for the first time in a real soft, easy
manner. "Marine, you see how it is, don't you?" And the
kid actually nodded his head. "Sure, you do. See, you
probably think we get more to eat than anyone because
we're the supply unit and all that stuff they fly in goes

through here. You probably think it's okay to get a little for you and your buddies, huh?'' The kid just kept nodding his head. ''Well, son take a look around here. You see any fat Marines in this bunker?'' The kid looked around at us with big, wide eyes, then shook his head. ''That's because we only take our share. In fact, we get fed last. Do you think you deserve more than any other Marine on the base?'' The kid shook his head. ''I told the corporal to shoot you, but I think he didn't because he feels we're all in this together. Do *you* feel we're all in this together?'' The Marine nodded his head. ''Maybe I ought to let the corporal take you out back, where you can settle it. Then one of you can have the ration.'' The Marine shook his head. ''Well, are you going to do this anymore?'' The Marine shook his head. ''Look, you can't do this anymore. Pass the word around your unit that we're not keeping anything back from anyone.'' The kid walked out of there, all put back together. What psychology!

☆

Capt EARLE BREEDING
Echo Company, 2/26 (Hill 861A) _____

I was relieved as Echo Company commander on March 8 and ordered to the battalion staff to take over as logistics officer. However, I kept hanging around on the hill until Battalion told me I absolutely had to turn Echo Company over to my relief. That was around a week after I was supposed to take off.

The first chopper I could get off 861A was a medevac, which took me straight to Dong Ha, where the 3rd Marine Division forward command post was set up. I got off the chopper looking like I'd just been through a battle. Almost right away, the division sergeant major came running out to tell me that the division chief of staff was upset because my uniform wasn't neat. The sergeant major took me down to the supply hooch, but the supply sergeant didn't want to give me fresh utilities because I wasn't a member of his battalion. The sergeant major told him he would if he wanted to live. Then, a short time later, I went into the

Officers' Club for a drink. Naturally, I kept my helmet on. Some staff captain started going on about how, since I had not uncovered, I would have to buy everyone a round. Then they wanted to take my pistol away. Next, I went up to the showers. Some lieutenant colonel I met there began telling me how tough they had it at Dong Ha. He even showed me a little bitty shrapnel hole in the corner of the plywood shower hooch. I agreed with him that he was really seeing the war.

Chapter 10

Hill 881S

LCpl PHIL TORRES
India Company, 3/16 _____

I landed at the Khe Sanh airstrip on February 14 and was immediately sent to help man the perimeter lines with Lima Company, 3/26. There was very little movement on the lines; everybody had to stay under cover, everybody had to wear flak jackets and helmets. Heaven help anyone caught without his flak jackets and helmet on. This was the first time since I had arrived in Vietnam, a few days earlier, that I worked with a loaded weapon. Occasionally I heard a spurt of small-arms fire or a barrage of "freight trains" coming in overhead, with explosions nearby. I kept thinking, what the heck have I gotten myself into? It was never-ending. A tent would get hit, some stored ammunition would go off, a Marine would be hit by shrapnel, rockets would hit the base.

On my second day at Khe Sanh, February 15, all the new guys were told to test-fire their weapons, to make sure they were okay. Then some of us were assigned to India Company, which was on Hill 881S. Others were assigned to Mike Company, also on Hill 881S, and Kilo Company, which was on Hill 861. As we boarded the CH-46 helicopters, there was a lot of talk about 881S. Even before I had left the States, people who were coming back from Nam were talking about 881S—about blood and guts, and all the glory. Fear started creeping in as we were told that helos were being blasted right out of the air as they tried to land on the hill. They told us that our chopper would take all kinds of fire when it tried to land—mortars, machine guns, and small arms. They told us we would *not* be getting 122mm rockets because of their trajectory. We heard about .51-caliber machine guns ripping through the helos, cutting Marines in half. The likelihood of becoming a casualty at this early stage was very high.

There was a lot of noise, a lot of commotion, as we arrived to land on the hill. I understand that there was a .51-caliber trying to cut the chopper down, that we came very near to losing the chopper and all the troops in it.

As soon as the chopper hit the ground on the hill, we had to move about a hundred meters, run from the saddle between India and Mike companies to the top of the hill, which was India Company's area. That had to be the roughest hundred meters I ever crossed. I was scared, there was a lot of noise, a lot of gunfire, I didn't know which way it was going, or who was firing what. I was told that the enemy was going to wipe us out. I believed everything I heard. Machine guns were shooting at us, and there were snipers in the treeline on the next hill over who were shooting at us, trying to pick off the people trying to get off the helicopter.

I met my new company commander, Capt Bill Dabney, just as I finished crossing the hundred-meter open space. He was a big Marine—a giant Marine—who didn't seem scared of anything. This guy looked like he could eat rocks. He wasn't getting down, he wasn't doing anything. He was just out there, making sure we were going to the top of the hill all right and putting us into the trenches. He was not

standing in the trench, he was standing outside, pushing us
in.

Cpl TERRY STEWART
Mike Company, 3/26 _____

The day-to-day life on Hill 881S was a combination of
many things, the most notable of which were the frustra-
tions of being confined in a static position and unable to
carry the fight to the enemy, the loneliness, the dreary,
sometimes ugly weather, and the feeling of uselessness. The
morale, however, was very high in spite of the many
negative factors that could have—should have—dominated
our spirits.

For the most part, we spent our days talking of home,
girls, cars, girls, food, girls, sports, girls, and, most important, girls. Quite often the talk was serious—of family and
loves won and lost. The war and the home front's attitudes
were also heavy topics. I can honestly say that every man
I'd spoken to felt "right" about being in Nam.

There was maintenance to perform, as well. This was
basically tending to our weapons and equipment, and the
constant work we performed on our fortifications and
trenches.

We had a couple of small, Japanese-type transistor radios
in the group, but batteries were always a big problem. We
managed to rig a squad-radio battery and some comm wire
to run the radios. The scratchy music was like a live concert
to us. Mostly we listened to Hanoi Hannah.

We nearly always had some kind of a battle with the rock
apes. These feisty primates would sneak up on us and
frighten the living shit right out of us. I know of one case
where one literally did just that. The damn thing got up on a
moonless night and grabbed hold of the muzzle of a man's
rifle. When he did, he screamed like a woman being raped
and jumped up and down. The Marine, frightened beyond
description, screamed, let go of his bowels, and then pulled
the trigger. The two of them screaming and the rifle going
off on a long blast alerted everyone on the line. Instantly,
men were up and firing, believing that somewhere in the

pitch blackness we were being attacked by the whole North Vietnamese Army. It was frightening, but funny as hell when it was over.

We had a bit of a ritual with the flag ceremony each day. This we shared with India Company, too. In the saddle between our two ends of the hill there was a place we called No-Man's-Land. Set out there was a radio antenna that we rigged as a flagpole. it wasn't very high. The NVA had No-Man's-Land zeroed in with their 82mm mortars real good. They could hit anywhere in the saddle that they wanted to. Each day, two Marines would crouch in the trench just before 0800 and then dash out to raise the flag. As soon as they cleared the trench, we could hear the enemy mortars fire. The two men had exactly twenty-two seconds to get out there, raise the colors, salute, and get back before the rounds impacted. This same ritual was performed at night. The NVA rarely fired more than just two rounds, and not once did anyone ever get hurt during Colors. There were some close calls, but not hits.

LCpl PHIL TORRES
India Company, 3/26 _____

We lived like moles, never leaving the trenches or bunkers. We were constantly digging—it never stopped—day and night, filling sandbags, digging trenches, carrying food. We were always laying German Tape concertina wire, which was very dangerous to work with because it was covered with razor blades. At least six separate strands surrounded the entire hill. There was about a hundred meters of clearance between the concertina and the trenches. We built homemade bombs from 106mm recoilless-rifle shell canisters filled with C4 plastic explosive, machine-gun links, expended M-16 cartridges, anything we could find. We put the bombs down by the concertina wire and ran a Claymore mine detonator line back to the trench.

We normally slept by day because the enemy could see us if we went into the trenches during the day. If they did see anyone, all hell would break loose. One person stepping out into the trenchline could bring in a whole barrage of mortars. Every morning the hill would be above what seemed to be a cloud. That was nice because the enemy was not able to see us and we would be able to come out of the trenches, see what needed fixing, and fix things up a little. As the sun heated up the air, the fog went away, the enemy was able to see us, and we had to stay in the trenches or bunkers. So we did most of the work by night. It was strange, living that way. It was difficult to sleep during the day, so we listened to the radio, to Hanoi Hannah. The 122mm rockets could not hit the hill because of their trajectory, but everything else could—mortars, artillery, machine guns, small arms.

I received a lot of mail, more than the average trooper. I would write a letter to my mother, and she would dramatize my letter—adding words here and taking them away there—and take it down to the Spanish newspaper in New York City, and they would print the letter with my address. I had all kinds of people—young females—writing to me. At times, I got as many as fifty or more letters from various states and even some from outside the United States. Most of them were Hispanic women who were proud to have one of their own fighting for the United States. They sent me pictures and body measurements and cute little lines asking me to look them up when I got back. That definitely picked up my morale, got me through some of the rough times.

☆

Capt BILL DABNEY
India Company, 3/26 ───────────────────────

We had a probe one night. We had several minor probes, but this, as best we could tell, was about a platoon-size probe, and the only thing we got out of it was the fact that the average Marine can throw a Mark-26 hand grenade downhill a hell of a lot better than the average NVA can throw a Chicom grenade uphill. It was a pretty one-sided sort of thing. I don't think we had two or three guys hurt. That was a pretty steep hill.[1]

LCpl PHIL TORRES
India Company, 3/26 _____

Because of the heavy concentration of enemy in the area, we were not able to send out patrols, but one of the things we constantly had to do on 881S was go out to man the listening posts. We went 200 or 250 meters outside the perimeter, about a quarter the way down the hill. The first time I went out, my third night on the hill, I almost didn't make it back. Sometime during the night, either us or some enemy snipers or an enemy patrol made some movement in the area near us. The people on our own lines, up the hill, decided to throw a couple of hand grenades in the direction of the movement. The grenades landed pretty near us. Luckily, we had a mortar crater that the three of us managed to squeeze into. Normally, a mortar crater wouldn't hold one person, but we managed to find room for three. Some of the grenades were landing a couple of meters away.

☆

Cpl TERRY STEWART
Mike Company, 3/26 _____

We sometimes played games with the NVA. One game was "Maggie's Drawers." Maggie's Drawers is what Marines call the red flag that is waved across the face of a target at the rifle range when the shooter completely misses the target. Well, we made a large bull's-eye target from a sleeve that went over a case of C-rations. One side was split, and the cardboard was folded out so that it was quite large. We propped this up just above our trench, in a place not too near any of the bunkers. We put it up just for the hell of it, with the hope that one night when the NVA hit us, we would catch a stray round. The target sat there for a few days without anything touching it. Soon we all forgot about it. Then, one afternoon, we received a single sniper round. That wasn't unusual, so we all just sort of ignored it. The first round was followed by another and, a few minutes later, another. Again, not too unusual, except that the rounds were all hitting in the same place. Someone yelled that they were shooting at our target, and everyone made a dash to get close enough to see. It was foolish. If one mortar round had hit in the trench on either side of that stupid target, it would have wiped out half of the platoon. But we all wanted to see the sniper try to hit our target. One of the guys slid into position under the target. He hastily fashioned a sort of Maggie's Drawers from a rag and a piece of stick. After the sniper fired again, the Marine waved the flag to indicate a miss. Actually, the sniper had hit the lower edge of the target with his last round. I guess that this really pissed off the sniper and one of his friends. The sniper sent us three or four quick rounds with his SKS, and then his pal cut into us with a quick burst of .51-cal fire. Those .51s are huge rounds and no joy to be anywhere near when they were fired in your direction. The bunch of us scattered like bugs in the kitchen when the lights come on.

A few days later, after talking about our little game and having a laugh, one of the men was moving down the trench to return to his bunker and, for no apparent reason, jumped onto the berm and began waving his arms and yelling, "Get me, you motherfuckers." He had no sooner gotten the words out of his mouth than the big machine gun barked and a round nearly took the guy's head off. The platoon corpsman kept him alive for two whole days. He died just as medevac was coming in.

RESUPPLY

LCpl PHIL TORRES
India Company, 3/26 _____

A lot of chopper pilots got scared when they caught a lot of fire. They often released their external loads a little too soon or a little too late, and a lot of the food landed outside the India Company perimeter, in enemy territory. We had to send out patrols at night, secure the area, and get our food. Sometimes we had to fight for our food because the enemy wanted it, too. Many times, we had no food or water.

Sometimes, days passed with no resupply whatsoever, and all the food would run out. When that happened, we scrounged through packs and bunkers to see what kind of food we hadn't wanted earlier. When we ran out of that, we went through the trash pit to get the little cans of jelly, peanut butter, and cheese most guys threw away. We had fights over those little cans. Marines offered fifty dollars, a hundred dollars for a can of food scrounged from the trash pit. Usually, the Marine with the food laughed and said something like, "What am I going to do with money? I don't need money; I need food." I know people who ate C-rat cigarettes, just to get something on their stomachs. At the time, none of us knew that Captain Dabney had quite a bit of food stored underneath his bunker. It was there for a *real* emergency. He would have taken care of us.

Capt BILL DABNEY
India Company, 3/26 _____

At the beginning of the monsoon season, about the end of October 1967, we were issued rainsuits, sized a certain mix of small, medium, and large. About the middle of February, it was cold up there at night in those hills, foggy. I sent down a request for some more rainsuits. "Don't have them, not available," was the reply. Actually, I had to put an order out to the company, directing that anything they ordered through Sears or Mom had to be olive drab, because mothers were sending them air-sea-rescue-orange things.

I brought this up to the supply officer, a major or lieutenant colonel down at the 3rd Marine Division Command Post, and he said, "Well, when a guy rotates, take the rainsuit from him and give it to his replacement." Now, does this tell you something about the supply system? I didn't have anybody rotating. They all went out on stretchers or in body bags. And I have yet to discover a way, when a round goes through a man, to keep the son of a bitch from going through his rainsuit first! But the supply system didn't think that way.

Socks. Goddamn, I hate to think of how many messages were sent, asking for socks. "Hey, you guys got socks in your basic issue." No. "Give us some socks, I want two pair of socks per week per man." "Wash the ones you have." "With what?" Two helos a day to bring water to wash eighty-nine-cent socks! In *that* antiaircraft environment! But they never took it that far in the supply system. The supply system was just a supply system. Nobody programmed socks. They figured everybody over there for just a year and the number of pairs of socks that was issued out to be able to do it. No shit. But here we're sitting on this damn hill with no water and with troops standing in those lines night after night. We had trenchfoot, infection, jungle rot, all that stuff. Couldn't get any socks, never did get any socks. Maybe it was just my battalion, I don't know. Get some more water? Well, it took a helicopter for two canteens of water per man. And that wouldn't have been enough to wash one pair of socks. Ask a helicopter pilot whether he would rather haul up fifteen pounds of socks or 5,000 pounds of water! That kind of thing. I still haven't gotten over that.

Stretchers. Same thing. They couldn't seem to understand that the operational requirement for the guy that was hit was all that mattered in the end. For example, dustoff birds—medevac—carried spare stretchers. But we didn't evac with dustoff birds up on the landing zone. For one thing, when we got hit by NVA, we got hit hard. Too many medevacs for a regular medevac bird. For another, we usually needed an emergency resupply of ammo after the first-round bell, and had it planned and staged. So we put our wounded on the logistics bird, a CH-46 usually diverted from another mission. But they didn't carry spare stretchers. What now? We couldn't just dump the poor guy on the floor of the bird just so we could keep our stretchers! So, a dozen or so hit, and our company had no stretchers. Ever tried carrying a 200-pounder with a sucking chest wound in a poncho under fire? It takes four men—men needed up front! Two can do it with a stretcher. We sent messages asking that spare stretchers be carried aboard CH-46s for one-on-one trade during medevacs. They don't weigh that much and don't take up much space, broken down. Nothing ever came of it, though.

I never had a supply officer visit us. You know, they stay in warehouses. The stuff is all on the shelves real nice, but it doesn't help people! We put a requisition in for 60mm firing pins because they were wearing out and we were shooting mortars, 200 to 300 rounds a day. Couldn't get the goddamned things. Sent a gutsy, thieving Pfc down to Danang with a bottle of Scotch that he'd scrounged up from someplace. He went to the Naval Support Activity, Danang, and found a chief petty officer who would machine those damn 60mm mortar firing pins on a lathe in return for the Scotch. Because the supply system said there weren't any in the system. Shit, make them! That's a pretty bottom-line sort of thing! Our flak jackets were falling apart—rotting. Sent down for forty or fifty replacements. Got a message back saying, "Send down the unserviceable ones and we'll survey them!" Yeah!

Slings and nets for helo external loads: Once we realized what the NVA could do to us, and that didn't take long, all supplies came in external. After two or three resupplies, five or ten birds each, we had a bunch of nets and slings on the hill. We'd get a message to stage them for pickups and reuse. We'd send back that it was too risky. We'd get a message back to have them ready for pickup or they couldn't resupply us anymore. So we complied. We lost three helo support teams doing that, two or three men each, and one bird, a CH-46. You see, the bird had to come in and hover exactly over the load, in the wind blowing across the crest, under .51-caliber and AK-47 fire, while the poor bastard from the helo support team stood, outlined against the skyline, on top of the pile, and married the sling to the cargo hook. If he didn't get hit by them firing at the bird, he'd marry, jump off, and run like hell for the nearest hole as the bird beat it out of there. They—the helo support and helo folks—both knew that the 120mm mortars were already on the way. We didn't always make it. One bird took a few rounds of .51 through the Plexiglas between the front seats just as the Marine was marrying the sling-loop to the hook. Well, the bird launched as if it had been shot from a slingshot, sling engaged, with the HST man still standing on the load. He tried to jump off, but his foot got caught in a net, and he rode down to Khe Sanh hanging upside down by one foot under the load, while his buddy with the radio, now deep in a hole, tried to tell the pilot what had happened! I guess the guy made it, but he never came back up the hill. I'm not sure I blame him! Now I don't know what nets and slings cost, but it was damned sure less than the cost of six Marines and a CH-46! And while we didn't have enough nets and slings in the Air Wing to avoid those risks, the fat cats were still driving Cadillacs at Miami Beach and the civilians at the supply depots were still beating the 1600 whistle out the gate. But I guess that'll never change.

Body bags. Couldn't get them. Ever watch rats crawling in and out of ponchos holding what's left of two men hit by a 152? The troops did! They were up there five days. Weather socked in. Ripe. We were told we couldn't bury them. We did anyway. Had to. Also told we couldn't send the bodies out external. Too risky to bring a bird down and load them. Too many men in one place. Took too long. So we buried them under piles of nets and slings and sent them out anyway. We did that several times. We'd tell the pilot after he'd lifted off. Those guys understood. The rear didn't.[2]

LCpl PHIL TORRES
India Company, 3/26 _____

We lived like animals. We couldn't take any baths, we rarely shaved, we never had haircuts, we rarely changed clothes. We lived like moles: in by day, out by night. The only morale booster we had was mail. Sometimes they brought us hot beer, but any consumable item raised the morale, even hot beer. In our imaginations, it was ice cold. We craved for sweets, for anything that was different than the C-rats.

HM3 DAVID STEINBERG
Indian Company, 3/26 _____

There was some obscure rule that if you're not paid within ninety days, you can leave combat. So they dropped us our pay.

□

HILL 861

Pfc ELWIN BACON
Kilo Company, 3/26 _____

The days following the January 21 attack on Hill 861 turned
into weeks and months of a complete fortification program.
Tunnels were built, and sandbags completely surrounded the
hill. Days were filled with sandbag details or other working
parties. We dug a system of tunnels that would have allowed
the enemy to completely overrun our hill without their
seeing one Marine. Supplies could be brought from the
landing zone to the command post totally underground. We
gradually built up one hell of a wire system and placed
mines with 55-gallon drums of chopper fuel over them, to
be set off by command from our bunkers if needed.

Hill 861 became a turkey shoot for snipers on both sides.
We had to stand watches on a point looking north. If we saw
any rockets being launched from the DMZ, we had a direct
line with the main base at Khe Sanh. All we had to say was
"Incoming," and the sound of sirens bellowed out from the
valley to the south. Boredom became a daily thing, except
for the nearly hourly mortar attacks that we began to tell the
time of day by.

One day I was looking out toward the northern ridge of
the hill next to us and saw someone watching us. I knew he
was well out of distance to shoot him, and besides, we
had orders not to fire unless we got permission from the
command post. (Fire control, right?) Anyway, I knew he
saw me, and the only thing I could think of was to wave to
him. He disappeared immediately, but looked up once more
before departing completely.

Another time I was on early-morning watch and was
eating breakfast when I spotted a head directly across from
mine. The NVA had a radio on his back and was watching
our hill very closely. I got down off the top of my bunker
very casual-like and went to my lieutenant's hut. I took his

glasses and set them on my helmet. The lieutenant looked through and identified my find. He sent me down the trenches and up the back side of the hill to the 106mm recoilless-rifle position and had them sight in on the dude. They were about to fire on the target when a 3.5-inch rocket tube went off. It turned out that the lieutenant had had them try to get the dude with it, but they missed. Anyway, the 106 fired on the same position and had a direct hit, but I never knew if we got the guy or not—thanks to the lieutenant.

Hill 861 became an island that was surrounded by a bunch of bees that were just waiting to get their stingers into us. Supplies were very hard to get in to us. Enemy fire took down some of the choppers, and I just knew those bastards were eating my cake from home and reading my mail. We were down to half a canteen of water a day and one box of C-rations each. It got to the point that Marines were sneaking out in front to search for food in the old crater we used as a garbage dump. It would drive us crazy at night because the rats would make so much noise in the garbage dump. We were never quite sure what kinds of rats were out there.

During the day we had a bird's-eye view of everything that took place in Khe Sanh, to our south, on Hill 861A, directly to our east, and up to the DMZ, to our north. Between the daily rocket attacks on Khe Sanh and the ever-increasing jet attacks on positions in every direction, we grew to be very nonchalant about the whole thing. Many times we took our chances by fixing the wire and mines out in front of our positions.

Many a night we stayed awake watching the B-52s working away around us, and that old standby, Puff the Magic Dragon, burning up the midnight oil and a lot of ammo. Puff was one of the principal deterrents of enemy buildup in that area. The short-timers were reluctant to leave the hill because of the chopper problem and the constant shit that was hitting Khe Sanh. At least we were only getting hit with mostly mortars and, once in a while, an RPG.

I began to get very disturbed over our lack of actually doing anything about the situation. We were not trained to just sit and take that kind of shit, day after day, with no way to get back at those bastards. The guys were doing anything to break the monotony. We played football in the opening landing zone until someone would holler "Incoming." Then everyone would hit the trenches. Some guys would run around the hill naked in the heavy rain, singing songs. I spent some time making toy rockets out of the pop-up illumination canisters and loose increments from mortars, and sent them across to the next ridge. To the NVA we must have seemed crazy, and I think they were right. Stir-crazy.

From time to time, in the evening, we would hear the NVA hollering at us from a distance. We had a Marine who spoke Vietnamese, and he would holler back at them. I never understood the conversation, but we all got a chuckle out of it.

There was a guy who flew overhead in a spotter plane and dropped some cartons of cigarettes down to us. I think his son was on the hill with us. We all appreciated the efforts that were made to get us some kind of supplies.

Sgt MIKE STAHL
4.2-inch Mortar Battery, 1/13 (Hill 861) _____

Water was a very big problem. When they couldn't get it in to us by helicopter, and we ran out, we had to send a heavily armed water detail to a stream at the bottom of the hill to fill canteens. That was always good for a few casualties.

There were always a few fresh NVA bodies in our wire. When the food situation got really bad a few times, some of us crawled out to retrieve the rice bags all of them carried. It was that grim.

Chapter 11

SSgt HARVE SAAL, USA
FOB-3 _____

Early on the morning of March 20, about 0200, my recon team departed the FOB using a starless sky to cover our movement. The mission was a basic area recon. We moved several kilometers from camp and awaited first light. With the first hint of dawn, we began moving. At full light we entered a large defoliated mass of hilltops. We felt that we had NVA trackers on our trail.

All of a sudden, all hell broke loose. *Thump! Whoosh! Blam!* We were under NVA mortar fire. We were forced to move toward a hill without vegetation. Then, *Bam! Bam!* —the launching of two 122mm rockets. *Boom! Boom!* —they impacted in our area. Geez, I thought, they're shooting *rockets* at a small recon team; they must have millions of them! *Thump! Whoosh! Blam!* More mortar shrapnel whistled through the air.

I called in to a prearranged frequency and call sign which had been coordinated between myself and the Marine operations and artillery planner. I needed help to get that mortar fire stopped, even just a delay of a few minutes—anything! I had one wounded Bru, and I knew we would take more casualties if we didn't get some help soon. I made the recon team start moving through an opening and up to the edge of the defoliated hill. I tried the radio again.

I finally got through to a Marine artillery officer, told him where the NVA mortar was located, and that we needed artillery fire placed on that location. He said, "Mission cannot be fired." I frantically asked, "Why can't you fire?" He said, "There's friendlies in that area!" It took me only a split second to realize what he had said and another second to notify him that those friendlies were us.

The Marines never did honor my request for artillery support that day. One Bru gave his life that day for the defense and security of that Marine officer, who was safe to hide inside a bunker and drink his hot cocoa and make life-or-death decisions.

☆

Cpl DENNIS MANNION
Charlie Battery, 1/13 (Hill 861) _____

March 20, 1968

Hey Man—
    No incoming in 48 hours. We've been getting fucking A-number-one air support the last few days (mainly because of clear weather) and that's the stuff to keep the mothers down.
    NBC was here yesterday, spent the night, and left this morning. Three guys, very Hollywood. Loud talk, many discussions about this or that shot or background, lights, action, camera, Act III, Scene 201. Bullshit. Made me sick. Supposed to be doing a special on the hill. They did cover the hill pretty well.
    One incident. Funnier than hell. The 106mm recoilless rifle is a mother (bigger than the 105mm cannon I shoot). It's recoilless—all the blast comes

out of the breech and can kill or maim you if you're
standing 100 feet behind it. The tube is nine feet
long, weighs 215 pounds. On top is a singleshot
.50-cal. You fire the .50-cal, watch the tracer hit—
adjust the .50-cal. onto the target—and the 106 will
hit the same hole. Okay, the photogs want a live
shot of the 106—to catch the backblast. They're
in a line. A tall, loudmouthed, skinny asshole has
the camera on his shoulder, eye glued to the sight.
"Okay, shoot," he says. Our 106-man fires the
.50-cal. *Bang!* One correction to the left. (They're
shooting at a possible bunker.) Another .50-cal.
Bang! A last correction. *Bang!* At this moment, as
our 106 man's hand is closing the distance between
the top of his finger and the firing button, the
asshole cameraman yells out, "What the fuck! I ain't
seeing any smoke at all. Is it broke?" *Wham!* I
laughed till I couldn't, then laughed some more.
When the dust, dirt pebbles, and debris settled,
there's our friend, flat on his fucking ass, camera
about ten feet away. By that time, I'm laughing so
hard I fall into my bunker, weeping with hysteria.
Oh, God—only two or three times in my life have
I laughed so hard. I laughed till I was sick. So
beautiful.

One thing they did get was some fantastic flicks
of Phantom jets dropping the heavies in close. Keep
a lookout for the special. I don't know if I'm in it
or not. The only time they were close to my hooch,
I was in the middle of a fire mission—25 NVA in
the open. We knocked down thirteen or so.

MARCH 21

Capt HARRY BAIG
26th Marines Target Information Officer _____

[Bravo Company, 1/26] was directed to dispatch a platoon
patrol into the trench system, south of Gray Sector, at dawn,
to determine what had happened to the enemy. The Fire

Support Coordination Center developed a fire plan to protect
the patrol. In essence, this plan was an offensive version of
the defensive boxes. Nine batteries of artillery participated.
Marine artillery formed the primary box and the rolling
barrage. The Army's 175s and [radar-guided] air formed the
sides of the secondary box, which fell on those pieces of
ground that overlooked or could influence the patrol area.
The patrol moved out seventy-five meters behind the rolling
barrage into the sides of the box. Then, as the patrol
continued to advance, the entire primary box also advanced,
with the patrol inside it and the rolling barrage also inside it
and in front of the patrol. Outside the primary box, as usual,
the secondary box's sides opened and closed over the terrain
like an accordion.

During the ninety minutes of the patrol [0630 to 0800],
over 1,300 rounds—shell mixed and fuse mixed—were
fired. Whether or not this was too much support for too
small a force may be debatable. A measure of its success
lies in the fact that, though the enemy made an attempt to
retaliate (two volleys of mortars, which were quickly
stopped), not a man was injured as a result of direct enemy
action.[1]

26th Marines Command Chronology _____

Several enemy explosive devices were found and blown
in place. During the patrol, 14 rounds of incoming 82mm
mortar fire caused three friendly WIA (evacuated) and six
friendly WIA (not evacuated).

MARCH 22

Capt JIM LESLIE
26th Marines Assistant Communicator _____

We decided that one of the communications teams needed
a new bunker as theirs had taken a direct hit which
injured a few Marines. Our project was to build them a
new bunker between artillery barrages.

Material to build a sturdy bunker was not available, so

we utilized the "field expedient," which is anything that is available. We had plenty of empty 55-gallon fuel drums, sandbags, and red dirt, but the thing we needed most was wood for frame construction. The best material on hand was the runway mating or eight-foot-by-eight-foot aluminum pallets used by helos to deliver our C-rations. We decided to steal some of the aluminum pallets from the airstrip. However, they were so much in demand that the military police had stationed a man near the pallets to keep other Marines from stealing them.

My well-thought-out scheme was, as the guards changed each day about 1800 in the evening, at about dusk, I would take a jeep, trailer, and three young Marines and drive down the runway, throw twelve aluminum pallets on the trailer, drive up the runway about fifty meters, and get away through the barbed-wire fence.

Just at 1800, the guard left for chow, as we anticipated. We casually drove the jeep and trailer along the side of the runway, pulled up beside the stack of pallets, and loaded on twelve—valued at $5,000 each. A young private who jumped in the driver's seat as the other three of us jumped on top of the pallets cautiously started to drive down the runway. Simultaneously, as the guard yelled for us to stop and fired a couple of warning rounds into the air, the NVA started dropping in mortar rounds about twenty yards behind us. The young private at the wheel had never driven a stick shift before; he didn't know how to go faster. As the next mortar round landed a little too close behind us, I leaped from the trailer to the backseat of the jeep and pushed the private over to the passenger side. At the same time, the other two Marines on the trailer jumped into the backseat of the jeep.

I pushed the pedal to the metal and jammed the transmission into second gear. At that point, all of the pallets went flying across the runway behind us like a loose deck of cards. We escaped without injury and went back the next night to grab the pallets.

The Seabees dug a large fifteen-foot-by-twenty-foot hole in the ground with a bulldozer and we built our

$60,000 mansion in the ground. We used ten of the twelve pallets below ground level and built a second roof by placing dirt-filled 55-gallon drums on the first roof and covering them with the two remaining pallets. Concealed by sandbags, this second roof created a false ceiling or dead space. If an artillery round hit, it would explode between the first and second roofs and only give the Marines inside a headache. This bunker took at least three direct hits during my tenure, and no one was ever injured.

☆

1stLt NICK ROMANETZ
Charlie Company, 1/26 _____

Our company gunny, GySgt John Grohman, was living in my bunker with me because they didn't want the company commander, exec, and gunny in one place in case it got hit by incoming. On March 22 we got the word that we could expect an incoming artillery barrage that night and a possible ground assault on the combat base. When we were put on Red Alert for the evening, Gunny Grohman told me he thought it would be best if he went up to the command post. The command post was brand-new because the old one had been blown up about a month earlier. It was strong; its roof had an initial row of runway matting, then two or three rows of sandbags, then 55-gallon drums filled with dirt, and then another row of runway matting with more sandbags on top. The idea was that a round with a delay fuse would go through the top row of matting and sandbags and detonate prior to reaching the bunker. It also had good beams inside; it was real sturdy.

26th Marines Command Chronology _____

   At 1830, the KSCB came under heavy fire.

1stLt NICK ROMANETZ
Charlie Company, 1/26 _____

Capt Walter Egger, Gunny Grohman, 2ndLt Paul Bush [company exec], and the company radio personnel were in the bunker by then. The command post took a direct hit. Captain Egger, Lieutenant Bush, and Gunnery Sergeant Grohman were all killed.

Also that night, one of my platoon's bunkers took a direct hit, probably from a 122mm rocket. There were three Marines inside the bunker. Two were killed, but, strangely, the third one came out without a scratch.

We were on Red Alert when the rocket hit. Everyone was supposed to be in their fighting positions, with their helmets and flak jackets on, and weapons at the ready. Yet, when we excavated the bunker the next day, the two dead men were found in an upright position, sitting there with no shirts, no helmets, and no flak jackets on. I found this to be very unusual because the two dead Marines were "salts"—old timers—each with about two months in-country.

Eventually I heard through scuttlebutt that the two salts had been sitting up smoking dope. The new guy had his helmet and flak jacket on and he was lying down flat in the bunker when the stuff was coming in. Lucky guy. He was too green to break the rules.

☆

LCpl PHIL MINEER
Bravo Battery, 1/13 _____

On March 15, the scuttlebutt going around had said that our intelligence people thought the major NVA units around Khe Sanh were withdrawing. That lightened things up a little. The only reason we believed it was because we went about three days and only received about twenty rounds. Just little harassment stuff; a pop here and pop there. But on March 22—just like on February 23—over a thousand rounds came in. We answered it. It never let up, and we never quit firing back.

We called the Charlie Battery executive officer, Lieutenant Eberhardt, "Mister E." He was a good guy. The best. We'd have done anything for him. He wasn't even from my battery, but he'd come down to the gun, break out rounds with us, and work just like the regular sweathogs.

He was a gymnast, on rings. He had the biggest forearms I ever saw. He'd move his fingers and all the muscles in his arm would ripple. He was a gym teacher and a guidance counselor, too. He kept my head right a few times. Mister E and Sergeant Whiteknight, also from Charlie Battery, were right there when the ammo dump blew. We were firing the battery and they were hauling stuff out of there. I saw Whiteknight with smoking rounds in his arms. They threw that stuff on a truck and Whiteknight drove it out of the area. It could have blown up anytime.

Soon we had to stop firing and lay low in the bunkers. The rounds in the dump were cooking and popping. We heard them going off. The worst part was feeling the concussion, when it compressed my chest and I could feel my diaphragm move. The bunker walls were thick, and we were all taking it pretty well. Some of the teargas had gone up, and we were all sitting there and the gas was getting us. Of course, we had all left our gas masks in our sleeping bunkers. We had a 5-gallon water can and dunked pieces of parachute to hold over our mouths and noses. It worked pretty good—if you stayed calm. But one of the new guys snapped out. Just like in the movies, he stood up and started screaming hysterically, "I'm gettin' outta here!" I just looked at him and said, "Whatta ya doin'?" There was terror in his eyes, and tears rolling down his cheeks. I said, "Where the fuck are you gonna go? You gonna go outside the bunker and catch a taxicab? Come on!" LCpl Thom Keaton, our section chief, and I held him. Every time the rounds hit, he shivered. It reminded me of the first time I had been rocketed at Con Thien. After that, the kid didn't have a whole lot of fear.

Soon after the ammo dump went, one of the guns took one right in the center. The rounds on the parapet went, and they set the gun on fire. The guys in the crew were hurt pretty bad. It was raining, the gun was on fire—we were trying to get foam on it—rounds were coming in, and we were trying to get the crew evacuated to Charlie-Med. One guy had a real bad abdominal wound; we were holding his intestines in and had a poncho wrapped around his chest. It was too far to Charlie-Med to hump him on a litter, so we got a Mighty Mite and loaded him on. But there was too much mud. We were trying to hold him on the Mighty Mite, but it kept sliding from side to side and we kept slipping. The rain mixed with the kid's blood, and it was all over the place. In the end, we finally got him to Charlie-Med. Later they told us he made it, he survived.

26th Marines Command Chronology _____

Damage assessments for the 1,049 rounds of incoming received revealed two 105mm howitzers damaged and temporarily out of action and one 105mm howitzer destroyed. Approximate ammunition losses were 300 rounds of 81mm mortar, 2,163 rounds of 3.5-inch rockets, 700 M-72 LAAWs, 800 rounds of 105mm white phosphorus, 100 rounds of 105mm "firecracker," 28 boxes of VT fuses, 10 boxes of point-detonation fuses, and an undetermined amount of Class II ammunition and pyrotechnics.

MARCH 23

Cpl ALLAN STAHL
Logistics Support Unit _____

It was the worst day of the siege for me. We heard that an NVA trench under the base had caved in, that an attack was imminent, that the NVA were coming. There would have to be a posted walking guard in each company area at all times, twenty-four hours a day. The Logistics Support Unit had to post a noncommissioned officer and another Marine to walk the area on two-hour watches.

Our area included the supply dump, which was piled high with boxes. They were piled up like skyscrapers. At night, that was a *spooky* place. I have never been more frightened in my life than when I was walking patrol in the middle of the night in the supply dump.

I had a shotgun and I was with another communicator. It

was obvious to me that we were sacrificial lambs. Our duty was to fire a round to alert everyone else as we died. I had the equal horror that everyone in the combat base was armed and looking to shoot at moving shadows—*any* moving shadows, like us.

It was eerily silent except for occasional artillery fire. As I walked, I expected someone to jump out of literally every corner. There was no relaxation at all. Finally, I had enough. I couldn't do it anymore. I was in charge, so I took charge. We got down in a corner, where we had protection, and sat there and breathed to muster every bit of courage we could put together. Then we took another walk, and then we stopped to pull ourselves together. The guy with me kept raising his weapon to shoot at shadows, but he never fired. Finally, after four or five times, we stopped walking altogether.

When I got back, they told me to unload the shotgun so I could turn it over to the next man. I tried, but I didn't know how to work the pump on the thing. I realized that I couldn't have fired the shotgun.

LCpl PHIL MINEER
Bravo Battery, 1/13 _____

They came down with a Red Alert. That meant "Everybody awake for as long as the alert lasts." They took guys from the artillery and put them on line with the grunts. We were all assigned a field of fire. That evening I heard that an NVA sniper got hung up in the wire. A lot of tripflares went up, and they shot him. He was hanging on the wire in the morning. We were waiting to hear the bugle and watch the 304th NVA Division come swooping in on us. We were ready for them, but the attack never materialized.

Next morning, when I got relieved from my position out on the perimeter, I went back to my bunker, sat down, and wrote four letters. After I wrote them, I put them in the bottom of my seabag and instructed my buddies to make sure the seabag got home if anything happened to me. One letter was to an old girlfriend—my first love—one was to my mother and father, one was to my aunt, and the last was to my brothers and sister. I just said the things a guy would say when he's ready to die.

MARCH 24

1/9 Command Chronology _____

At 1130, a platoon patrol from Alpha Company dispatched a squad to the northwest to reconnoiter the area. Contact was made resulting in two friendly KIAs from heavy small-arms fire from an estimated fourteen NVA in well-constructed bunkers and fighting holes. A second squad was sent to reinforce this squad. In the resulting fire fight, three more friendly KIAs were sustained, and four WIAs. The enemy strength increased to an estimated thirty NVA, and twenty more were spotted moving down the ridgeline.

Pfc LAWRENCE SEAVY-CIOFFI
Bravo Company, 1/9 _____

After recuperating from the wounds I suffered defending the Alpha-1 outpost on February 8, I returned to 1/9 in mid-March and was reassigned as an artillery forward observer scout with Bravo Company, 1/9.

I was manning an observation post outside the northwestern perimeter line of the Rock Quarry when the patrol was ambushed. I was watching as Huey helicopters came in. One of them was shot down about 300 yards west of the observation post. It didn't quite crash; it hovered down slowly. One guy jumped before it hit the ground. He was lucky the helicopter didn't topple over on him. Other helicopters had to come in and rescue the crew.

1/9 Command Chronology _____

Friendly tanks, artillery, mortars, and Huey gunships were used in support and, coupled with fire from the two squads, resulted in 31 NVA KIAs (confirmed), four bunkers, and two 60mm mortar positions destroyed.

MARCH 25

LCpl RAY NICOL
Bravo Battery, 1/13 _____

On March 25, I was repairing one of the three howitzers in
the battery that had been damaged on March 22. The recoil
mechanism was acting up, and I was the only one left in the
battery who knew how to repair it. The gun was nearly
repaired when I got shot through the right elbow. I remember seeing a red tracer after the bullet left my arm. I ran into
the next gun pit, which was below the ground, to avoid
being hit again. At first, I didn't know I had been shot.
There was no pain right away, and very little blood.

I was taken to Charlie-Med for treatment and to await a
medevac to Dong Ha. By nightfall I was in tremendous pain
as the shock wore off. I had to have a shot of painkiller.

Late the next day, during a lull in the shelling, a chopper
came in. I got aboard with six other marines. I was more
afraid at that moment than I had been at any time during the
siege. As the chopper gained altitude, the NVA gunners
started firing at us. We could see tracers going by the open
door, and I could feel them impacting on the aircraft. But
we managed to get away.

At Dong Ha they changed my battle dressing, gave me
another shot for the pain, and then cut off all my clothes.
They even cut off my new boots. Then they put me on a
stretcher and covered me with a sheet. All they bothered to
clean was my wounded arm. The rest of me was incredibly
filthy. Red dirt was stuck to every part of my body.

Just before dark, I was flown to Phu Bai for further
medical attention. They operated on my arm there and put
me to sleep for a whole day. Then I was flown to Danang.
They kept me in a transient ward until the next morning and
sent me to Japan aboard a C-141. After being shipped
around to several hospitals in Japan. I reached Great Lakes
Naval Hospital on Easter weekend.

MARCH 26

Pfc LAWRENCE SEAVY-CIOFFI
Bravo Company, 1/9 _____

Each night I manned a sensor receiver, and each day I was accompanied by a fire team and a radioman to man one of two Bravo Company daytime observation posts located well outside the perimeter wire.

The northwestern Bravo Company observation post, which I manned, was within sight of the battalion main perimeter. We left the perimeter at about 0730 each morning, in the fog so we couldn't be observed, and worked our way to the top of the little hill. I spent the day moving around the top of the hill, scouting possible NVA positions with my binoculars, trying to see over and between patches of trees and elephant grass to spot enemy movement to the north. We left around 1630, as it began to get dark.

On March 26, we left at 0645 through a rolling fog and were nearing the top of the hill when the pointman, right in front of me, heard movement and saw an NVA soldier putting on his helmet.

The pointman had an M-79, which he leveled and fired at a target only fifteen or twenty feet away. The thing clicked, and the pointman cursed and opened it up. It had misfired. He put another shell in while I took a grenade out. As soon as the pointman got the M-79 reloaded, Chicoms began raining down on us.

Cpl BERT MULLINS
Bravo Company, 1/9 _____

I heard a whispered voice on the radio asking me if there was supposed to be anybody else out there on that hill. I said, "Negative." Only a few seconds passed before I heard firing in the distance. Immediately, over the radio, I heard more firing when the handset was keyed by the radioman. He was yelling that there were NVA out there.

Pfc LAWRENCE SEAVY-CIOFFI
Bravo Company, 1/9 _____

The bullets were kicking up all around us as we pulled back
to the bottom of the hill. It was a miracle we didn't take any
casualties. I figured there was a squad of NVA up there,
fifteen or twenty. But there were a lot more than that.

Cpl BERT MULLINS
Bravo Company, 1/9 _____

I told the radioman to get out of there, immediately. This
was actually beyond the realm of my authority, but it felt
right at the time. They managed to get back down off the
hill.

Pfc LAWRENCE SEAVY-CIOFFI
Bravo Company, 1/9 _____

We took cover in some brush at the foot of the hill, but
more bullets starting kicking up dust on our flank. Someone
looking over at the treeline to our right said he saw flashes
from an automatic weapon. Apparently it was an L-shaped
ambush.

We moved back farther as bullets kicked up all around us.
We continued to move back, three men at a time, while the
other three fired up at the hill and the automatic weapon on
the right. We leapfrogged back into a ravine, but they could
see us from the top of the hill. One of the grunts said that he
heard movement farther down the ravine. The NVA could
have been flanking us, so we again leapfrogged back toward
the 1/9 perimeter. My radioman took a round in the radio,
but we took no casualties. I don't understand why no one
was hit.

We made it back to the 1/9 lines and explained what had
happened. They had heard the fight, but no one had been
able to see what was going on.

1/9 Command Chronology _____

Two squads from Bravo Company were deployed to
regain the observation post.

Pfc LAWRENCE SEAVY-CIOFFI
Bravo Company, 1/9 _____

I decided to accompany the assault force back to the observation post. We had been unable to get any artillery support, so I had no reason to go out again. But I did.

We made it to the base of the hill and one squad moved up the slope. I stayed back with the other squad. I saw a head up there, had it right in my sights, but someone told me not to shoot yet. We waited and then moved up. As we did, we took Chicoms and mortar fire.

As we pulled back from the base of the hill, a Marine near me was hit by mortar shrapnel. I yelled over and over for the corpsman, but he didn't come.

Cpl BERT MULLINS
Bravo Company, 1/9 _____

All our corpsmen carried smoke grenades taped to the strap of their aid bags so they could mark a zone for medevac helicopters. The corpsman with the assault group had a green smoke grenade taped to his aid bag. When he was killed by a mortar round, the smoke grenade ignited. It was a pitiful sight; we all knew what had happened.

Pfc LAWRENCE SEAVY-CIOFFI
Bravo Company, 1/9 _____

Everyone around me was pulling back, and I was left alone with the wounded grunt. He was hit in the chest and I didn't know what to do. He said, "Don't leave me here." I asked him if he could stand, and he said he could, so I helped him up. The grunts were regrouping and I kept asking where the corpsman was. I asked the wounded Marine if he could walk, and he said he could, so I walked him back to the edge of the battalion perimeter and called for a corpsman to come down. They brought a poncho and carried him up the hill.

I had a piece of shrapnel in my arm, but I picked it out and avoided treatment. It would have made my third Purple Heart, but I couldn't turn myself in after seeing the condi-

tion of the Marine I had helped. My wound just didn't seem
like much.

1/9 Command Chronology _____

One reinforced squad assaulted the hill and was taken
under fire by enemy small arms. The enemy strength at
this position was estimated to be of company size, heavily
armed, and in well-prepared positions.

Cpl BERT MULLINS
Bravo Company, 1/9 _____

It was an eerie sight. It was like watching a real, live war
movie taking place in front of me. In the distance I could
see the group of Marines form a line and work their way up
the hill. All of them threw grenades when they got close to
the top. I saw the grenades explode and then the men were
firing their rifles as they worked their way up to the top of
the hill. They eventually took the hill, but they suffered
several killed and wounded in the process. It was unnerving
to me.

1/9 Command Chronology _____

Maximum supporting arms were utilized against the enemy while the platoon returned to the perimeter. The
contact resulted in the confirmed killing of 26 NVA and
the capture of one AK-47 rifle, one RPG round and
launcher, and five Chicom grenades. The unit sustained
three KIAs and 15 WIAs.

MARCH 27

Capt HARRY JENKINS
Mike Company, 3/26 (Hill 881S) _____

The first casualty Mike Company incurred after I arrived on
March 22 and took command on March 24 occurred on
March 27. It was a fully moonlit night, and my Marines
were out working at various assigned details. Pfc Irwin

Sobel was working on the north side of the perimeter, digging to try to improve his fighting hole. All of a sudden, he was engulfed in a tremendous explosion.

Cpl TERRY STEWART
Mike Company, 3/26 (Hill 881S) _____

I was returning from the platoon command post and heading down the trench to my squad area when there was a terrific explosion just behind me. There was a slight turn in the trench just behind me and that alone is the only reason I am here today. As soon as I shook off the shock of the explosion, I jumped to my feet and ran back toward the command-post pit. It was damaged, and I could hear our platoon guide moaning in pain. I called for a corpsman, and the call was passed on down the trench. At the same time, I heard a man screaming just behind me, from over the wall outside of the trench. I stood up and glanced over. There was a guy flopping around crazily in the concertina wire. I noticed that he kept falling over and flailing with his arms. What I didn't notice right away was that he had no legs; they were blown off at the hips. I jumped the trench and raced out to him. I reached the man at the same time as one of the corpsman. Snipers had already started to ding at us, but the darkness kept their shots from being accurate. We got the man back to the trenches and I turned him over to the doc. I then ran to my squad sector to prepare for who knew what. At that time, we didn't know what had caused the explosion; we thought it may have been a rocket and the beginning of another attack.

Capt HARRY JENKINS
Mike Company, 3/29 (Hill 881S) _____

We thought initially that an incoming round had landed in the hole with Private First Class Sobel, but it was really probably a dud round that had been buried there from some time in the past. Sobel's shovel or pick struck the round, and it went off.

Sobel lost both feet in the blast. A corpsman got to him very quickly and tried to arrest the bleeding. We dragged

him down the hill to the landing zone, and initiated a
medevac.

Night medevacs were extremely dangerous and very difficult to put together, especially as far out as we were. It took
us a while to get the request back through channels, but
finally word came back from the combat base that an H-34
was on the way along with a gunship escort. We put Sobel
on a poncho and the corpsmen were working on him
frantically, trying to keep him alive. When the helicopter got
there, we put Sobel on board and the helicopter immediately
took off into the night. The last I heard was that Sobel died
on his way to Charlie-Med.

Chapter 12

Capt HARRY JENKINS
Mike Company, 3/26 (Hill 881S) _____

During the day, our 106mm gunners lay still and searched the hills opposite Hill 881S for targets. One day at the end of March, the lance corporal commanding the 106 on the south side of our hill indicated that he thought he had spotted a sniper's position but wouldn't be able to tell for sure until the sniper moved or we received another resupply mission, in which case all the snipers would become active.

The gunner waited two days, until we got the word that an aerial resupply would be coming in. He told me that he would watch the position at which he thought the sniper might be to see if there was any movement out there. As it turned out, it was a sniper's position. The gunner saw the NVA move around in what was apparently a sniper hole. As soon as the helicopters came in and began their approaches on the central landing zone, between India and Mike companies, the sniper began to shoot at them. Our gunner cranked off a 106mm round which went right into the sniper's spiderhole.

There was a huge explosion from the recoilless rifle's backblast and a great shower of dirt on the hill. That scared the hell out of the pilots, who all waved off, thinking the landing zone was under artillery attack. They came in after we assured them that it was just the 106 going off to protect their interests.

☆

Pfc ELWIN BACON
Kilo Company, 3/26 (Hill 861) ———————————

During the last few weeks on Hill 861, things seemed to lighten up a bit. The enemy mortars subsided considerably, but we still were reminded on occasion that they had not left completely. We had communications with Hill 861A, and were doing daily patrols between the two points. However, I have always felt a little guilty about asking some of my squad to go down on one of the first trips between the two outposts. I had received word that someone from my hometown was down there, so I asked permission to go down and see him. I was allowed to go get our mail if I could get some guys to go with me. An Echo Company Marine was supposed to lead us through their minefield outside the wire, which he did, but one of my buddies set off a charge. It resulted in his death, and several others were seriously wounded and had to be medevacked out. To make the incident worse, my reason for going came to nothing; the friend had left a week before to go on his R&R.

☆

Pfc JIM PAYNE
Charlie Battery, 1/13 (Hill 881S) ———————————

On the day I rotated off Hill 881S in late March, a bunch of us short-timers were hunkered down in the trenchline near the saddle, facing the Mike Company hill. While we were waiting, Captain Dabney walked down and joined us.

One of the Marines was muttering a prayer as fixed-wing aircraft came screaming in low and smoked up the entire area. A minute or so later, two CH-46 approached and began descending down onto the southern side of the saddle.

Captain Dabney was grimly pacing back and forth when the moment came to scramble out of that particularly deep section of trenchline and run for those waiting choppers. I leaped up to the top of the trench but lost my footing. As I was falling backwards, the captain grabbed the seat of my trousers and gave me a hell of a fling back out of the trench while shouting, "Get out of here, Marine, and don't you *ever* come back!"

Amid smoke and incoming, I ran about fifty yards across No-Man's-Land and boarded the nearest helicopter before it lifted off. The second CH-46s got hit and those poor boys went down somewhere near Hill 861. The chopper I was on took several rounds while departing, and in my last violent act as a U.S. Marine, I emptied my sixgun into Hill 881N. A few days later, I was a civilian.

☆

Capt HARRY JENKINS
Mike Company, 3/26 (Hill 881S) ⎯⎯⎯⎯⎯⎯⎯⎯⎯⎯⎯

We got a call one day at the very end of March that three resupply helicopters bound for Hill 861 were being diverted because of bad weather and heavy incoming over 861. The understanding was that we could keep whatever the bird dropped off.

The three helicopters with external loads came winging in as part of the normal Super Gaggle air show, dropped their loads, and took off without incident. They left three pallets on the landing zone.

HM3 DAVID STEINBERG
India Company, 3/26 (Hill 881S) ⎯⎯⎯⎯⎯⎯⎯⎯⎯⎯⎯

We didn't know what the hell it was. It turned out to be filled with Foremost ice cream.

Capt HARRY JENKINS
Mike Company, 3/26 (Hill 881S) _____

It turned out that the ice cream was supposed to be dropped
at Hill 861 *and* Hill 881S, but we got it all. There was
almost enough ice cream to feed an entire infantry battalion.

We divided all that ice cream up between men who had
been living on one C-ration per day, many of whom had not
eaten any rich foods for months.

LCpl PHIL TORRES
India Company, 3/26 (Hill 881S) _____

We got melted ice cream, but it was beautiful, it was
delicious, it was the best ice cream I ever had.

HM3 DAVID STEINBERG
India Company, 3/26 (Hill 881S) _____

We ate ice cream until we all had the shits. The diarrhea
was unbelievable.

1stLt FRED McGRATH
Bravo Battery, 1/13 _____

Chow was a challenge. How do you make C-rations appetiz-
ing day after day? Occasionally we would get some B-rations,
but never enough to break the monotony. Besides, by the
time they got around to us, usually only mayonnaise was
left. I hate mayo! The C-rations in 1968 still contained
white bread, so you could invent a fairly tasty sandwich
with a little imagination. But I found that, after a while, one
or one and a half rations per day was all I needed or wanted.
Unfortunately, for one of our Marines, that was not the case.

Not all Marines were comfortable with the situation at
Khe Sanh. We had a Marine who did not cope too well. To
relieve the pressure, he ate. And ate. By the time we
discovered the problem, he weighed so much he could not
walk. His ankles would not support him. He had eaten a
case of C-rations a day. I think each *meal* was 1,600

calories. That times twelve meals per case is just too much. Combined with little or no exercise, he just ballooned. He had to be medevacked. I ran across him at Camp Pendleton about seven months later. Even though he had lost weight by then, he still tipped the scales at 280. We discharged him. His overweight condition was a direct result of what a Navy psychiatrist had diagnosed as anxiety neurosis. The Marine was afraid of dying. But then, so was everyone else. And everyone else dealt with their fears differently.

☆

HM3 BILL GESSNER
Delta Company, 1/9 _____

We had an incident that punctuated my experience with drugs in Vietnam—which was none. One of our platoons received a replacement. On his first or second night, he lit a joint (marijuana) and offered it to the man he shared a foxhole with. That man excused himself and came back with a couple of other guys. They gave him a lecture about dope in the field. He told them to "mind your own business." They broke both of his arms, and we never saw him again.

☆

HN ROD DeMOSS
1/26 Battalion Aid Station _____

During the siege, my papers came through for R&R in Sydney, Australia. I had been waiting seven months for this R&R, but I was almost too scared to take it. There weren't many planes landing, and what few planes did land never stopped. If you got on one, you had to run to catch it as it made its turn to take off. Also, the plane was a magnet for mortar and rocket rounds. Several times, as I waited out by the runway, I was tempted to say "Forget it." I was taking a big risk just being there, and then I was going to have to worry about coming back under the same circumstances. But I made it onto the plane, which took a few rounds just a few feet from where I was sitting. I had a hell of a time in

Sydney for six days, then I was flown to Danang and tried to get a flight back to Khe Sanh. I caught three different airplanes before I could make it back. The first two planes flew all the way to Khe Sanh, but they wouldn't land due to heavy shelling. Finally the third flight landed and I had to jump off because it wouldn't stop. Most of the pilots were leery of landing because, while I was in Sydney, a C-123 was hit and crashed on the airstrip. I was a nervous wreck by the time I made it back. I was on my way from the airstrip to the 1/26 Battalion Aid Station when I heard a *zing* and saw dirt fly up on a sandbag next to me. I had almost been hit by a sniper.

Sgt DENNIS SMITH
Bravo Company, 1/26 _____

One of the Marines from Los Angeles took his R&R in Hawaii, bought a ticket home, and spent a few days watching us on the TV news. Then he returned to Khe Sanh. We asked him, "Why didn't you stay back in The World?" He said he got to thinking about his brothers back at Khe Sanh and knew we wouldn't make it without him, so he came back.

MARCH 30

Capt KEN PIPES
Bravo Company, 1/26 _____

We had been planning to go back out and retrieve the bodies of 2ndLt Don Jacques's patrol pretty much from the day they were ambushed, on February 25. It quickly shaped up as a company raid outside the lines—get out there, get the bodies, and get into the perimeter. It had to be Bravo Company. We wanted to do it. We *had* to do it. I don't think any of us would have settled for anything else.

The planning was ongoing, but the execution kept getting delayed. I don't know why it was delayed. There was a lot going on. The fact that we were given the go-ahead at the end of March might have had to do with intelligence information that said the NVA was pulling back.

We knew exactly where the bodies were. We had aerial photographs, and they were monitored daily by aerial observers.

It got to the point where we had rehearsed going through the trenches. We were going to be relieved on the line early in the morning by Bravo-Recon. We had our routes laid out. We had a couple of intermediate objectives. 2ndLt John Dillon's 2nd Platoon was going to move first, then 2ndLt Pete Weise's 1st Platoon. I was right behind Pete, and 3rd Platoon was behind the command group.

We were relieved, as planned, hours before dawn. It was very crowded in the trenchline as we followed the route we had rehearsed in the dark at least two or three times. The lead platoon somehow got fouled up in one of the turns in the trenchline. It took time to get that straightened out, but we got to our jump-off point inside the wire and launched the raid.

HM3 DICK BLANCHFIELD
Bravo Company, 1/26 _____

"You bloody bastards," was all I could think of when I heard the lieutenant tell us that we—Bravo Company—would be going out beyond the perimeter at 0530 in order to try to locate some dead Marines killed weeks before and pick up their remains, which were in the middle of NVA-held territory. What bullshit was this after seventy-four days of rockets, artillery bombardment, and constant mortar attacks spewed upon us?

The men of Bravo Company had been assigned a mission, and I knew, as an ex-Marine and now a Navy corpsman, they would, as ordered, follow it through to the best of their ability. The company was at least one-third below strength, maybe more. Many of the men had been wounded two or three times in the siege. Many of the men's feet were infected, many were weak from poor diet, and some were on the verge of mental breakdowns.

I kept asking myself that night, while waiting for "jump-off hour," why, after all these past days of hell and madness, should Bravo Company go out on this suicide mission, knowing that we would walk into hell with no air support

and only fifteen minutes of artillery cover before battle?
Why? Because some general or colonel decided to test his
map-pinned, board-strategy thinking with the lives of the
men of Bravo-Company as his chess pieces.

HN ROD DeMOSS
1/26 Battalion Aid Station _____

On March 29 we were called together by the battalion
surgeon, Dr. Harvey DeMaggd, and told of the plan for
Bravo Company to go out and recover the bodies from the
massacre in February. Dr. DeMaggd told us that corpsmen
would be needed to set up a forward aid station just behind
the firing line. He said that he was going and that he wanted
volunteers. I volunteered. I had treated some of the wounded
following the February ambush and I felt like I had to
volunteer. That's not saying I wasn't scared as hell.

Capt HARRY BAIG
26th Marines Target Information Officer _____

Captain Pipes asked for and received [a rolling artillery box
barrage]. Marine artillery formed the primary box and the
rolling barrage. The Army's 175s and [radar-guided] air
formed the sides of the secondary box, which fell on those
pieces of ground that overlooked or could influence the
[combat] area. The [company] moved out seventy-five meters behind the rolling barrage into the sides of the box.
Then, as [it] continued to advance, the entire primary box,
with the [company] inside it and the rolling barrage also
inside and in front of the [company], also advanced. Outside
the primary box was, as usual, the secondary box, whose
sides opened and closed over the terrain like an accordion.
Added to the support were the fires of six heavy and
medium machine guns, employing overhead-and-direct-fire
techniques. After ten minutes of continuous fire, with Bravo
Company advancing swiftly behind the rolling barrage inside the moving primary box, the diverging movement of
the platoons caused the sides of the box, on order of Captain
Pipes, to collapse so that he could accomplish his mission.

The fires of the two boxes were shifted to other targets to prevent reinforcements from reaching the battle area and to suppress the fires of enemy mortars and artillery (the latter were very badly handled.)[1]

Capt KEN PIPES
Bravo Company, 1/26 _____

Our artillery fire went off, as planned, long before we moved outside our wires. In fact, it had been going on for days so it wouldn't draw undue attention to our move. Also, the morning fog was obscuring our position.

At 0600, shortly after first light, Dillon's 2nd Platoon went out and, unopposed, seized the first intermediate objective at 0615. As Dillon moved, a CIDG unit from FOB-3 moved out deep off our right flank, down along a ridgeline southwest of their perimeter sector. Their job was to shield our flank.

As soon as Dillon reached the first objective, the rest of the company moved to the line of departure and prepared for the next phase of the assault. The main body of the company was held up at the line of departure for nearly an hour because rolling fog obscured our objectives and routes of advance. The main body jumped off at 0725 and quickly linked with Dillon's 2nd Platoon. As we did. Dr. Harv DeMaggd and the medical folks moved up to the first objective and set up an aid station in a big bomb crater.

HN ROD DeMOSS
1/26 Battalion Aid Station _____

We had no sooner gotten out of the perimeter than the fight started.

Capt KEN PIPES
Bravo Company, 1/26 _____

At 0750, I requested ten-minute prep fires on all our objectives. When the main body of Bravo Company jumped off from the first objective at 0800, there was a lot of fire and action going on to our front. Hand grenades were thrown as I moved out with the two assault platoons, 1st and 3rd. Second Platoon remained in reserve at the first objective, covering us and our withdrawal route. We followed a rolling barrage by no more than seventy meters. Flamethrowers and demolitions were used to clear NVA strongpoints.

I had set up a plan with the 106s inside the wire so that I could call and adjust preplanned fire on various targets to our front. I also had contact with the 81s. Bravo Company's 60mm mortars were on the intermediate objective, and I had my artillery forward observer, 1stLt Hank Norman, right beside me. We had plenty of on-call fire support.

We got out 500 or 600 meters, to our limit of advance, overrunning several NVA positions on the way. In the process, however, we took a lot of fire ourselves. Looking up, I could actually see their mortar rounds coming in on us. Dozens of them. Most fell in among the assault platoons.

As I was talking to someone on the radio, one of the mortar rounds hit right on top of my command group and three or four others hit around us. Everyone was hit. I was knocked down and my radio operator had his arm very badly mangled. Also, 1stLt Hank Norman, my artillery forward observer, took a lot of shrapnel from the one that landed on top of us. Hank had his flak jacket unzipped and took a large piece of shrapnel through his chest. I was dazed; it took me a few moments to realize what had happened. When I knelt down beside Hank, he was expiring. I told him to hang on, that I'd get a corpsman up, but by the time I finished speaking, he was dead. I held him for a bit, but we had to move on. I had also been hit by shrapnel down through my arm and down through my chest cavity, but my wounds felt minor, so I stayed with what was left of the command group. Everyone except myself and the forward air controller's radiomen was out of action. Several of our radios were damaged or out and we had to switch frequencies to get comm reestablished. When we did, I called my exec, 1stLt Ben Long, from the reserve—2nd—platoon area. Ben, who brought up two squads of 2nd Platoon, helped me reorganize and evacuate the wounded, and then we resumed the advance.

HM3 DICK BLANCHFIELD
Bravo Company, 1/26 _____

Contact was made with a North Vietnamese unit to my left—I was with the 1st Platoon, on the far right—and soon afterwards my platoon was engaged full force with the North Vietnamese. Mortars and automatic fire erupted on us, and casualties were quickly sustained by the 1st Platoon. The terrain was barren due to B-52 bombings, making cover almost impossible to find, except for bomb craters. My platoon had lost contact with the 2nd and 3rd Platoons, and the fighting was man-to-man, with no quarter given.

Marines were yelling, "Corpsman, Corpsman," which meant a Marine was hit and needed me to keep him alive. I ran, ducked, dropped, and kept moving until I jumped into a bomb crater filled with two dead North Vietnamese soldiers, a wounded Marine with his brain matter dangling out of his head, another Marine with his left arm almost blown off, and six other Marines huddled together, firing. At first glimpse, I thought the Marine with the severe head wound was dead, but his eyeballs were just barely moving, so, after treating the Marine with the arm wound, I bandaged the head wound and placed him on a stretcher.

The other Marines and I knew we could not stay in the bomb crater long, so we decided to make a run for the ridge. With some luck, we would connect up with the other platoons. We placed the Marine with the head wound on the stretcher and started working our way slowly up from the crater. But by this time the enemy mortars were falling in and around us in a steady volley.

We were just about to reach the top of the crater when, all of a sudden, a mortar landed right on top of us. The blast knocked me back down into the crater with a murderous pain in my left shoulder and hand. I automatically looked up to check on the others. They were all down. Two of the Marines' heads were blown off, and the others were motionless.

I checked my left arm and hand and knew that I was badly hit and losing blood rapidly. The pain was intense. I gave myself a morphine shot in the right upper leg and realized that if I remained in the crater the North Vietnamese would soon be upon me. I decided to give it a try and started climbing out. It took me two tries to get out of that death-filled crater, and when I reached the top, I stood up and looked all around me. My only thoughts at that pain-filled moment: My God, what an absurdity, what an absurdity!

Pvt DONALD RASH
Bravo Company, 1/26 _____

[NAVY CROSS CITATION] For extraordinary heroism while serving as a rifleman with Company B, First Battalion, Twenty-sixth Marines, Third Marine Division, in connection with operations against the enemy in the Republic of Vietnam. On 30 March 1968, while conducting a reconnaissance in force near the Khe Sanh Combat Base, Company B suddenly came under a heavy volume of small-arms fire from a numerically superior North Vietnamese Army force occupying fortified positions. Although the majority of the hostile fire was directed at his squad, pinning down his companions, Private Rash disregarded his own safety as he unhesitatingly left a covered position and launched a determined assault against the enemy emplacements. Ignoring the hostile rounds impacting near him, he fearlessly advanced across the fireswept terrain, boldly throwing hand grenades and delivering a heavy volume of rifle fire upon the enemy force. Although continuously exposed to intense hostile fire, he resolutely continued his vicious attack until he had destroyed five enemy positions and killed numerous North Vietnamese soldiers. When his company was subsequently ordered to withdraw while under accurate enemy mortar fire, he steadfastly remained behind, and as he delivered suppressive fire to cover the evacuation of casualties he was mortally wounded. His bold initiative and resolute determination inspired all who observed him and were instrumental in his company accounting for 115 North Vietnamese soldiers confirmed killed. By his courage, intrepid fighting spirit, and selfless devotion to duty,

Private Rash contributed immeasurably to the accomplishments of his unit's mission and sustained and enhanced the highest traditions of the Marine Corps and the United States Naval Service. He gallantly gave his life for his country.

Capt KEN PIPES
Bravo Company, 1/26 _____

When we reached the limit of advance, I called back to report that we needed some more help, that we had not reached most of the bodies we had been sent to retrieve. I was told that there was no one else to send out. I replied that we would do the best we could, but that the fire was building up. Shortly after that, I was directed to break contact and bring back as many bodies as I could. So far, we had recovered only two of the dead, but we began breaking contact, as ordered. We also had one prisoner and some captured gear, several mortars and heavy machine guns that had been overrun. We began leapfrogging back over the ground we had just attacked through.

Capt HARRY BAIG
26th Marines Target Information Officer _____

When the Marines eventually retired, after having successfully accomplished their mission, the primary and secondary [artillery] boxes closed back with them. The fires of the machine guns and four 106mm recoilless rifles contributed heavily to the overall outcome of this operation.[2]

HN ROD DeMOSS
1/26 Battalion Aid Station _____

I went to the aid of a Marine whose arm had a tourniquet applied to it. I lifted the arm up to inspect the wound, and it seemed like a gallon of blood poured from it.

The Marines who brought in the body of another Marine were beside themselves because the dead man had only a few days left in-country. Now he would be going home in a body bag.

Capt KEN PIPES
Bravo Company, 1/26 _____

The night before we went, Pfc David Anderson came up to
me and said he had about ten days left in-country and that
he just didn't want to go. Anderson was a good Marine, a
fellow who had done everything he had been told to do. He
said he had some bad premonitions. I explained that we
needed everybody we could get and that he was an experienced machine gunner, that we needed him. He said,
"Okay. I can understand that. I just wanted to talk to you,
Skipper, and let you know what my feelings are. I'll be
ready to go." Dave Anderson stayed behind to cover the
final withdrawal from the reserve area with his machine
gun, and he was killed.

Cpl KENNETH KORKOW
Bravo Company, 1/26 _____

[NAVY CROSS CITATION] For extraordinary heroism while
serving as Mortar Section Leader of Company B, First
Battalion, Twenty-sixth Marines, Third Marine Division,
in the Republic of Vietnam on 30 March 1968. During a
search-and-destroy operation in the vicinity of the Khe
Sanh Combat Base, Company B suddenly came under
intense small-arms and mortar fire from a well-entrenched
North Vietnamese Army battalion. Fearlessly exposing
himself to the hostile fire, Corporal Korkow quickly
deployed his mortar section into firing positions and,
moving about the fire-swept terrain from one squad to
another, directed heavy barrages of accurate fighting against
the enemy, destroying four fortified bunkers. Alertly
detecting a hidden mortar site which was pinning down
elements of his company, he advanced to a position
dangerously open to enemy fire and, employing his own
mortar, singlehandedly destroyed the hostile emplacement. As the battle intensified, Corporal Korkow repeatedly
disregarded his own safety as he moved from one position
to another, encouraging his men and directing their fire.
Observing a Marine fall wounded by an enemy explosive
device, he selflessly rushed into the hazardous area and

assisted his injured comrade to an aid station established to the rear of his company. Although seriously wounded while returning to the forward area after assisting more casualties to the aid station, Corporal Korkow resolutely continued to encourage and assist his men and comfort the wounded until he was medically evacuated. His intrepid fighting spirit inspired all who observed him and contributed immeasurably to the final defeat of the numerically superior enemy force. By his uncommon valor and selfless devotion to duty in the face of extreme personal danger, Corporal Korkow reflected great credit upon himself and upheld the highest traditions of the Marine Corps and the United States Naval Service.

HN ROD DeMOSS
1/26 Battalion Aid Station _____

Finally, it was over. We were told to pull back to the combat base. It seemed like we just kind of straggled back.

I helped three Marines carry a wounded Marine back. As we got close to the perimeter, a senior corpsman came out and took my place. I walked on and caught up with Dr. DeMaggd. I heard a couple of sniper rounds zing past us, and as we got back into the base, mortar rounds hit on both sides of us. That scared me silly.

When I got back, one of the other corpsmen told me about what he had seen going on out there. He could see it from where he was, inside the base, but I was right in the middle of it and hadn't seen a damned thing.

Capt KEN PIPES
Bravo Company, 1/26 _____

When we got back in, I was still a little dazed from the mortar rounds that had hit my command group halfway through the advance. I knew I was bleeding, but there were so many others in worse shape that I didn't pay much attention to my wounds. As soon as the company got settled in, I went down to Battalion to report. When I got there and threw my helmet down, a piece of shrapnel the size of my index finger fell out from between the helmet and the liner.

I hardly noticed. The gunny from the 81mm mortars asked me if I wanted some coffee, and I said okay. Later he told me he gave me a cup with a little coffee and the rest bourbon—twice. I didn't even know it; I thought it was good coffee. He found the piece of shrapnel and asked me what it was. I said I didn't know and, for the first time, looked at the helmet. It had a big hole just above the center of the forehead.

After we debriefed, I went up to the Battalion Aid Station to have my wounds treated. Dr. DeMaggd got most of the shrapnel, but when he probed a deep one at the point of my shoulder, I got sick. He told me he couldn't get that piece out, that he would have to leave it in there. The shrapnel was about two inches from my heart.

The remaining Marines killed during the Jacques patrol of February 25 were recovered by Delta Company, 1/26, on April 6. After jumping off in much the same way as had Bravo Company on March 30, Delta Company encountered zero opposition.

☆

1stLt JOHN KAHENY
1/26 Combat Operations Center _____

It was very difficult to get back into Khe Sanh in late March, following my special emergency leave at home. I would have thought that it would be easy, what with all the flights in to pick up the wounded, but not many airplanes were landing and it was difficult to find out where the medevac choppers were leaving from.

On March 30, I went to the battalion rear at Phu Bai because I knew that if I got the payroll from Disbursing that I would get priority seating on any aircraft. So, as the "pay officer," I got priority on a CH-53. When I got to the helo pad, I hooked up with Captain Champion, who just wanted to get in to Khe Sanh to take over Bravo Company. Nothing was going to stop him. He was a rather large man who pushed and shoved everybody out of the way to fight his way onto the helicopter leaving for Khe Sanh.

The helicopter dropped us off at the landing zone. The place had been battered by incoming during the forty-five days I had been gone. All of the buildings were flattened, so the only way I could get my sense of direction was by looking at the hills to figure out which way was east and west. I led Captain Champion to the 1/26 command post and was greeted there by the survivors. I could sure tell they had been living underground for the six weeks I had been gone.

☆

HM3 BILL GESSNER
Delta Company, 1/9 _____

March 30, 1968

Dear Dad:

I got some goodies for you. Delta Company caught eleven in the grass just outside the wire yesterday. We got five confirms and the jets got the other six. Clean sweep.

I got a banana clip full of the 7.62mm shorts that they use in the AK-47. That's a total of 31 that I have for you now. The slug itself is brass-jacketed. They look very cheap. Well, anyway, I have the K-44 round, too. A Chicom grenade (disarmed) that we got yesterday, and the magazine itself. I have some war souvenirs. I'll be sending the round out in small groups. The Chicom and the banana clip I'll have to carry out.

Well, I'm okay and out of news so I will close.

P.S. Just got the plaque [for Captain Schafer]! It's just great. Pop, thanks a million. I'll tell you what he says after we give it to him.

MARCH 31

HM3 BILL GESSNER
Delta Company, 1/9 _____

At 1630, I gave the skipper, Capt Fran Schafer, the going-away plaque I had ordered through my father. He was flabbergasted. All he could say was "I'll be damned!" He showed it to the company exec, who said there were newsmen there. One of them took pictures.

At 1830, some new men were getting a pep talk from Captain Schafer while Weapons Platoon was carrying ammo from the command post to their area. A mortar round wounded one of the men in Weapons Platoon. He wasn't seriously hurt, but he needed a stretcher, so I went down to the company sickbay to get one. Captain Schafer decided to come up and talk to the wounded man. After we loaded the man on a stretcher, we were mortared again. We all were okay except for the wounded man on the stretcher, who had again gotten a minor wound, and, when he rolled into the trench, his foot got stuck in the damn stretcher. Also, the Weapons Platoon commander got a small wound in his shoulder. Captain Schafer told me to stay and bandage the lieutenant, then he got four other men to load the enlisted Marine back in the stretcher and take him to the battalion aid station. They got about fifteen meters when some rounds dropped all around them. Three Marines were killed. Captain Schafer and two more Marines ran out to help them. Another mortar round killed all three of them.

We all loved the CO, and there were a lot of prayers said and tears shed for that man.

1stLt NICK ROMANETZ
Charlie Company, 1/26 _____

We had some NVA out in front of our lines, firing a mortar from time to time. We could never see them, but we could see a puff of smoke whenever they dropped a round into the tube. They fired on us every day, in the mid- or late afternoon. We always saw the puff of smoke and heard the tube pop, so we always had time to yell and get everyone out of the way in their holes. The 60mm mortar rounds were nothing unless they fell right in your hole with you.

Sgt Arnold Ferrari reported in to the company in mid-March. He was assigned to my platoon, and I made him my right guide. He was a junior-college student from California, a Reserve who volunteered for active duty in Vietnam. He was a football player, handsome, a good physical specimen. He had his heart set on winning himself some kind of medal. He spoke to me quite a bit about it; he wanted to know when we were going to go out and fight the enemy—hand-to-hand—and quit just sitting there and taking a pounding like we were doing.

Unfortunately, on the afternoon of March 31, the NVA mortarmen popped a round in when nobody was looking. The thing came out of nowhere and exploded in the trench. I heard a yell for a corpsman and ran down there. It had gone off knee-to-waist-high, right where Sergeant Ferrari was standing. One of his legs was blown off and the other was hanging by a thread. There was no blood; the heat of the exploding round had cauterized the wounds. When we picked him up to put him on the stretcher, the other leg fell off. The troops put both legs on the stretcher and carted him off. He was white-faced and moaning. I looked at the boy and knew he wasn't going to make it. I got a call on the land line that Sergeant Ferrari had died at the hospital. Shortly after he was taken away, we found his boot lying outside the trench. It still had his foot in it, so we buried it in front of the line.

PART TWO

BREAKOUT

*April 1–18,
1968*

Chapter 13

OPERATION PEGASUS

MGen JOHN TOLSON, USA
1st Cavalry Division Commanding General _____

On January 25, I was directed to prepare a contingency plan for the relief or reinforcement, or both, of the Khe Sanh base. This was the first in a chain of events that was later to emerge as Operation Pegasus.

The mission was threefold:

- Relieve the Khe Sanh Combat Base.

- Open Highway 9 from Ca Lu to Khe Sanh.

- Destroy the enemy forces within the area of operations.

This was the basic concept of operations: The 1st Marine Regiment, with two battalions, would launch a ground attack west toward Khe Sanh while 1st Cavalry [Division] would air-assault the high ground. On D-plus-1 and D-plus-2, all elements would continue the attack west toward Khe Sanh; and, on the following day, the 2nd Brigade of the 1st

Cav would land three battalions southeast of Khe Sanh and attack northwest. The 26th Marine Regiment . . . would attack to secure Hill 471. The link-up was planned at the end of seven days.

It became evident during the planning that the construction of an airstrip near Ca Lu would be a key in the entire operation. This airstrip, which became known as LZ Stud, had to be ready well before D-Day.[1]

Work on LZ Stud began on March 14 and a 1,500-foot-long, 600-foot-wide airstrip and associated facilities were completed by March 26. Between March 26 and D-Day, April 1, elements of the 1st Cavalry Division thoroughly reconnoitered the route of approach—generally along Highway 9 between LZ Stud and Khe Sanh—and an integrated fire-support plan was prepared. NVA positions along the route of approach were identified and targeted for reduction or bypass. Preassault air and artillery preparations were intensified from March 26 onward. As overall commander of Operation Pegasus, General Tolson ordered Colonel Lownds to participate by means of breakout sweeps from the static positions at and around the combat base.

26th Marines After Action Report ———————

Operation Pegasus opened with exact enemy dispositions uncertain. The 304th NVA Division remained located to the south of Khe Sanh Combat Base, and east along Highway 9, with the 325C Division remaining to the west and north of Khe Sanh Combat Base.

APRIL 1

MGen JOHN TOLSON, USA
1st Cavalry Division Commanding General ————

At 0700 on April 1, 1968, the attack phase of Operation Pegasus commenced as two battalions of the 1st Marine Regiment . . . attacked west from Ca Lu along Highway 9. The 11th Marine Engineer Battalion followed right on their heels. At the same time, the 3rd Brigade of the 1st Cavalry [Division] was airlifted . . . into LZ Stud in preparation for an air assault into two objective areas farther west. Weather delayed the attack until 1300, when the 1/7th Cavalry [1st Squadron, 7th Cavalry Regiment] . . . air-assaulted into LZ Mike, located on prominent ground south of Highway 9 and well forward of the Marine attack. The 2/7th Cavalry went into the same LZ to expand and develop the position. The 5/7th Cavalry . . . air-assaulted into an area north of Highway 9 approximately opposite LZ Mike . . . Both landing zones were secured and no significant enemy resistance was encountered. A battery of 105mm howitzers was airlifted into each landing zone and [3rd Brigade headquarters was moved] into the northern landing zone, LZ Cates. . . .

The bad weather of D-Day was to haunt us throughout Operation Pegasus. Seldom were we able to get in high gear before 1300. . . . [2]

APRIL 2

MGen JOHN TOLSON, USA
1st Cavalry Division Commanding General _____

On D-plus-1, the 1st Marine Regiment continued its ground attack along the axis of Highway 9: Two Marine companies made limited air assaults to support the regiment's momentum. The 3rd Brigade air-assaulted the 2/7th Cavalry into a new position farther to the west while the other two battalions [1/7th Cavalry and 5/7th Cavalry] improved their positions [LZ Mike and LZ Cates]. The 2nd Brigade . . . moved into marshaling areas in preparation for air assaults the next day, if called upon.[3]

1stLt JOE ABODEELY, USA
Delta Company, 2/7th Cavalry _____

[DIARY ENTRY] 0645. We air-assaulted to the top of this mountain. It's jungle and grassy. I jumped from the chopper and hurt my arm.

As we walked along, I smelled the distinctive, unforgettable, sweet odor of burned flesh. Someone nearby had gotten napalmed.

[DIARY ENTRY] I could see bomb strikes off in the distance as the sky lit up and the ground shook.

1000. The sun is out. We're on a high mountaintop surrounded by a river on three sides. Today, Delta Company is to air-assault to a new location to set up there. We just got a [logistics] ship with food and water. It was nice sleeping last night.

1720. Delta Company led the air assault to where we are now. My platoon led the ground movement. We found a site for a .51-caliber antiaircraft gun. Also, some of my platoon found some NVA ammo and grenades. Now we're waiting to see where we'll set up. We're hot and tired.

APRIL 3

MGen JOHN TOLSON, USA
1st Cavalry Division _____

Our initial thrusts had met lighter enemy resistance than expected, so the 2nd Brigade was thrown into the attack a day earlier than the original schedule, with three battalions moving into two new areas south and west of our earlier landing zones.... They met enemy artillery fire during the assaults but secured their objectives without serious difficulty. We now had six air cavalry battalions in enemy territory.[4]

1stLt JOE ABODEELY, USA
Delta Company, 27th Cavalry _____

[DIARY ENTRY] 0953. We are sitting in the jungle right now. The 3rd Platoon hit some NVA a little while ago. They got one of their men KIA.

The 3rd Platoon had run into a light machine gun in the trees. The dead man, a sergeant, had gone to get it and they shot him. He was actually still alive when the battalion operations officer carried him back and laid him on the ground near us. I heard a gurgling sound and saw fluids dribble out of the sergeant's mouth. It was the first time I had seen anyone die like that.

[DIARY ENTRY] We're waiting for artillery to come in. There are huge bomb craters all around. I can hear helicopters circling the area now. There are trees, high grass, and ferns all around.

1808. We moved to this hill (Hill 242). NVA mortared us. We had ten or eleven WIA. NVA have surrounded us now. One platoon from another company tried to bring us food and water but got pinned down. I hope we make it through the night. We dug in and made overhead cover.

We were surrounded. No one could get in or out, so we set up a perimeter and built fortifications. We put our ponchos out to collect water and drank what we could get. Another platoon tried to come down the road using Mechanical Mules, but they got several people killed and pulled back. That night we received a lot of incoming, but there were no explosions. I heard on the radio that other parts of the battalion were experiencing the same thing—lots of incoming that wasn't detonating. We didn't know if it was gas or delayed fuse or bad fuses. We could hear things crashing in, making impact but not going off.

APRIL 4

MGen JOHN TOLSON, USA
1st Cavalry Division Commanding General ———————

[The 2nd Brigade] assaulted a battalion into an old French fort south of Khe Sanh. The first contact resulted in four enemy killed. The remaining uncommitted brigade [1st Brigade] was moved into marshaling areas.[5]

1st Lt JOE ABODEELY, USA
Delta Company, 2/7th Cavalry _____

[DIARY ENTRY] 1540. We are now back at [LZ Cates].
1800. I have my platoon in position on the perimeter.
As we came back today, we picked up a couple of dead
and wounded who tried to get supplies to us yesterday.
When we got back here, we saw more dead and wounded.
The 2nd Platoon leader of Charlie Company was killed.
One medevac chopper was shot up. The NVA here are
dangerous. I don't like this area. I hope we all get out
alive. I got a card from a friend today which cheered me
up. We didn't have any food or water yesterday and for
most of today. Everyone is tired.

☆

*With the relief forces only days away from the combat base,
the breakout phase of Operation Pegasus began on D-plus
3. 1/9 was ordered to sweep across the hills south of the
combat base. Three companies of 1/9 jumped off on April 4.
The first objective was Hill 471, an important terrain
feature due south of the combat base and overlooking
Highway 9.*

HM3 BILL GESSNER
Delta Company, 1/9 _____

I felt naked when we left the holes and trenches behind and
moved to the battalion's first objective.

Delta Company was in a blocking position on the west,
and Alpha Company conducted the main attack. As we
moved into our blocking position, we had to cross a finger
on a ridge that exposed us to the artillery in Laos. The NVA
took advantage of that, and pounded us. Somehow, we
didn't take very many casualties.

1/9 Command Chronology _____

At approximately 1500, following an air strike, Alpha
Company initiated its assault on Hill 471 across a narrow

approach with Delta Company providing a heavy base of fire. Alpha Company assaulted Hill 471 with the 2nd Platoon in the lead, the 3rd Platoon in trace prepared to take the right half of 471, and with the 1st Platoon in reserve. The assaulting elements slowed down near the top of Hill 471 due to heavy enemy small-arms fire and grenades. Alpha-1 was sent to move through Alpha-2 and continue that assault. At approximately 1530, Alpha-3 secured the left half of Hill 471 and provided fire support for Alpha-1 and Alpha-2 to secure the remaining portion of Hill 471. Hill 471 was secured at approximately 1600.

Cpl BARRY THORYK
Alpha Company, 1/9

[NAVY CROSS CITATION] For extraordinary heroism while serving as Machine Gun Section Leader with Company A, First Battalion, Ninth Marines, Third Marine Division, in connection with operations against the enemy in the Republic of Vietnam. On 4 April 1968, Corporal Thoryk was participating in a company assault on Hill 471 near Khe Sanh, when his platoon came under an enemy grenade attack and intense automatic-weapons fire. Although he sustained multiple fragmentation wounds in the initial moments of the attack, Corporal Thoryk refused medical aid and singlehandedly launched an aggressive assault against an enemy machine gun position, killing three of its defenders. Having expended his ammunition, he quickly obtained an enemy weapon and delivered fire at two enemy soldiers, killing them as they ran from their position. With complete disregard for his safety, Corporal Thoryk continued to maneuver forward, retrieving enemy hand grenades and throwing them at several hostile positions as he advanced. His courageous actions and steadfast determination were instrumental in seizing the enemy-occupied hill and inspired all who observed him. By his intrepid fighting spirit, bold initiative, and selfless devotion to duty, Corporal Thoryk upheld the highest traditions of the Marine Corps and the United States Naval Service.

HM3 BILL GESSNER
Delta Company, 1/9 _____

Alpha Company had its hands full. Battalion called for medics to go to help on the objective. I went by myself instead of sending a platoon medic. The NVA were still firing a lot of artillery as I took cover near the assault position. When I had a chance to look up, I saw dozens of khaki-green lumps at the foot of the objective, and I thought, "They must *all* be hit!" Then I realized that I was looking at their packs. They dropped them at the bottom of the hill. In the assault position, I found enough wounded men to exhaust my supplies, so I went to the Battalion Aid Station for more. The battalion surgeon told me to go back to Delta Company, so I did.

1/9 Command Chronology _____

On April 5, Alpha Company, 1/9, and Charlie Company, 1/9, were situated at Hill 471. H&S Company, 1/9 and Delta Company, 1/9 were on an adjacent hill.

At 0430, April 5, Charlie Company came under a heavy enemy counterattack by an estimated two NVA companies. Fighting was intense, with small arms, automatic weapons and heavy machine guns, grenades, and RPGs in their assault. The enemy was well disciplined. It was observed that the NVA were uniformly dressed in green utilities and steel helmets and well equipped. The enemy broke off their assault at approximately 0630 and retreated to a hill southeast of Hill 471. From this position, they continued sporadic small-arms, mortar, and RPG fire in Hill 471. The fire was returned by 1/9 elements who maintained fire superiority over the enemy. As a result of the attack on Charlie Company, the following enemy equipment was captured: 1 60mm mortar with ammo, 13 machine guns, 4 RPGs, 28 AK-47s, 30 AK-47 magazines, 3 SKSS, 13 drum-type magazines for automatic weapons, and other miscellaneous gear. 1/9 killed 148 NVA (confirmed) and captured 5 prisoners. By 0800, the enemy had ceased their small-arms fire on 1/9's position.

Total friendly casualties sustained by 1/9 on April 5 were 1 KIA, 21 WIA (serious), and 7 WIA (non-serious).

The abortive attack on 1/9, apparently conducted by a composite unit drawn from all three battalions of the 325C Division's 66th Regiment, was the last serious effort by the NVA to keep Marine battalions bottled up at or around the combat base. Thereafter, all contacts achieved during the breakout phase of Operation Pegasus were against NVA rearguard elements, which were usually manning static defenses at key terrain features. After Hill 471, the remaining intact elements of the 325C and 304th NVA Divisions were perceived as withdrawing from the Khe Sanh plateau.

MGen JOHN TOLSON, USA
1st Cavalry Division Commanding General _____

On D-plus-4, the 2nd Brigade continued its attack on the old French fort, meeting heavy resistance. . . . The ARVN 3rd Airborne Task Force was alerted to prepare to airlift one rifle company from Quang Tri to link up with the ARVN 37th Ranger Battalion at Khe Sanh. Units of the 1st Brigade . . . entered the operation with the 1/8th Cavalry air-assaulting into LZ Snapper, due south of the Khe Sanh and overlooking Highway 9. The circle began to close around the enemy.[6]

1stLt JOE ABODEELY, USA
Delta Company, 2/7th Cavalry _____

[DIARY ENTRY] 1550. I got word today that our battalion may walk into Khe Sanh tomorrow. This could be disastrous. We've incurred a lot of killed and wounded since we've been here. I hope to God we make it alive. I've had a lot of close calls and I'm getting scared again. Everyone is scared of this area. The NVA are numerous and good fighters. We're digging in again for tonight.

1720. Jets keep circling this hill. There are also a lot of choppers in the air. Artillery keeps pounding the surrounding areas also. I hope the NVA move out. They ambush a lot here.

APRIL 6

26th Marines Command Chronology _____

> 0700: 1/26 executed a morning assault on an NVA trench
> and bunker complex located parallel to the access road
> which runs southeast from KSCB to Highway 9. Delta
> Company seized the objective against light resistance,
> policed the battlefield, and returned to KSCB at approxi-
> mately 1200. The remains of 21 Marine bodies were
> recovered, accounting for all those declared as MIAs on
> February 25. Enemy casualties were 6 NVA KIA (con-
> firmed).

MGen JOHN TOLSON, USA
1st Cavalry Division Commanding General _____

On D-plus-5, the 1st Marine Regiment continued its operations on high ground north and south of Highway 9, moving
to the west toward Khe Sanh. The heaviest contact on that
date was in the 3rd Brigade's area of operation as the 2/7th
Cavalry . . . continued its drive west on Highway 9. Enemy
forces blocking along the highway offered stubborn resistance. In a day-long battle which ended when the enemy
summarily abandoned his position and fled, the battalion
had accounted for 83 enemy killed, one captured, and 121
personal and ten crew-served weapons seized. The troops of
the 1st Cavalry Division were airlifted to Hill 471, relieving
[1/9] and permitting them to drive toward Hill 689, some
4,500 meters to the northwest. (This was the first relief of
the defenders of the Khe Sanh.) Two companies of [Calvary]
troopers remained on [Hill 471] while two other companies
began an attack to the south toward the Khe Sanh hamlet.
    The 1st Cavalry forces on LZ Snapper were attacked by an
enemy force with mortars, hand grenades, and rocket launch-
ers. The attack was a disaster for the enemy, and twenty were
killed. At 1320, the 84th Company of the ARVN 8th Airborne
Battalion was airlifted by 1st Cavalry Division aircraft into the
Khe Sanh Combat Base and linked up with elements of the
37th Ranger Battalion. The lift was without incident and
marked the official link-up by forces at Khe Sanh.[7]

The ceremonial ARVN link-up was barely mentioned in official Marine Corps documents relating to the siege, and all but overlooked by individual Marines at the combat base.

1stLt JOE ABODEELY, USA
Delta Company, 2/7th Cavalry _____

[DIARY ENTRY] 1400. Well, we tried to walk from this LZ [Snapper] to Khe Sanh, but we had to come back as the two forward companies received effective fire. Now our company is supposed to air-assault to within 500 meters east of Khe Sanh. This is a glory push to see who can be first to walk into Khe Sanh. I hope we make it. We have many reporters with us.

The reporters thought this was going to be a parade down Main Street. They were with us for a little while, but they moved on when nothing happened.

As the Cavalry sweep and Marine road-clearing operation drew closer to Khe Sanh, the battalions of the 26th Marines became more actively engaged in patrolling and preparing to mount sweeps across the northern and western ridgelines overlooking the combat base. The first order of business was to locate close-in NVA units and clear them from the immediate area. Especially active in this regard were 1/26, at the combat base, and 2/26, at Hill 558. Also, once relieved of Hill 471, 1/9 began a sweep westward along the 689 ridgeline.

APRIL 7

26th Marines Command Chronology _____

0800: The 37th Ranger Battalion conducted a sweep in front of their position and discovered trenches, bunkers, and a large amount of ammo and equipment. . . . The Rangers also found 70 NVA KIA (confirmed) believed to be results of supporting-arms fire directed on enemy sightings during the last two days of March.

MGen JOHN TOLSON, USA
1st Cavalry Division Commanding General _____

On April 7, the [ARVN] 3rd Airborne Task Force air-assaulted three battalions into positions north [of Highway 9] and east of Khe Sanh to block escape routes toward the Laotian border. Fighting throughout the area was sporadic as the enemy attempted to withdraw. U.S. and ARVN units began picking up significant quantities of abandoned weapons and equipment. The old French fort, the last known enemy strongpoint around Khe Sanh, was completely secured.[8]

1stLt JOE ABODEELY, USA
Delta Company, 2/7th Cavalry _____

The 2/7th Cavalry's order of march from LZ Snapper to Khe Sanh had my 2nd Platoon as the last unit of the follow-up company. However, when the lead company met opposition, it was decided to leapfrog Delta Company over the fight and on down to Khe Sanh. Since we were the last unit in the column, we were the first to be picked up. That put us at the head of the column.

Cpl TIM SNELL
Hotel Company, 2/26 _____

During the late afternoon, about an hour before dark, our rear command post got word that an Army unit had started up one of the nearby hills and had gotten caught in a vicious crossfire. We had seen the activity on the hill, but it wasn't noticeable until after dark, when the tracer rounds showed up much better. We didn't know who was on the hill, but we did know that they had their hands full. We were told that they had been allowed to advance halfway up the hill against token resistance, but once they were halfway up, the enemy, who were hiding underground, popped up in front, turned on them, and attacked. Artillery support was out of the question due to the position of our people, literally on top of the enemy in both directions. The Army unit was in a terrible spot, but it fought valiantly.

As soon as the situation was reported by their radioman, medevac was called in. When our first sergeant said they needed volunteers to help with the medevacs, only three or four of us were willing to go because of the incoming. The word came that they wanted us at the landing strip to wait for the choppers to arrive. We all jumped into a jeep and headed down to the strip. It wasn't long before we heard the *thump-thump* of the choppers. It was starting to get dark by then, and we got the word that the pilots needed someone to help guide them in. We had had trouble earlier in the day with snipers, and that was on everyone's mind, so no one wad really too anxious to jump up and stand out in the open to direct the choppers and dodge incoming rounds at the same time. Finally, I said I would guide them in. There was no argument over my decision. When the first chopper was in sight, I ran up on the landing strip and started to direct it as best I could. None of us had any formal training in landing planes, but we knew that we could do whatever it took to get them in safely.

As I stood out there all alone and wondering if I was doing a good enough job, I got a sudden surprise. The first chopper turned on its landing lights and scared the *hell* out of me. But he turned the lights off again and continued landing. Next thing I knew, he was on the ground and the wounded began to unload.

As soon as the chopper touched down, the other Marines with me were on the strip, ready to do their best to help the wounded. The thing that struck me was the total lack of concern some of the wounded had for themselves. If they could walk on their own, they told us, "I'm okay. Take care of the ones who need help." These men had holes in their shoulders, legs, and arms, but they were most concerned with their buddies' well-being instead of their own.

Another thing that struck me was the care we took to ensure that the dead were treated with dignity and respect. They were not thrown around like used baggage. Instead, we laid them on the edge of the strip until all the wounded had been cared for. I was so proud to have had a small part in bringing these brave men in safely, and to have seen the care we all shared for each other.

Every one of these medevac choppers landed and departed safely.

1stLt JOE ABODEELY, USA
Delta Company, 2/7th Cavalry _____

[DIARY ENTRY] 1045: We air-assaulted to an open area on
a mountaintop and received light sniper fire. We found an
NVA complex with rockets, mortars (tubes and ammo),
AK-47s, and all sorts of material. I have a sharp AK47,
which I hope to keep. We are to go to Khe Sanh.

The complex was huge, bunkers everywhere. It was
right on Highway 9, near the road that branched off to the
Lang Vei Special Forces Camp. We found some bodies in
the bunkers, and tons of equipment. One of my men
found an old French bugle. He made a tassel for it out of
parachute cord and gave it to me. The same trooper
created a sensation that afternoon when he shot a cobra he
found in the trenches with the unauthorized .38-caliber
snub-nosed revolver he carried.

After he finished sending off all the captured gear we
weren't going to keep, we marched down the road off
the mountain toward Khe Sanh. We found other bunkers along the way, but nobody was there. We found
rucksacks, medical supplies, ammunition, and a few
bodies.

[DIARY ENTRY] 1700. We are at Khe Sanh, camped
outside the east entrance on Highway 9.

We saw some Marines there, going to a garbage dump.
They were really surprised to see us. The Marines had not
been able to go down the road we were on for about two
months.

APRIL 8

1stLt JOE ABODEELY, USA
Delta Company, 2/7th Cavalry _____

[DIARY ENTRY] 1130. Today, Delta Company was the
first to walk into Khe Sanh on Highway 9 in two months.
My platoon was the first in.

There was a Marine captain standing there at the gate. I must have looked interesting to him. I had all my normal equipment on, but I also had my bugle and the AK-47 I had picked up the day before.

We were the cavalry, so, as we were walking in, my company commander asked if I could play the bugle. I told him I had played trumpet in my high school band. He asked if I could play "Charge." "Sure," I said, and I blew the cavalry charge as we walked in.

I walked up to the marine captain, saluted him, and said, "Sir, Lieutenant Abodeely reports with the 2nd Platoon, Delta Company, 2nd Squadron, 7th Cavalry, to relieve you." He gave me a disdainful look and said, "Lieutenant, your people will take this position, from here to there." No "Hi, how are you"; "Thanks"; "Welcome"; "We've been waiting for you"; "We're glad to see you." Nothing. I thought that, under the circumstances, he was being an asshole.

MGen JOHN TOLSON, USA
1st Cavalry Division Commanding General _____

At 0800 on April 8, the relief of Khe Sanh was effected and the 1st Cavalry Division became the new "landlord." The 3rd Brigade airlifted its command post into Khe Sanh and . . . the 2/7th Cavalry successfully cleared Highway 9 to the base and linked up with the 26th Marines.[9]

LCpl PHIL MINEER
Bravo Battery, 1/13 _____

We saw newspapers that said the 1st Cavalry Division opened the road and rescued us. But, by the time the Air Cav arrived, guys in the base were moving around in the open, sitting in the air, joking. It was done with by the time the Air Cav came in. They filled the sky with helicopters and a few walked in with a general and a bunch of news photographers. They were posing like, "Here we are. We saved you." That is a bunch of bullshit. One newspaper said we were so glad to see them that we were throwing

C-rations to them. Absolutely! I was standing on top of my bunker with cans of ham and lima beans—what the Marines called "ham-and-mothers" because they tasted so good— and I was throwing them *at* the Army troops. I didn't want those guys anywhere near me. I could see that attitude.

1stLt ERNIE SPENCER
1/26 Intelligence Officer _____

Charlie must have said, "Hey, let's watch the U.S. Army embarrass those little fuckers at Khe Sanh." When the doggies get there, everyone else is pulling out. The Marines feel it is just about over.[10]

1stLt NICK ROMANETZ
Charlie Company, 1/26 _____

When a bunch of Air Cav guys set up in front of our lines, they set their tents up above the ground. They got a couple of mortar rounds that night. I'm sure no one was hurt because there were no medevacs flying, but I bet they dug in the rest of the time they were around Khe Sanh.

Cpl ALLAN STAHL
Logistics Support Unit _____

The fun was over. The face of the war changed. Suddenly, all night long we were under an umbrella of flares. That offended our macho.

We had been eating one C-ration per day, and there was a time when we had had to ration water. Now the siege was lifted, and things were looking up.

An Army unit set up right down the trenchline from us. Starting right away, the Army flew in hot chow in insulated ration cans, something we hadn't seen in months. We were so hungry when we saw this that we went over and asked to get in their chow line. The sergeant in charge said, "We feed our people first. Come back later." Fair enough. We went away for a while and then returned. At that moment, the sergeant we had seen earlier had a ration can in his hands and was dumping mashed potatoes on the ground. "Hey," I called, "we'd like some of that chow." The guy got a real surly look on his face and turned his can up. "There," he offered as the last of the potatoes fell to the ground. "Fucking Marines need to eat off the ground."

As the inevitable shouting war got louder, the guy I was with picked up some food that had been set aside and dumped *it* on the ground. "If we don't eat it, nobody eats it." With that, three Army guys came at us. The sergeant stepped up to me and I let loose on him. I'm no fighter—I had only had my first lesson a few days earlier—but he rolled. Then we took off running and giggling.

It was tense with the Army from that moment on. We were ordered to stay clear of the Army.

Capt BILL DABNEY
India Company, 3/26 (Hill 881S) _____

There wasn't really a hell of a lot of fighting out there when the siege was lifted as such. The Air Cav came in with all these buzzy helicopters and things. They went hill-hopping, but they didn't go down in the valleys much. But there was just not a hell of a lot of fighting. I think the North Vietnamese just melted away.[11]

MGen JOHN TOLSON, USA
1st Calvary Division Commanding General _____

The 3rd Brigade elements occupied high ground to the east and northeast of the base with no enemy contact. Now it became increasingly evident, through lack of contact and the large quantities of new equipment being found abandoned on the battlefield, that the enemy had fled the area rather than face certain defeat. . . . Operations continued to the west.[12]

APRIL 9

MGen JOHN TOLSON, USA
1st Cavalry Division Commanding General _____

On April 9, all of the 1st Marine Regiment's objectives had
been secured and Highway 9 was repaired and secured with
only scattered incidents of enemy sniping. Enemy mortar,
rocket, and artillery fire into Khe Sanh became increasingly
sporadic.[13]

☆

1/9 Command Chronology _____

0720: 1/9 on Hill 689 received 18 rounds of enemy 82mm
mortars resulting in 2 KIAs and 14 WIAs. An artillery
mission was fired on the enemy mortar position and no
further rounds were received from that location.

LCpl MIKE GUESS
Charlie Company, 1/9 _____

Each squad took turns sending a guy about twenty-five
yards to the rear, right off the front lines, to guard the CO
and communicators. When we took a defensive position on
Hill 689 on the night of April 8, it happened to be my turn.
They decided to dig into a B-52 bomb crater. The officers
and communicators were toward the back of the crater, and I
dug a fighting hole within the bomb crater. I got up to take a
leak and had just gotten back into my hole when the first
round of the morning came in. It got me; tore me up pretty
good—lower legs, waist, back. The thing that scared me
was the smell of the powder. I had been hit or had close
calls twice before. I got sick to my stomach all three times
from the powder smell. It all went so fast and the metal was
so hot that I didn't feel any pain at first. Just that smell. But
I was lucky. The mortar round had landed at the rear of the
bomb crater and killed all the communicators back there. A
corpsman got back right away and wrapped me up real
good, but that was the start of a fire fight, and they couldn't

get me out on a chopper right away. I don't know how long I sat out there because I kept phasing out and they kept waking me up.

I finally got on the medevac chopper, but I was the only *wounded* guy. Everybody else was in body bags, but I was wrapped up in my poncho liner up to my neck. There was a gunner shooting out the side of the chopper. He was shooting away and shooting away and shooting away until they finally got the chopper away. I was just lying there, in and out of consciousness. One time, as I came to, the gunner was leaning in the door of the chopper with his foot up, lighting a cigarette. I said, "You got another one of those?" I thought the guy was going to jump out of the chopper. I guess he thought everybody on the chopper was dead. He came over, gave me a cigarette, and shot the breeze with me.

They got me to an aid station somewhere—I don't know where—and they cut out as much shrapnel as they could. I spent the night there, the only wounded guy on the ward. I knew I was dirty—everybody around me for three months had been dirty—but I didn't realize how filthy I was until a doctor came in and made this poor Air Force medic give me a sponge bath. I felt sorry for the medic.

Cpl BERT MULLINS
Bravo Company, 1/9 _____

Bravo Company stayed to hold the battalion perimeter at the Rock Quarry while the rest of the battalion went to Hill 471. As soon as the rest of the battalion left, we pulled into a smaller perimeter and went to work policing the whole Rock Quarry position.

The 1st Air Cav came up and relieved us at the Rock Quarry. We were all packed up and ready to go. They marched out of Khe Sanh, right up the road to us.

We had stockpiled quite a bit of canned orange juice in our position before the battalion pulled out and left us. There were cases of it because we had gotten a little tired of it after a while. The first Cav trooper to reach the juice staked a claim and started *selling* it to his buddies as they filed past the cache. Those of us who saw the incident absolutely could not believe we were seeing a guy making money off his own buddies. I was there only about another thirty minutes, but from the time he started until the time I left, he was still selling cans of orange juice.

I saw my first thirty-round M-16 magazine there, when the Cav came up. An officer had one in his M-16, which he put down next to me. If I had had about thirty seconds, I'd have been the first Marine I knew with a thirty-round magazine, and he'd have been an Army officer with a twenty-round magazine.

We cut a direct path across a low area in order to rejoin the battalion on Hill 552. As we moved, we came upon a stream, at which point it was decided that everyone should have an opportunity to take a bath. We took about an hour, and we got the entire company bathed in the stream—our first baths in over two months. After we all got through bathing, we marched upstream and found a thoroughly decomposed elephant lying right in the stream.

On the way from the bathing pool, I saw the devastation caused by the B-52 Arclights. There were massive craters and shredded trees all around. It was a sight to behold.

By the time we got to Hill 552, the other three companies had already moved to Hill 689, a higher hill. There was not enough room for the whole battalion on 689, so Bravo formed a separate perimeter on Hill 552.

☆

1stLt JOHN KAHENY
1/26 Combat Operations Center _____

Pegasus was a very strange operation. The Army came in and we assumed we would be sent somewhere to be refitted. But we ended up being in the center as the 26th Marines pushed the NVA back toward Laos. The battalion did not see much action during the operation. We went out just short of Hill 881S and took some casualties, but we didn't see any NVA. They hit us with long-range recoilless-rifle fire.

On the way toward Hill 881S we had to go through what was known as Leech Valley, which the Air Force had seeded with gravel. This was supposed to expire after so many days, but they apparently gave us the wrong expiration date. That held us up.

1stLt NICK ROMANETZ
Charlie Company, 1/26 _____

We broke out along the 784 ridgeline. The whole time we were out there—a week or ten days—I only saw a half-dozen NVA. I did see a lot of prepared positions. But I really had to wonder if the great numbers that were surrounding us were really out there. There were a lot of dead animals. We took a few enemy mortar rounds, which unfortunately killed a company radio operator. Also, some-one put some bum dope on our guns, and a Marine artillery unit put some white phosphorus on a friendly unit and caused some casualties. The 1,000-pound bomb craters were impressive. We also came on an area where there were toe-poppers [gravel]—little chemical packets that went off like a big firecracker if enough pressure was applied.

Pfc ROBERT HARRISON
Alpha Company, 1/26 _____

The Air Cav relieved us from our position on Hill 950 and we rejoined Alpha Company for the purpose of conducting a combat sweep west of the main base. We were walking through abandoned NVA positions when we noticed thousands of small bags, about the size and shape of teabags, scattered on the ground. LCpl Jack Bibbs picked one up and it blew two of his fingers off. Jack was one of my best friends. He was from Texas, and was nineteen years old. He got married before he came to Vietnam. His wife delivered a baby girl while he was on Hill 950 with us. Jack had to be medevacked, and the rest of us tried to avoid stepping on the bags. This was impossible and quite a few were stepped on, but they didn't penetrate our boots. Interspersed among the small bags were chrome balls about the size of softballs. We kept moving trying to leave the area before nightfall and it became impossible to see them on the ground.

We later learned that the bags and chrome balls were

dropped by óur planes. They were small booby traps called "gravel" by the Air Force. The gravel was intended to hinder enemy movement, especially during the night. What is odd is that we were not told to expect this type of booby trap. It was the first time any of us had seen anything like it.

APRIL 10

MGen JOHN TOLSON, USA
1st Cavalry Division Commanding General _____

The 1/12th Cavalry . . . under the 1st Brigade, seized the Old Lang Vei Special Forces Camp . . . against light resistance.[14]

Operation Pegasus/Lam Son 207A was terminated much sooner than expected. When told on April 10 by LtGen John Rosson [commander of the Provisional Corps, Vietnam] to initiate extraction and start planning for an immediate assault into the A Shau Valley, it all came as a complete surprise. One immediate result was that I had to cancel a large number of air assaults that were scheduled for that afternoon, which would have extended our activities a considerable distance in all directions from Khe Sanh.[15]

☆

Pfc ROBERT HARRISON
Alpha Company, 1/26 _____

It was near midday on April 10, and Alpha Company was moving in column through dense terrain. The pace was fast, considering the amount of equipment everyone was carrying, and some people had trouble keeping up with the column. Private First Class Pruitt was in front of me; he was one of those people having trouble. Our platoon commander, 1stLt Maxie Williams, came back from his position near the front of the 3rd Platoon to offer words of encouragement to Pruitt. Then he moved back to his original position in the column. This was the last time I saw the lieutenant alive.

The column was moving when suddenly there was an explosion. We halted, and there were cries of "Corpsman,

up!'' My fire team was called up to help. We moved to
where the explosion had occurred and found that a booby
trap had gone off. I don't know for sure what type of booby
trap it was. Lieutenant Williams was killed outright and
Lance Corporal Higuerra, the lieutenant's radioman, was
wounded. The company commander called in a medevac.
The chopper arrived and we put the lieutenant and
Higuerra on it. The column re-formed and began moving
again.

☆

Cpl ALLAN STAHL
Logistics Support Unit _____

The sergeant in charge of the ammunition supply point had
boasted days in advance that he was going to throw us a
spaghetti dinner, and he came through. I have no idea where
he got the spaghetti and sauce, but he did it. We got a big
old cauldron going out in back of our bunker. We even had
beer. It was glorious. The only thing that put a damper on it
was when one of the guys who didn't drink tried to *sell* his
beer for ten dollars a can.

APRIL 11

MGen JOHN TOLSON, USA
1st Cavalry Division Commanding General _____

Highway 9 into the Khe Sanh Combat Base was officially
opened on April 11 after Marine engineers had worked day
and night to complete their task. In eleven days they had
reconstructed more than fourteen kilometers of road, repaired
and replaced nine bridges, and built seventeen bypasses.
Many sections of the road had to be cleared of landslides
and craters.[16]

APRIL 17

CHANGE OF COMMAND

Col BRUCE MEYERS
26th Marines Commanding Officer _____

I was serving as Operations Officer of the 9th Marine Amphibious Brigade, whose actual headquarters was at Okinawa, but all of whose units were deployed in Vietnam. As the brigade operations officer, I began coming to Khe Sanh in August 1967. My last visit as brigade operations officer was in January 1968, just before the "siege." I then assumed command of the 2,200-man Special Landing Force Alpha, where I was aboard the helicopter carrier *Iwo Jima*. In that unit, I had a Marine battalion landing team and a Marine Sikorsky H-34 helicopter squadron. We were making amphibious raids along the coastline from Danang north to the Cua Viet River, on the DMZ. In that my landing force assets were 9th Brigade assets (under operational control of MGen [Tommy] Tomkins, the 3rd Marine Division commander), I was in-country daily to visit my units, and on a number of occasions I went into Khe Sanh with my H-34s, which sometimes flew resupply and medevac runs for the 26th Marines.

Dave Lownds and I had been battalion commanders together in the 2nd Marine Division, and we had known each other for years. He was my predecessor as 9th Brigade operations officer.

When the brigade commander called me by scrambler radio from Okinawa, I was in my sea cabin aboard the *Iwo Jima*, just having returned from the mouth of the Cua Viet River. The general asked, did I "want a regiment?"

As the youngest colonel in the Marine Corps, having been a grunt my entire career—twenty-six years at that point—I had obviously aspired to a regiment as the capping of infantry command. (I had commanded a platoon at the close of World War II, a rifle company in Korea, had been first commanding officer of 1st force Reconnaissance Company as a major, and a battalion commander in the Mediterranean 6th Fleet as a lieutenant colonel.) I replied, "Hell yes,

General." We arranged for me to turn over command of my landing force in the morning, and by 1100, I was dodging the 12.7mm antiaircraft in the early-morning Khe Sanh fog aboard the first chopper I could get.

Dave Lownds and I walked the perimeter that day, April 11, and his staff gave me briefings on the situation. The next morning, April 12, we had a very brief change of command about the time the usual morning fog lifted (to avoid being targets for the gunners on Co Roc Mountain). Dave took off by chopper for what later proved to be a trip to the White House to receive his Navy Cross and the 26th Marines' Presidential Unit Citation.

☐

CHANGE OF MISSION

MGen TOMMY TOMKINS
3rd Marine Division Commanding General _____

I don't think it was General Westmoreland's decision to abandon Khe Sanh. He was out of town, in the United States. General Creighton Abrams, who had already been designated as his relief, held a meeting at Phu Bai, I believe, and announced that we were going to get out of Khe Sanh. I was charged with the phase-out of the Marines and the dismantling of the base.[17]

Col BRUCE MEYERS
26th Marines Commanding Officer _____

I was told that the future of Khe Sanh as a forward base in I Corps was under reconsideration. My mission was to roll back Khe Sanh Combat Base proper and all installations. . . . My mission was twofold: tactically to patrol actively and aggressively with the regiment with four battalions in the field—the 1st, 2nd, and 3rd Battalions of the 26th Marines, and the 1st Battalion, 9th Marines. The second portion of the mission was that of a logistic retrograde of all material located at Khe Sanh Combat Base on back to the Force Logistic Command echelons for necessary repair after the

heavy artillery and mortar and rocket attack damage. The
instructions were to completely demolish Khe Sanh Combat
Base after taking everything usable. The mission was to be
accomplished by a phased reduction in size of the operations
base of the battalions in the field. Initially, the close-in
battalions would draw into the base, assist in the demolition
of the base, extracting all unnecessary material for the
future mission of a light screening and reconnaissance base,
and then eventually closing down the ring around Khe Sanh
until eventually the final elements would be phased out predominantly by use of air.[18]

MGen TOMMY TOMPKINS
3rd Marine Division Commanding General _____

When General Westmoreland returned and took control again,
he was quite adamant that Khe Sanh would not be abandoned
until such time as General Abrams was in the chair, that he,
Westmoreland, felt it was necessary to retain Khe Sanh.[19]

APRIL 13

Col BRUCE MEYERS
26th Marines Commanding Officer _____

In the early-morning hours of April 13, the 26th Marines
received additional guidance indicating there would no longer
be a retrograde action and that Khe Sanh Combat Base was
to continue in existence with a heavy and very active
patrolling, screening, and reconnaissance series of missions...
going out from the Khe Sanh Combat Base proper.

Upon receipt of this additional guidance, our planning
continued and progressed for a battalion-by-battalion relief
of the 26th Marines, including the attached 1st Battalion,
9th Marines, by other battalions of the 1st Marine Division.[20]

Maj TOM COOK
26th Marines Assistant Logistics Officer _____

I left Khe Sanh on a CH-53 with the advance party to Dong
Ha. When we got there, I had a lot of troops to get fed, but

no one knew we were coming, and no one knew where we could stay. It wasn't fun. As I worked, I happened to start noticing that people were looking at me funny. And then I noticed why. I was orange. My face was orange. My uniform was orange. I looked at my troops, and they were all orange. All the other people had green uniforms on. It was the funniest feeling I ever had in my life. I was an orange person and the rest of the world was green.

Chapter 14

THE EASTER OFFENSIVE
APRIL 9

On April 9, for the first time since its Christmas sweep, 3/26 was to be reconstituted in its entirety preparatory to a series of planned sweep operations centered on Hill 881S. The battalion headquarters, weapons detachments, Lima Company, and Mike Company's 3rd Platoon were to be flown to the hill from the combat base, and Kilo Company was to be flown from Hill 861.

LCpl CHARLIE THORNTON
Lima Company, 3/26 ⎯⎯⎯⎯⎯⎯⎯⎯⎯⎯⎯⎯⎯⎯⎯

I recuperated from my wounds over a period of about thirty days, but I was released from the hospital ship about two weeks earlier than I felt I should have been. The ship was supposed to sail from Vietnam to the Philippines, so the doctors discharged all of us who were within a couple of weeks of full recovery. I was still extremely weak, and my wounds were very tender. The sutures had been removed only two days before my release from the ship. I returned to

Khe Sanh by helicopter, which landed without drawing any
incoming. The pace in general was much less tense than
when I had been medevacked in March. Everyone greeted
me enthusiastically.

Within days of my return, we saddled up, destroyed the
bunkers that had been our homes for the past several
months, and simply walked out of the perimeter toward Hill
881S.

Pfc LIONEL TRUFANT
106mm Platoon, 3/26 _____

The day they externally loaded our 106 out of the combat
base to Hill 881S was the first time in Vietnam I put on a
pack and carried heavy equipment. I had two cans of ammo
for our M-60 machine gun, the tripod, plus my own personal gear, and my M-16. I had never packed a backpack
before; I didn't know how to pack it. Nobody told me how
to do it because Marines like boots to find out the hard way.
So, I packed the machinegun ammo down at the bottom of
the backpack. We waited for the helo a long time, and the
weight of the pack was just killing me.

While we were waiting for our ride, a helo from the 1st
Air Cav landed and this guy without a flak jacket on got out.
He walked around like he was thinking, This ain't shit. I
could feel the tension and see the looks on the faces of all
the Marines there. We resented it. We had been sitting up
there, playing Russian roulette with the artillery for the last
two months, watching our buddies get blown away, get hurt,
get constantly harassed, facing psychological stress and
physical stress every day. And here was this guy, walking
around like it wasn't shit. For all we knew, he might have
been in the thick of shit, too. I could see the resentment all
the way from our staff sergeant on down.

A CH-46 landed and we loaded aboard. Then we flew to
Hill 881S. My first impression of Hill 881S was that it
looked like an anthill. When the helicopter started going in,
we were sitting in two rows, across from one another. The
gunner opened up and the word was that the landing zone

was "hot." When the helicopter hit the ground, I felt like we were the wagon train, 881S was the fort, and 881N was the Indians. They were shooting at us, and our guys were shooting back at them. We started running off the helicopter, and all the weight in the bottom of my pack was just kicking my ass. The first thing I was looking for was a trench. I was running downhill toward a trench and finally got into it. The shooting kept going on. They kept shooting 82mm mortars at us, and our 81mm mortars kept shooting back. Small-arms fire was hitting everywhere.

Next we had to climb to the top of the hill. The weight in my pack was killing me. On the way, it started raining. When I got to the top of the hill and finally took my pack off, it felt like I didn't have a lower back or buttocks.

Hill 881S was very different from the combat base, where we dug into the ground and built a top over us. On the hill, the Marines were inside the ground. In most cases, living quarters were dug into the ground off to the side from the trenchline. The first living quarters they put us in were literally underneath the ground. There was barely enough space to sit up. It was dark. The setup was more of a community thing than at the combat base because the trenchline went all the way around the hill; there were more people going back and forth than in the combat base, where we were isolated in our own holes. They got hit by a lot of rockets and mortars, but not as much artillery as we had had at the combat base.

Pfc ELWIN BACON
Kilo Company, 3/26 _____

Just prior to our leaving Hill 861 for good, we received more food and ice cream than we could ever eat. Actually, it got a lot of us sick because we had gone so long on short rations that our stomachs couldn't take it.

We received the word that we were going to push on Hill 881N the next day. The word passed down the line that we were to get our shit together and prepare for the worst. They expected heavy resistance to our advance.

We were given extra C-rations and a special package for

each squad consisting of soap, cigarettes, writing paper, and that sort of thing. We knew that most of the stuff would have to be left behind, but the evening was mostly spent getting the gear together and feasting on everything we liked best out of the extra rations. Most of us made hogs of ourselves, but we thought this might be our last big meal.

In the early-morning hours, we began a systematic transfer from Hill 861 to Hill 881S, which was the jumping-off point for the operation. We were placed in teams and given instructions on when to move up to the landing zone. The anticipation that we would get mortared was correct. When the choppers came in to pick us up, we received some incoming, which put everyone more on edge. The holes around the landing zone were packed with men.

When it was my squad's time to load up, we heard the sound of incoming and ran back to the hole. Then we heard someone didn't make it. He had fallen down. A round landed between his legs and did a real number on him. They carried him to the chopper with us and set him down in front. Both of his legs were gone below the knees, and he had tourniquets made of web belts on both stumps. He was just sitting there, nonchalantly viewing his situation and shrugging his shoulders like he didn't care. Either he was in shock or he just knew his duty was over. I thought I might be in a position like that in the near future, and I wondered what my reaction would be.

We made a diversion to Khe Sanh Combat Base to unload the wounded man, and I got my first glimpse of the base since before the start of the siege. The place was completely covered with fresh dirt, and everything in sight was damaged. I felt very uneasy while the chopper was being unloaded. I just knew the rockets were on the way in, but nothing happened.

After we landed on Hill 881S, we moved to a small ridge and dug in. Our first chance to see what we were in for came while we spent a few days on the ridge. We could see up along our route of advance. It gave us a lot to think about, but it seemed to help morale.

☆

LtCol JOHN STUDT
3/26 Commanding Officer _____

The perimeter around Hill 881S was expanded: the high
ground immediately to the north, Pork Chop Hill, was
occupied and close-in patrolling was initiated. An extensive
complex of abandoned enemy fortifications was uncovered
within 300 meters of the defensive wire. Pork Chop Hill
was covered with interconnecting fortifications but was
evacuated by the enemy without a fight following extensive
air attacks, including CS gas.[1]

APRIL 10

Capt HARRY JENKINS
Mike Company, 3/26 _____

We got word from Battalion that the restriction on patrolling
outside the wire had been lifted. The first thing we wanted
to do was clear and screen the areas around the base of the
hill, mainly to the north and west. To help us do this, I put
together a reconnaissance patrol and requested that scout-
dog teams be brought in to cover the patrol's point position.
I was able to get one dog to the hill, a big, beautiful sable
German shepherd named King.

I was also worried about the Marines I would be sending
out on patrol. Many of them had lost their physical conditioning
after being cooped up on the hill since late January, and no
one had eaten properly in weeks and months. The troops
were not really in condition to go out and hump those hills.
So I decided to try to do as much as possible within the
limits of what I thought the troops could handle. The result
was a series of patrols beginning at the west-end gate on
Mike Company's end of the hill.

The first mission was to scout around the entire base of
the hill to determine what was there. The first patrol, with
King on the point, went out on the afternoon of April 10
and quickly came upon a series of North Vietnamese positions

—fighting holes, spiderholes, caves, trenches, and so on—all around the north side of Hill 881S. Fortunately, they were not occupied, but it appeared that the positions had been prepared in anticipation of an attack on 881S as well as for protection against air strikes. Marines on top of the hill didn't know there were NVA living at the base of the hill and, in some cases, beneath the hill itself.

As the patrol proceeded, King alerted his handler with increasing frequency that there was something ahead of the patrol. Finally, the handler let the dog go. King took off into the bushes and a big fracas commenced. Apparently, King jumped an NVA soldier. There was a lot of yelling and growling, and then the dog and the NVA went crashing off through the brush. When the handler called King back, he promptly returned and the patrol deployed and screened the area to the west, about three hundred meters out. They found one AK-47 on the ground, but nothing else. The patrol returned to the top of the hill that evening.

A second patrol was sent out four hours after the first patrol returned. It went off down the same trail toward the positions at the base of the hill and set up an ambush.

APRIL 11

Cpl TERRY STEWART
Mike Company, 3/26 _____

As I was on my third tour, I was elected to lead the patrol. We waited until late that evening, around midnight, and departed the wire on the western end of the hill. We went straight down off the side of the finger and moved ever so slowly and cautiously. Without telling me, my platoon commander, 2ndLt. William Ammon, had dropped off two men to act as a rearguard to cover our back door. The rest of us, with me as point, continued on down. We carried only our rifles, a few extra magazines, and a couple of grenades. We wore soft covers. We were light, silent, and mobile.

As we neared the foot of the hill, we heard very faint sounds. It wasn't determined what the sounds were; they were indistinct. At the bottom of the hill we could smell the smoke from the enemy's cooking fires, and there was rustling in the bushes to our front. As there were only about eight of us and we had no idea what we were up against, we pulled back. I whispered to the lieutenant that we should pull back a hundred meters and figure out how to go on from there. It was agreed.

The usual practice would have the patrol simply invert so the tail would become the lead. If this had been done, there would not have been any problem. However, the lieutenant had me lead the way back up; we just sort of snaked around. I put the man who was behind me at point and just told him to retrace our steps back about 100 meters and then stop. Neither of us knew about the rearguard, which was expecting us to return along the same track. They did nothing as we approached, but my pointman, when he was right on top of them, noticed a boot sticking out from a bush right next to him. He was quite startled when he touched it and it moved. He opened fire with a long burst.

The remaining member of the rearguard was several feet away. When I dived off the track and sought cover, he ended up directly in front of me, not more than ten feet away. I heard the bushes rustle as he turned to see what was going on. I almost opened up on him, but something held me off; something didn't feel right. Even though all this happened so suddenly, there was still only the one M-16 that fired a burst. If we were being ambushed or had jumped the enemy, there surely would have been more firing. Anyway, in a second or so, I heard an American voice whisper, "Are you all right?" I knew then that the person in front of me was a Marine. At first I thought that somehow the patrol had gotten twisted around. Safeties were clicking and I just knew that all hell was about to break loose, so I loudly yelled to cease fire. The person just in front of me in the bushes called my name and we finally got control of the situation.

Unfortunately, Pfc Charles Finley, the poor guy whose boot was sticking out from the bush, lay very seriously wounded. We quickly got him into a makeshift stretcher that we prepared using our shirts, and started up the hill. It was rough and steep and miserable. I know it had to have been very bad on the wounded man. We all had to take turns

carrying him. It was exhausting work. We were also frightened because we were making incredible noise going up; we
were easy targets for any NVA that we had attracted. I fell
back about twenty-five or thirty yards after my turn on the
litter. I lagged the rest of the way back to cover the others. I
cannot be sure if it was imagination born of fear of if we
were followed, but I believed that I heard pursuers and saw
fleeting, ghostlike shadows only a short way behind me. If
they were real, I can't imagine why they did not try to take
us.

We got Finley up the hill in a few hours. After a few
more hours, it was nearly dawn and a medevac arrived. This
was very dangerous for everyone. When the bird was
coming in, the NVA gave us all they had. Small arms,
rockets, and mortars came at us and the bird. But whoever
was flying that thing had a set of nuts that were definitely
fourteen-karat gold-plated lead. Knowing that he couldn't
land on the saddle, the normal landing zone, because the
NVA had it zeroed in, he hovered just off our positions on
the north side of the hill and backed the baby right up to us.
The ramp hit the side of the hill and two men walked Finley
into the bird and then hopped off. The bird took off. We all
thought that it was a clean mission. Later we learned that
the bird had evidently sustained a serious small-arms hit and
crashed on the way out. I heard that all on board were lost.

Finley had studied in the seminary and had taken a leave
to join up and volunteer for Vietnam so that he could learn
the lessons that it would have to offer him.

Capt HARRY JENKINS
Mike Company, 3/26 _____

Our third patrol off the hill included King, the scout dog,
with the point element. It went off on April 11, about seven
hours after the ambush patrol was aborted. The patrol was
moving along without having made contact when, for some
unknown reason, our 4.2-inch mortars on Hill 861 struck in
the immediate vicinity. A white-phosphorus marking round
landed upslope of the patrol, and the second marking round

landed right behind the patrol. We sustained three relatively
minor casualties from phosphorus burns. King was also
burned, more seriously than the three Marines. Scout dogs
were considered so valuable that King rated the highest
priority for medevac, and an H-34 was immediately dispatched
to get him—and the burned Marines. We received another
scout-dog team that evening.

APRIL 12

Col BRUCE MEYERS
26th Marines Commanding Officer _____

Major General Tompkins gave me broad guidance and
directed me to "move out from the perimeter at Khe Sanh."
On April 12, my first day as regimental commander, I
visited every unit on the surrounding hills (1/26, 2/26, 3/26,
and 1/9, as well as my two ARVN battalions). LtCol John
Studt, battalion commander of 3/26—he had been a Pfc in
my rifle company in Korea—requested permission to retake
Hill 881N from his battalion's position on 881S. I gave
approval, and my staff worked closely with his. In one day
and one night of intense requests, we had laid on every
possible bit of air and artillery prep that we could. Lieutenant Colonel Studt wished to avoid the mortar fire and direct
automatic-weapons fire from 881N that had previously struck
his units (India and Mike companies) on 881S.

APRIL 13

LtCol JOHN STUDT
3/26 Commanding Officer _____

On April 13 the commanding officer, 26th Marines, ordered
3/26 to attack 881N the following day. Detailed plans had
already been prepared, including an extensive fire-support
plan, as a result of an earlier warning order.

It was estimated that an NVA battalion was defending the
881N complex, with numerous strongpoints on the interven-
ing ground between 881S and 881N. In addition to organic

weapons, the enemy was supported with 12.7mm antiair-craft guns, 120mm mortars, and 122mm/140mm rockets. Moreover, the entire operation was within easy reach of his 130mm and 152mm artillery in Laos. After evaluating his various capabilities, two questions were of primary concern.

Would he use his artillery/rockets against us, or would our attack progress rapidly enough to disrupt his capability to adjust fires on our maneuver elements?

Would he reinforce? After all, we were threatening his primary rocket site for attacks on the Khe Sanh Base.

3/26 possessed all its organic elements plus the normal reinforcing units: shore party, engineers, scout-snipers, and two scout-dog teams. In addition, we had six .50-caliber machine guns taken from downed helicopters. Fire support would be provided by LtCol Jack Hennelly's 1st Battalion, 13th Marines, at the Khe Sanh Combat Base; three 105mm howitzers were actually located on top of 881S, a handy but hazardous arrangement. The 175mm gun batteries at Camp Carroll would reinforce 1/13, and finally, our traditional Sunday punch would be provided by Marine fixed-wing.

Col Bruce Meyers . . . assured us of priority of fire for all supporting arms.

Drawing heavily on Captain Dabney's familiarity with the terrain and on the keen mind of my operations officer, Maj Matt Caulfield, we developed a plan involving the following key factors:

1. Maximum maneuver forces. We would attack with three full rifle companies and one rifle company minus. Hill 881S would be manned only by H&S Company and one rifle platoon. Captain Dabney, now a major selectee, had been relieved of his company a few days earlier by Capt Lawrence Luther. Captain Dabney would command 881S and control our organic fire support. If the bulk of the battalion became too heavily engaged to make it back by night, no one was better qualified to defend 881S with limited forces if it came to that. Moreover, although Captain Dabney apparently lived a charmed life, his luck had about run out. With his predilection for exposing himself at the thickest point of any fire fight, it would have been a tragic

conclusion to the ten-week siege of Hill 881S to lose the man who had contributed so much to its successful defense.

2. Maximum organic fire support. All the battalion's supporting arms would be organized into a provisional weapons company:

Eight 81mm mortars, organized in two sections with separate fire-direction centers to permit firing two simultaneous missions.

Eight 106mm recoilless rifles positioned on 881S to provide direct fire against point targets to the north. They were to prove invaluable for precision destruction of enemy forward-slope bunkers during the attack.

Six .50-caliber machine guns.

Three 105mm howitzers.

Three 60mm mortar sections from Lima, Mike, and India companies. Kilo Company's mortars would support them from Pork Chop Hill.

3. Surprise. Since the slightest observable movement invariably brought mortar fire on 881S, just getting through the wire and off the exposed slopes of 881S was a problem. The obvious answer was night movement. On the night of April 11, security patrols worked their way into positions covering the entire route to each company's attack position. Remaining concealed and motionless in daylight, they would serve three functions: reconnaissance, security for the battalion's movement to attack positions on the night of April 13-14, and guides for each company's night movement. Dog teams would also move with the company points until initial contact was made.

4. Maximum stand-off destruction of the enemy prior to infantry assault. This was key to the whole operation and required maximum use of supporting arms. Fire support was planned in great detail, by the book. Every known and suspected enemy position was pre-plotted for "on-call" fires. Lieutenant Colonel Hennelly's guns at Khe Sanh Base would be firing with the long axis perpendicular to our axis of advance, an ideal arrangement. Fixed-wing strikes could then be run on deeper targets simultaneously with artillery missions, with air attacking parallel to the artillery trajectory.

Heavy prep fires by artillery and [radar-guided] bomb

runs by aircraft would commence at midnight, April 13. Each objective would be heavily prepped just in advance of attacking infantry while aircraft hit deeper targets.

Finally, company commanders would exercise extreme care to avoid getting lead elements pinned down close-in to heavily resisting enemy strongpoints. In other words, they would do everything to counter Charlie's favorite tactic of knocking down our lead elements so close to his position as to prevent our further use of supporting arms. If heavy enemy fire was still encountered following our planned preps, the attacking companies would pull back and further supporting arms would be employed prior to infantry assault. Since the ground was not to be held, the mission was to inflict maximum casualties on the enemy with minimum loss of Marines.

5. Maneuver. The battalion would attack with three companies up, moving along three roughly parallel avenues of approach to 881N. The command group, with the fourth company (minus) as battalion reserve, would move in trace of the center company. If particularly strong resistance was encountered by any assault company, an adjacent company would be maneuvered to turn the flank of the strongpoint and/or deliver supporting fire. The reserve could be employed in any direction.

6. Speed. This was important to capitalize on surprise before the enemy could react by reinforcing or adjusting his heavy mortars or artillery or the attacking battalion. 3/26 was given one day to complete the operation.[2]

☆

Pfc LIONEL TRUFANT
106mm Platoon, 3/26

After moving our 106mm recoilless rifle around the top of Hill 881S a few times, we set into a permanent position next to the landing zone. We had eight 106s up there—the four guns that had been up there the whole time, the two we brought up from the combat base, and two more from Hill 861. At that point, they told us that we were up there to help take Hill 881N.

I could see the NVA hill. It was like we were all on one side and they were all on the other side. As soon as we got our guns set in, we started firing on their hill. It was the first time we had really had a chance to fire our gun. The 106 gunners who had been on 881S told us how to use the recoilless rifles up there. Several times we used them to blow away mortar positions, or against snipers. They had us use the .50-caliber spotting rifle attached to the 106 to fire spotting rounds so we could plot in targets.

We just knew something big was coming. There was a great sense of anticipation. We had been taking all that shit all that while, and now we felt like giving some of it back.

Cpl DENNIS MANNION
Charlie Battery, 1/13 (with Kilo, 3/26) _____

Kilo Company left the hill early on Saturday morning, April 13, and cautiously walked downslope using trails into the draw between Hill 881S and Hill 881N. We dug in there with Marines from other companies. Having had the experience of Hill 861, we were really fearful of getting attacked. We dug good, deep, covered foxholes and cleared fields of fire with machetes. No one I know of slept that night.

APRIL 14

Col BRUCE MEYERS
26th Marines Commanding Officer _____

During early-morning darkness of Easter Sunday, April 14, LtCol John Studt and the major portion of his battalion wound through the ''gate'' in the wire and into attack positions.

LtCol JOHN STUDT
3/26 Commanding Officer _____

Security patrols covering the approach routes to attack positions had reported no enemy contact. Artillery preps commenced at midnight and continued throughout the night, with emphasis on bunker-busting, large-caliber rounds: 155mm and 175mm. Since heavy shellings in this area were not unusual, it was not anticipated that the enemy would necessarily be alerted to our attack. Known enemy positions to the south and west were also hit to further confuse the enemy as to our intent. . . .

The approach routes had been carefully studied by key personnel the previous day. Security elements along the routes acted as guides and joined their units as they passed.[3]

Capt HARRY JENKINS
Mike Company, 3/26 _____

The night of April 13–14 was very clear, with a three-quarter moon. It was very easy to see as Mike Company left the perimeter and moved down the hill into its attack positions. Starting at midnight, we worked down off the finger, into the ravine, carefully picked our way through the NVA positions at the base of the hill, and moved into our attack positions. The scout dog with the point platoon alerted its handler a few times as the company moved through the NVA positions, but nothing happened. As the point broke out of the brush and mounted a bare knoll, the dog gave a strong alert. The pointmen saw movement and opened fire. Screams were heard and the point moved forward to clear the area. All we found were two NVA packs. We did not find the people involved, or any signs that we had inflicted casualties. Lima Company, which had moved off Hill 881S right behind us and had veered off to the west at the bottom of the hill, made no contact of any kind. Neither did Kilo Company, which followed Lima and veered off to the east.

As soon as we got into the attack positions, I told my troops to lie down in the grass and get as much rest as possible. I was still very concerned with their physical conditioning. The terrain was steep, and if it was a hot day, a tremendous amount of physical exertion would be required. I wasn't sure how they would do.

LtCol JOHN STUDT
3/26 Commanding Officer _____

By 0530 all companies were in position; Lima and Mike companies were putting out scout elements with dog teams toward their first objectives. Just before first light, approximately 0545, both Lima and Mike companies' scout elements had made contact with the enemy's outposts on the approaches to Objectives 2 and 3. As the familiar staccato of AK-47s and NVA machine guns suddenly erupted to the front, we all knew that the surprise was over; the battle was on and it would be a fight all the way. Thanks to early warnings by the dogs, only one scout was wounded.

Mortars were adjusted on the enemy positions, and they were quickly overrun. The battle began to unfold exactly as planned.

Artillery was adjusted on Objectives 2 and 3 while mortars covered Objective 1. By now an aerial observer was on station and directing fixed-wing air strikes on Objectives 4 and Alpha.

As Lima moved out against Objective 3, they received heavy automatic-weapons and small-arms fire. They held up while further preps were called with 81s and 106s.[4]

LCpl CHARLIE THORNTON
Lima Company, 3/26 _____

As we moved, we suddenly came under fire from a strong force of well-entrenched NVA. They had occupied a small hill and built a very strong defensive position of bunkers. As we tried to advance up the hill, we were turned back by heavy automatic-weapons fire and other small-arms fire.

The bunkers were well-concealed and we had trouble determining from where the fire was coming. I was the gunner of a 60mm mortar, which we moved back to a hill approximately fifty yards to our rear in order to improve our line of sight. Artillery had begun to support our position, but they were unable to destroy the bunkers or even slow down the fire we were receiving. I set my mortar up without using the sight because the angle of the hill made the line of sight impossible. I aligned the gun, pointing the barrel toward the targets by using my judgment and eyesight. The distance was very short, and the gun's trajectory was almost straight up. As we began firing white-phosphorus rounds to get on target, the NVA began to concentrate their fire on our gun. We fired high-explosive rounds until our ammunition was gone. We then moved forward to join the other Marines in assaulting the hill. My gun was later credited with five kills made by direct hits on the NVA bunkers

☆

Pfc ELWIN BACON
Kilo Company, 3/26 _____

We started the climb up Hill 881N by breaking the company up into platoon-size units. Although there was small-arms fire going on everywhere, we seemed to be lucking out. As the 2nd Platoon moved slowly up the hill, we heard reports of all kinds of sightings of enemy units running along the ridges in great numbers. They seemed to be avoiding us as much as possible. At least, they were trying not to get boxed in by the Marines.

As we gained ground, we found heavily used trails and bunkers throughout the area. I got the feeling that there were a hell of a lot of those dudes around there somewhere. We found all kinds of things—food, clothes, and belts. I thought of some of them running around trying to shoot at us while they were holding their trousers up.

Cpl DENNIS MANNION
Charlie Battery, 1/13 (with Kilo, 3/26) _____

It was a classic, company-on-line advance. As long as the terrain didn't dictate differently, we stayed on line. Artillery from the combat base was firing tremendous numbers of rounds in front of us. They fired whole grid squares at a time, using the time-on-target technique, in which all the rounds fired land and detonate at one time. More impressive and more helpful to us, however, were the 106mm recoilless rifles and .50-caliber machine guns lined up in the trench along the top of Hill 881S. They were able to fire directly over our heads, into the treeline 150 yards ahead of us, just churning the place up as we moved forward. As we advanced, they raised the elevation on those guns and kept on firing.

Capt HARRY JENKINS
Mike Company, 3/26 _____

As Mike Company started to push up to the final part of Objective 2, the pointman from one of the lead platoons was shot in the head and fell down on top of the position. The first thing we had to do was try to regroup and drag him back off the top of the hill. As we tried to do that, the NVA started rolling grenades down the steep portion of the hill, which was right in front of us. These caused people in the 1st Platoon to veer off to the right and I had to pull my command group back somewhat. We were able to get the casualty off the top of the hill, but he was already dead.

LtCol JOHN STUDT
3/26 Commanding Officer _____

Mike Company . . . ran into a reverse-slope defense, the first real surprise of the day. A grenade-throwing contest developed along the crest. It began to look like a long day! Mike was ordered to pull back 300 meters to permit the use of supporting arms. This was not easily done, as they now had one KIA on the crest and several wounded. Moreover, after months of being pounded by the enemy with little opportunity for the infantry to strike back, it was difficult to hold back the troops from premature assault. These Marines wanted to settle a score—and did before the day was over.[5]

Capt HARRY JENKINS
Mike Company, 3/26 _____

The 106s lined up along the top of Hill 881S cleaned off

Objective 2, in front of Mike Company, and after a lot of noise and confusion, we went back up the hill.

LtCol JOHN STUDT
3/26 Commanding Officer _____

As additional preps were delivered on Objective 2 and 3, Kilo Company moved on Objective 1 and then slightly north of Objective 1 to bring fire to bear on the reverse slope of Objective 2. Only sniper fire was encountered by Kilo Company.[6]

Cpl TERRY STEWART
Mike Company, 3/26 _____

I was lead for the whole movement, and I had Cpl Bob Saffle, my 1st Fire Team leader and his team, on point. I was right behind them. Halfway up the naked slope, we took vicious small-arms fire from several automatics. Bob's only two men were cut down without the chance to even fire a shot. Bob was pinned behind a small bush not twenty feet up to my left. Just ahead of him, I could see the muzzles of the enemy rifles sticking out of a well-camouflaged firing port. I called to Bob, but he was in a sort of shock; he wouldn't move in any direction. After several moments, I made a dash to him and pulled him back to a crater in which we could take cover.

Bob was crying and mumbling something about losing his whole team. He wasn't really very rational. I shook the shit out of him and he snapped right out of it. Once I had his attention, we decided that we had to knock out that bunker fast; the whole unit was pinned and, if we didn't get rolling, we could get flanked and end up in serious trouble. It was decided that we would both rush and draw the shooters to separate targets. This worked, and we got to spots that we knew were in areas that would be hard for anyone in that bunker to see. We were apart by maybe twenty-five yards, lying flat. The plan was for Bob to place sustained, well-aimed rounds directly into the firing port while I rushed from the right front and planted a grenade.

It looked like it was going to work, but as soon as I started to raise up to start my rush, a half-dozen Chicom grenades fell toward me. I guess we hadn't fooled anyone. I hugged the deck so low that an ant would have had to look down at me. I buried my head in my arms and slammed my legs together. I heard several of the grenades land near me, but the explosions I heard were not that awfully close. When the shock waves settled, I looked up. There were three duds within arm's reach of me. The remaining grenades had landed far enough away that I had escaped harm.

I wasted no time. Bob was keeping his end of the bargain, so I completed mine. I hit the bunker with a home run and went right on past to set up for the first men behind us. It was all over very quickly. We captured a couple of NVA from that hole. One was a warrant officer.

On the way up the hill, some poor guy was shaken real bad when an NVA round set off a LAAW he was carrying slung across his chest. The rocket went off and blew this poor bastard for a loop. Somehow he wasn't injured, but it must have made a devout worshiper out of him.

Capt HARRY JENKINS
Mike Company, 3/26 _____

We were able to go right over the top of Objective 2, consolidate our gains, and hold for further orders.

☆

LtCol JOHN STUDT
3/26 Commanding Officer _____

Lima Company now launched an assault on Objective 3. Approximately fifty enemy broke and ran to the northwest, where they were promptly brought under fire by artillery, then air. The rest died in their positions, some by the preps, the others by close-in fighting as Marines cleared the position bunker by bunker. In ten minutes Objective 3 was secured.

The spirit of the assault troops was typified by Lance Corporal Patterson, a cool, slow-speaking Kentuckian. As he led his squad into the enemy positions, an NVA sniper popped up ten meters distant and fired. Patterson was knocked down by a round grazing his skull. Finding himself still alive, he jumped up with his M-16. As the enemy soldier attempted to chamber another round with his bolt-action sniper rifle, Patterson cut him down with a burst of automatic fire, then continued the attack. As Lima Company moved back onto 881S that night, Patterson was sporting a bloody head bandage and a scopemounted NVA sniper rifle. After hearing the story, I asked him if he didn't feel pretty lucky. Patterson replied in a matter-of-fact tone that it all boiled down to his having cleaned his rifle the night before; Charlie apparently had not. In examining his trophy, Patterson noted that the NVA weapon had a cartridge jammed in a dirty chamber. Patterson, who had led his squad with distinction throughout the attack, was promoted to corporal on the spot.

Now that the high ground to both flanks was occupied, the enemy on Objective 2 decided it was time to pull out as Mike Company resumed the attack. Again the fleeing NVA were well covered with supporting arms.[7]

☆

Capt HARRY JENKINS
Mike Company, 3/26 ──────────────────────────

The battalion command group came up on my position surveyed the situation, and ordered Mike Company to continue the attack to the north. The game plan was for Kilo Company to continue on its axis toward Hill 881N itself. Mike Company was to attack straight downhill behind Objective 2 toward a large, wooded bowl in a low area between Objective 2 and Hill 881N. Lima Company was supposed to stay in its position to support Kilo or Mike if it was needed. India Company remained in the rear, as battalion reserve. We jumped off again shortly after noon.

LtCol JOHN STUDT
3/26 Commanding Officer ──────────────────────

Now a new threat developed. Observers on 881S reported

that, in addition to the enemy trying to pull out to the west, approximately one NVA company was apparently taking up supplementary positions on the southern slope of 881N (Objective A), obviously planning to hit Mike Company as they came down the reverse slope of Objective 2. This was beautiful! While Mike Company held on the forward slope, for the next hour the NVA on 881N were hit with everything: air, artillery, mortars, and, not least, Captain Dabney's 106s. It was an unparalleled employment of recoilless rifles. Clearing my observation post on Objective 2 by inches, Captain Dabney adjusted his powerful weapons directly on individual enemy positions, literally blasting the NVA out of their bunkers. With eight guns and hundreds of rounds stockpiled on 881S, the hill was a veritable land battleship. The enemy attempted to suppress this fire with 122mm rockets.[8]

Pfc LIONEL TRUFANT
106mm Platoon, 3/26 _____

We were peppering Hill 881N. The assaulting troops called in targets, and they were relayed to the guns from the battalion fire-control center through the 106 Platoon commander and our section chief, Cpl Gary Smith. When we fired, all we could see was the round going into trees and the trees getting blown out. We kept firing and hearing that the fire was effective.

We got a call from Corporal Smith that the NVA had just fired some 122mm rockets at us. Just as he finished talking, the rockets came in. When the first explosion sounded, I looked up and saw a body being thrown in the air. I knew who it was. It was Pfc Marvin Smith, the assistant gunner on the other gun in our section. Everybody on my gun just stopped. Then another rocket came in and exploded. That really stopped us. Our land line was out, we didn't know who was hit, we didn't know what was happening. After a minute or two, though, we started firing again. But the NVA had stopped our guns for a few minutes.

We kept firing until, finally, the word came down that

helicopters were coming in. We started carrying the wounded guncrew down to the landing zone. One of them was Marvin Smith. He had been hit across the face and across the midsection. Pfc Gary Smith, the section leader, had his knee messed up. Another guy had his ear blown off, and another guy had a stomach wound.

My emotions were mixed. I talked to the guy with the stomach wound while I was waiting to put him on the helicopter. I had tears coming out of my eyes, but I still did what I had to do. The one that impacted the most was Marvin Smith. He was a buddy. I hated seeing him like that. The helicopters came in, we put them on the helicopters, and then we went back to our guns and started firing again.

LtCol JOHN STUDT
3/26 Commanding Officer _____

Four 106 crewmen were wounded, but our counterbattery fire quickly removed this threat.[9]

Pfc LIONEL TRUFANT
106mm Platoon, 3/26 _____

One of the guns ran out of ammunition, but they needed ammo because they had a bunch of NVA caught in the open. I was an ammo man, so I had to carry two heavy rounds on each shoulder, running through the trenches to the gun that needed them. Mortars and rockets were still coming in, but we kept going.

The good thing about the 106s is that we could keep firing even when air strikes were coming in because their trajectory was so low. The mortars had to stop firing, but the 106s didn't. That meant we were free to fire immediately whenever the grunts got resistance from bunkers that were facing us.

Col BRUCE MEYERS
26th Marines Commanding Officer _____

The 106s and the .50s were used in a superb manner by the gunners in close coordination with Studt's lead elements. Always cautious of treelines, I remember seeing several treelines literally blown away, just yards in front of the advancing Marines. The barrels of the 106s got so hot at one point that we took turns joining the 106 crews in cooling the barrels by relieving ourselves and pouring water from our canteens on the steaming tubes.

☆

Cpl DENNIS MANNION
Charlie Battery, 1/13 (with Kilo, 3/26) _____

Kilo Company was on the extreme right of the battalion line. Because of a point in the terrain where it got real sleep, part of the company moved ahead while the other part got slowed down. I became extremely concerned because I knew what the artillery were doing. I was afraid the part of Kilo Company that was moving ahead faster would be hit by our own guns in an area I knew was going to be subjected to a time-on-target bombardment. I called the base and told them they had to shift the mission by 500 yards because I felt that part of Kilo Company was already on the fringes of the target grid square. The mission was shifted.

LtCol JOHN STUDT
3/26 Commanding Officer _____

By now it was all but over for Charlie. An aerial observer reported more NVA breaking from positions around 881N and running into the jungles to the west. Two flights of fixed-wing reported good target coverage, although no casualty assessment could be obtained due to the vegetation.

At approximately 1400, Kilo Company attacked 881N while Lima occupied the high ground just short of Objective 4, which was now deserted of live enemy. Mike Company, changing its direction of attack to the northwest to parallel Kilo's axis of advance, continued to mop up a vast complex of bunkers, tunnels, and storage caves between Objective 2 and 881N. Numerous bodies were found, mostly killed by supporting arms, which had caved in many bunkers. Two NVA wounded were also picked up, one an officer.[10]

Capt HARRY JENKINS
Mike Company, 3/26 _____

What we had was an entire bunker complex—freshly dug
holes, spiderholes, underground bunkers, all kinds of trenches.
There were enough positions in there to hold a battalion.
Fortunately, there was nobody in there.

Col BRUCE MEYERS
26th Marines Commanding Officer _____

As the advancing elements of 3/26 approached the hated
crest of 881N, some of the NVA defenders broke and ran.
My air officer heard from an air spotter, who asked for the
lead elements to hold up while he called an air strike in on
the fleeing NVA. However, with the exhilaration of nearly
regaining what had once been theirs, the lead elements fixed
bayonets and broke over the crest in a bayonet charge—
despite the request to hold up from Studt's operations
officer, Maj Matt Caulfield. The company commander said
that he "could not stop them."

Cpl DENNIS MANNION
Charlie Battery, 1/13 (with Kilo, 3/26) _____

There were numerous dead North Vietnamese, but not in
great quantities. They were scattered here and there, in
caved-in bunkers and trenchlines. I fired my M-16 at two
guys I saw running diagonally from my right. They went
down under a hail of fire.
   When we got to the top of Hill 881N, the smell of cordite
and gunpowder was in the air. The smell was just incredible, more than I ever experienced during my tour. The
torn-up landscape was something else.
   One of the Marines on top of the hill had a flag. Another
guy and I helped him up one of the few trees still standing,
and he hung the flag up there.

LtCol JOHN STUDT
3/26 Commanding Officer _____

At 1428, Kilo Company, meeting only light resistance,

swept across the scarred slopes of 881N and raised the National Colors.[11]

Pfc ELWIN BACON
Kilo Company, 3/26 ⸻

When we reached the top of Hill 881N, I was surprised that the resistance was so light. There were many wounded and some KIAs, but the NVA didn't seen interested in holding the hill.

Cpl TERRY STEWART
Mike Company, 3/26 ⸻

When we got to 881N we found an incredible mess. The hill had been devastated by B-52s, air strikes, and artillery. It was cratered like a moon, and all the trees were twisted and broken. It was an awesome sight. Some of their bunkers were sitting, ready to fall, at the very edge of bomb craters. I entered a couple. They were made of trees, dirt, and banana stalks.

Col BRUCE MEYERS
26th Marines Commanding Officer ⸻

I remember my burst of pride in seeing one of the leading Marines shinny up one of the shrapnel-torn trees and take a small American flag he had obviously been carrying in his pack for just such an event and raise the Stars and Stripes. That was the signal for the completion of the retaking of 881N.

The former defenders continued to retreat north on the reverse slope, on which we called an air strike, with excellent results. The battalion had been ordered to make a limited incursion, which they had done with success. They then began the planned withdrawal, bringing two slightly wounded NVA prisoners—one was an officer—whom I took back on my chopper to Khe Sanh for medical treatment and interrogation. There were 106 NVA killed in contrast to six Marines killed and nineteen Marines wounded and medevacked. We considered our "Easter egg hunt" to be a solid success. The night approach for the dawn assault paid off.

None of the subsequent actions pushing out from our original "siege" positions in the hills surrounding Khe Sanh had the success of LtCol John Studt's raid and subsequent withdrawal.

LtCol JOHN STUDT
3/26 Commanding Officer _____

Colonel Meyers, who had flown in during the height of the battle in spite of rocket and mortar fire hitting 881S, sent his congratulations. Throughout the attack he had personally ensured that the battalion received maximum fire support; this support, both artillery and air, was superb and a key factor in the success of the operation.

The final tally: 106 NVA bodies, two prisoners, numerous individual and crew-served weapons captured. No count could be obtained of the fleeing enemy killed by air and artillery in the jungles and eight-foot elephant grass to the west. Colonel Meyers personally landed near 881N and picked up the prisoners in his helicopter.

The cost: six marines killed and thirty-two wounded, nineteen of which were medevacs. The battalion closed back on 881S that evening under a dense, protective fog. It was an unforgettable sight to study the Marines of 3/26 trudging back through the wire on 881S. After months of static defense, they were near exhaustion; they were filthy, bearded (water was scarce), and ragged, in tattered remnants of uniforms; some of them wore bloody battle dressings. but they were loaded with captured NVA weapons, and they were all grinning. An old score had been settled![12]

Chapter 15

BGen JACOB GLICK
Task Force Glick _____

I was sent up here on verbal orders from Major General Tompkins, Commanding General of 3rd Marine Division. At the time I was sent up here, I was Assistant Division Commander of 3rd Marine Division. I was sent to be prepared to take command of the forces here upon termination of Operation Pegasus, which was being run by the 1st Cavalry Division.

On April 15, at 0800, the remaining forces from Pegasus passed to the operational control of the 3rd Marine Division, and, in turn, passed to my operational control.

My mission is to continue offensive operations in the . . . area, to mop up enemy forces, to locate and capture enemy material and equipment, and to continue operations with mobile and flexible forces using maximum air, artillery, and all nature of supporting fires.

There are still extensive enemy forces in this area. We

estimate ten to twelve enemy battalions, and our purpose will be to search out and continue to destroy enemy forces.

My initial mission when I came was to roll back the Khe Sanh Combat Base. The forces were going to be withdrawn from here, leaving only one battalion of highly mobile forces to be primarily a reconnaissance screen. That has since been changed, and my new mission is to remain here to continue the offensive operations against the enemy, to search him out and destroy him.[1]

Col BRUCE MEYERS
26th Marines Commanding Officer _____

The plan of withdrawal [includes provisions that on] April 15, 1st Battalion, 9th Marines, is to stay in position. . . . 3/26 will come into the base for lift-out the next day, April 16.[2]

☆

Cpl DENNIS MANNION
Charlie Battery, 1/13 _____

First Lieutenant Benjamin Fordham was about the same size as me—five-eleven, about 190 pounds—and liked to play football, like me. He liked to read, like me, and liked to talk about books, like me. In fact, when one of us got a book, he would read a chapter or two, then tear out that section and pass it on to the other until the book was gone. We shared a lot of books that way. And we shared some laughs about some of the books. As the Kilo Company artillery forward observer, I wasn't responsible to anyone except the captain, so I sort of got to free-lance all over the place. That allowed me to spend many hours with Lieutenant Fordham—bitching, planning, and speculating on the war, the Marine corps, the country, and life in general. Even though he was an officer and I was enlisted, we got pretty close.

We spent the night of April 14—following the Easter Offensive—on the saddle between Hills 881N and 881S. As we were being choppered off the saddle on the morning of April 15, Fordham's platoon had landing-zone security. Two of the rifle platoons had already been lifted out. As the company command group crawled to the edge of the zone, I happened to be stretched out in the dirt next to Lieutenant Fordham. As we watched the last two CH-46s approach, we both laughed and touched hands. We were on our way out!

Just as my chopper touched down, two good-sized rounds exploded in the scrub trees about 100 yards from us. We looked at one another and shrugged. As I ran past him, he yelled up to me to say that he would be right behind, on the last chopper. Four minutes later, I stepped off my chopper at the main base. I was greeted with the news that, as the lieutenant's men rushed for the last CH-46, two mortar rounds hit at the edge of the landing zone.

Lieutenant Benjamin Fordham was the last member of Kilo Company killed at Khe Sanh.

Capt HARRY JENKINS
Mike Company, 3/26 _____

When we were lifted off Hill 881S to the combat base by helicopter, it appeared that Mike Company's role in the siege had ended. We landed at the edge of Red Sector, just off the airstrip, and were told that we were to be lifted out of the combat base by helicopter later that afternoon.

The only cover I was able to find for the company in this area was the old trench that followed the perimeter between Red Sector and Blue Sector. It was only three feet deep at its deepest point. I spread the company along the trench for a distance of 250 meters. Shortly thereafter, we began undergoing an ordeal the likes of which Mike Company had not experienced the entire time it was on Hill 881S.

About 1300, the 37th ARVN Ranger was moving en masse from one end of the perimeter to the other, from east to west along the airstrip. The NVA artillery forward observers in the hills picked up the movement and we began to take artillery fire from the 130mm and 152mm batteries located at Co Roc, in Laos.

The initial incoming rounds impacted about midway along the runway. As the ARVN Rangers continued to move, still somewhat en masse, the NVA forward observers continued to adjust their artillery. Gradually, over a period of forty-five minutes, the artillery was continually adjusted and moved farther west, toward Mike Company.

After about an hour of this, the ARVN Rangers were almost at the western end of the runway and into our area, where they appeared to go to ground. At that time, the NVA artillery began firing for effect—entire batteries of four or six guns opened up with one or two rounds per gun. It just happened that, as they tried to blanket the area where the ARVNs were located, their artillery fell on us.

What occurred over the next ninety minutes was what I would call a mass artillery attack. We could hear the guns going off in Laos and had to sweat it out for ten or fifteen seconds before we could hear the shriek of the rounds coming in and impacting. Initially we were not harmed, but the artillery was eventually adjusted, shifted from the ARVN Rangers to where we were. We could not move, we could not dig, there was no place to go.

Dozens of artillery rounds fell within our area. By the time it was over, the majority of the troops of Mike Company were thoroughly shaken by the experience.

Cpl TERRY STEWART
Mike Company, 3/26 _____

I was assigned as an advance man. I had lost most of my men, and the remaining few were sent to other squads. I had the mailbag and was supposed to take one of the first birds out of Khe Sanh to Quang Tri to help get ready for the rest of the company. I was sitting well away from my unit, at the edge of the airstrip, when the big guns in Co Roc cut loose. My platoon commander, 2ndLt William Ammon, and my platoon sergeant, Staff Sergeant Harriman, were tucked up beneath a tank at the edge of the strip when a single round came in and hit just under the lip of the tank. It was a million-to-one shot that propelled both men out the other end like rifle bullets. The lieutenant was killed instantly and Staff Sergeant Harriman was critically injured.

Captain Jenkins got in touch with me since I was the next-senior man in my platoon. I rushed back to Mike Company under heavy artillery. I would get only a few steps

and have to dive for cover in the trenches that bordered the
strip. I couldn't move through them because they were packed
with men. At one point, I dived as I heard a round coming in
and landed right on top of another Marine. I hit him sort of
hard and knocked the wind out of him. As I was helping him,
he saw "MICH" on my helmet and asked where I was from. I
told him I was from Charlevoix. He said that he was from
Hudsonville. I mentioned that my grandfather was from there,
also. He asked his name and I told him. He nearly jumped
out of the trench. We had the same grandfather! The guy I
landed on was my first cousin, whom I had not seen since we
were about five years old. It was a very quick reunion and I
was off as soon as I heard the air was clear.

Capt HARRY JENKINS
Mike Company, 3/26 ——————————————————

The artillery attack disrupted the plans to get 3/26 out of
Khe Sanh on April 15. We had to spend another night in the
combat base. We dispersed into a number of abandoned
bunkers and spent a quiet night.

APRIL 16

Col BRUCE MEYERS
26th Marines Commanding Officer ——————————————

On April 16, the 3rd Battalion, 26th Marines, would fly to
Quang Tri; the 1st Battalion, 26th Marines, would come on
into the Khe Sanh Combat Base; and a battalion of the 1st
Marines would come up and relieve 2/26 in the northern tier
of hill positions.[3]

Pfc LIONEL TRUFANT
106mm Platoon, 3/26 ——————————————————

We flew back to Quang Tri on CH-53 helicopters. I felt
good, but I also felt bad because we had lost a lot of people.
Even though Khe Sanh was a bad place, it was like a lot of

other places—once I left it, I felt like I was leaving something there.

Pfc ELWIN BACON
Kilo Company, 3/26 _____

As we lifted off the ground, I was very tight and nervous about the whole thing. And just when we started to circle until the other choppers were airborne, more rockets came in. All of a sudden a loud bang came from the bottom of our chopper. My thoughts were, Oh, shit! The pilot took the bird down sharply, probably out of instinct, but he then leveled off. As I looked out of the window, I could see a flare floating down below. It seemed as though the rockets had hit a flare bunker, and one just happened to come up to meet us.

HM3 DAVID STEINBERG
India Company, 3/26 _____

Finally, almost at dusk, they brought choppers in for India Company. One of our guys had just been hit, and I put down my pack with everything I owned in it. I lifted the wounded Marine onto my back and carried him over to Charlie-Med. When I got there, a reporter stuck a camera in my face and asked, "What you got there?" I put down the wounded Marine and said, "I got my fist." And I punched the reporter in the face. I'm not that way, but I had a lot of emotions going on. Instead of helping me carry the wounded Marine across an open field, under incoming, all he wanted to do was take a picture and do an interview. My buddy came first.

When I left Charlie-Med, I saw the open back of the chopper. Someone yelled, "Come on, Doc. It's the last chopper out. We're gettin' outta here." The back of the CH-46 was open and the rotors were going. Over to the left was my pack. I had two choices: all the material things in my life that were in the pack, or getting on the chopper. I made a right turn and got aboard the chopper, which took off right away. I never saw my pack again, but my wallet reached me about two months later.

Pfc ELWIN BACON
Kilo Company, 3/26 _____

There was a small band and a number of people waiting
there to greet us. We must have looked as bad as we
smelled, and I noticed that most people kept their distance
from us. The band played while we stripped naked in front
of God and the world and walked through open showers,
which were set up like a bunch of coatracks. As long as we
were up there, I felt as though we were being treated like a
bunch of hogs getting washed for slaughter.

HM3 DAVID STEINBERG
India Company, 3/26 _____

It was dark by the time we got to Quang Tri. We had red
sand instead of red clay. The people of India Company,
3/26, had made it out of Khe Sanh. It was party time! We
had showers! They gave us new clothing! We shaved! They
had steaks for us, and beer! We drank beer and we ate and
the war was over for us. Everything was happy and gay. We
slept in tents right across from the Quang Tri airstrip. We
felt so secure and safe—until 0300. The eighteen survivors
of the original India Company on Hill 881S became twelve.
They rocketed us! Six of them were killed that night when
one of the 122mm rockets hit their tent. It was like they
followed us down to kill the rest of us off.

☆

HM3 BILL GESSNER
Delta Company, 1/9 _____

On the night of April 15, the [ARVN 3rd Airborne Task
Force] moved off their ridge and attacked south. One the
morning of April 16, 1/9 moved down off Hill 689 and over
the ridge vacated by the ARVN. Alpha Company was
leading, and Delta Company was last in the formation.
Alpha Company walked into a big ambush. The battalion
commander committed Bravo and Charlie companies right
away to relieve the pressure on Alpha Company, but the
NVA were too well positioned. Delta Company joined the

fight. We assaulted the southern slope and got up to the enemy's first foxholes, then we were stopped. The battalion commander, already wounded once, was wounded again while visiting the Delta Company command post. I put a dressing on him, and he continued on his way.

Our second attack was stalled by furious small-arms fire. I was crawling toward a hole when an NVA soldier stuck his head up to see. I froze. Fortunately for me, someone else saw the man and shot him. I pulled him out of the hole and climbed in. I was joined by a couple of Marines, and we decided we couldn't go any farther. Just then, our CO crawled by and told us to get moving—so we did. I crawled another few yards and tumbled into a bomb crater. The forward air controller and another Marine joined me. Then a wounded man crawled into the bomb crater with us. I was squatting over him to bandage his wounds when the lights went out.

When I came to, I sat up and checked the wounded man. He was dead. I looked around the saw the forward air controller lying on his back. I found he had a sucking chest wound and another less serious wound. The other Marine was dead. The forward air controller asked me to help him down the hill. When I started to drag him, I found out that I'd been wounded in the left leg. I put a bandage on the leg, and we started down to the rear of the hill. Battalion had designated a casualty collection point on a piece of level ground on the east side of the hill—so helicopters could land. When I got down to the casualty collection point, it was crowded with wounded. Some had been treated and others had not. I didn't see any other corpsmen there, so I stayed and treated the Marines on the pickup zone. During the day, small-arms and incoming artillery kept medevac choppers from extracting any of the wounded. Several choppers were shot down. Finally, after dark, choppers started taking casualties out. The CH-53s couldn't land on the hill; they had to hover while casualties were loaded. I helped load several choppers before my leg gave out. I rode out to Dong Ha and the 3rd Medical Battalion.

Before my letter arrived home, the Navy casualty reporter at Quonset Navel Air Station called my father at the house. He wasn't home, but my stepmother was. She asked,

"What is the call about?" The casualty reporting officer replied, "I can't tell you over the phone. When will Mr. Gessner be home?" Naturally, my stepmother assumed the worst. She told the casualty officer to come at seven that night. Then she called my dad and my fiancée. Dad tried to call the casualty officer back, but he couldn't get him.

When the casualty officer arrived, my fiancée and the whole family was there. He said, "Your son was wounded in the left leg in fighting near Khe Sanh."

My dad asked, "Well, how serious is the wound?"

"I don't know. But because he's still in Dong Ha, it means it's either really bad or not too bad at all."

After I heard about that, I refused a Purple Heart for another minor wound.

The April 16 fight involving 1/9 resulted in very heavy casualties: nineteen KIAs, thirty-six serious WIAs, an unknown number of minor WIAs, and sixteen MIAs. It took 1/9 days and cost more lives to locate and recover most—not all—of the MIAs, all of whom were from Alpha Company. An unknown number of NVA solders died in the action that involved, at the most, one NVA company.

☆

Pfc MIKE DeLANEY
Echo Company, 2/26 (Hill 861A) _____

We got word on April 14 that we were going to the combat base. Not that we were leaving Khe Sanh, but that we were leaving the hill, and we're leaving it ASAP. When they told us to start tearing down the hill, we said, "You gotta be kidding, when are we leaving?" They said, "Tomorrow morning." So, we asked, "What are we going to do tonight?" They told us to bayonet our sandbags—all of them—and pour them out into the holes, to tear up everything. We were being asked to spend the night on top of the ground, in the open. Nothing had ever slowed down; there was still shit happening all the time. That made everybody very uneasy. We had to think, Do we rejoice? We're getting off this hill, but is it any better where we're going? Nobody had the answers, just that we were leaving the hill. One minute we were very pleased, then we were scared to death. I had been fighting my ass off to stay on that hill, and now they were asking me to walk down it. They weren't going to chopper us off; we were going to walk off. I thought that was kind of neat because we were leaving by our own will.

We tore it all apart for a day and a half, and left it.

LCpl WILLIAM MAVES
Echo Company, 2/26 _____

Of the original sixteen or eighteen men in the company command group, all but me and the two corpsmen had left, one way or another. The CO and two others rotated, while the rest were either killed or wounded. We turned Hill 861A over to the Army when they were flown in, and we were to join the rest of the battalion on Hill 558. After ninety-two days without washing and wearing the same clothes, we were looking forward to bathing in the creek we knew flowed just outside the 558 perimeter. Several of us were in that creek the afternoon we got to 558, including me and my two corpsmen friends. We had just dug our hole together and had put a poncho roof on it for our last night in the Khe Sanh valley. Tomorrow, we were to fly out to Camp Carroll.

Thirteen of the two dozen or so of us bathing in the creek headed back toward the wire. I couldn't go just then. Doc wanted to, but the water was just too nice. I told him I would come back with the second group. The first group crossed the open ground in front of the wire, and Charlie dropped a salvo of three 122mm rockets. Of the thirteen Marines ready to leave, seven were dead, five were wounded, and one stood untouched except for shell shock. I sat in the creek, shaking, crying, and laughing. A second salvo of three rockets came in over our heads and into the trees, hurting nothing except the landscape. I remember a lieutenant asking me if I was all right or if I was hit. I could only stare at him and nod. Somehow, I felt all the rockets were aimed at me, that none of the originals were supposed to escape. The corpsmen were both dead, and Charlie had only

one more of us to get. I sat up that night in our hole,
wondering when they would come for me.

Midmorning the next day, April 17, I flew out of the Khe
Sanh valley, forever. I left alone.

APRIL 17

Cpl TERRY STEWART
Mike Company, 3/26 _____

After my platoon commander was killed by the artillery
attack on April 15, I was given the command of my platoon.
We were all the way at the end of the trench and the last unit
of 3/26 to be lifted out. At sundown, April 16, the fog started
to roll in and the birds were called off. As far as I knew, there
was just one pit of about thirty men left in all of Khe Sanh.
Mine. I was instructed to find a secure position and hold on
until daylight. I took the men to the Combat Operations Center
and we set up a very tight perimeter around there. We were all
on the line all night. I plotted more "on calls" than any
artillery battery could possibly fire, but I was assured that guns
were up and ready for us on a moment's notice. It was one
restless night. We sat with rifles in our shoulders all night,
ready to fight like we'd never dreamed of. After all, it was said
that there were 60,000 NVA in the area during the height of
the siege, and Lang Vei, down the road, had been overrun with
over 500 defenders guarding it. But the night passed with
nothing more than the scurrying of rats. We were used to
them, so it wasn't all that traumatic.

The next morning, April 17, the birds came in and started
to drop off men from another Marine regiment. I had my
men broken down into helo teams long before dawn, and we
wasted no time boarding the choppers as they emptied. I
was the very last man. I stopped only for a brief second to
look back at the base. It was a mess! Then I glanced out at
881S, way off in the distance. The fog was just lifting, and I
was struck by how beautiful the hill looked from where I
was standing. It was hard to imagine that it wasn't as
peaceful and beautiful as it appeared just now. I watched it
the whole time the bird was lifting off and flying away.

Cpl WALT WHITESIDES
3/26 Tactical Air Control Party _____

All were in high spirits since it was apparent that the worst of Khe Sanh was over. While it probably couldn't be called a victory, survival in itself was reason to be grateful. Several of the Marines I knew that had been on the hills for a long time were nervous about being in comparatively large spaces at Khe Sanh. One wireman, Pfc Tommy Williams, remarked to me that it was different, that he was used to listening for the pop of a mortar, not the distant boom of artillery or the sound of incoming rockets. Unfortunately, that day, Tommy was caught in an upright position and wounded by shrapnel. LCpl Toby Jackson and I tried to save him, but he was very badly wounded in the torso and abdomen. He bled to death before we could get a corpsman to the scene.

APRIL 18

Col BRUCE MEYERS
26th Marines Commanding Officer _____

The decision having been made to withdraw the 26th Marines as a unit from Khe Sanh, we airlifted out the few pieces of regimental equipment that were still operable. By then, Route 9 had been opened. We thus were able to use Route 9 to bring out the larger road-bound pieces of equipment, such as Ontos, tanks, and generators. However, the vast bulk of the regiment's equipment had been severely damaged during the siege.

I sent my two ARVN battalions out a day or two ahead of the regiment and used headquarters units and adjacent Marine units to fill the gap in the perimeter where the two small ARVN battalions had been. The major airlift of the 26th Marines was on April 18.

1stLt NICK ROMANETZ
Charlie Company, 1/26 _____

Helicopters bringing in a new battalion brought us out of Khe Sanh. One of the birds landed with its ass end at the edge of a minefield, with his belly straddling the triple concertina wire. Before anyone could do anything, he dropped the ramp and Marines came running out. They took at least two casualties when they tripped our own mines.

Flying out of the base, it still looked beautiful. There were a lot of pockmarks, but it looked pretty. My parting thoughts were that I could still remember how pretty the place looked when I was coming in. It was still pretty, but it was a moonscape pretty, with a lot of the jungle all torn up and the elephant grass gone. I was glad to leave it.

My platoon had about sixty guys in it throughout the siege. We had seven guys killed—a couple by snipers and the rest by incoming.

1stLt ERNIE SPENCER
1/26 Intelligence Officer _____

I take a seat next to the door gunner on the forward jumpseat of a CH-46. Half a rifle platoon has boarded with me.

As soon as we're at cruising altitude, the pilot removes his flight helmet and places it on his lap. Looking back at me, he says, "Relax, I'm going to get you out of this." He's got a big fucking John Wayne smile on his face.

I jump to my feet and lunge at him. "Fuck you! Fuck you!" I scream.

I watch that John Wayne smile melt. I'm not sure if he can hear what I'm saying, but I know he is bothered by my snarl. I stare at him until he turns his John Wayne ass around. He puts his helmet on and does not look back.[4]

Col BRUCE MEYERS
26th Marines Commanding Officer _____

On one of the last of the choppers making the withdrawal of the 26th Marines from Khe Sanh, I asked the pilot to make a final swing—out of range of potential 12.7mm antiaircraft fire. I remember vividly commenting to my regimental operations officer, "It looks like the mountains of the moon!"—a reference to the Arclight bomb craters that virtually ringed Khe Sanh and its surrounding hill outposts. I thought to myself that the earth and jungle torn up from the numerous B-52 missions was a superb visual example of how the concentration of American firepower—combined Air Force and Navy/Marine Corps close air support, supplemented by massed artillery—was the nemesis of General Giap in his frustrated attempt to replicate his victory over the French at Dienbienphu.

The bulk of the regiment—2/26 and 3/26—was airlifted to Quang Tri while 1/26 went to Dong Ha. The troops were given hot showers and a steak through the efforts of General Tompkins. Our first task was to reassemble all of the missing field equipment—trucks, jeeps, generators, and crew-served weapons—to replace those that had been either destroyed or damaged in the siege. All units in III Marine Amphibious Force were scoured, and many people surplus to the official unit tables of organization were pulled away and given to the 26th Marines. I am sure that many of my fellow regimental commanders had few kind words to say about this temporary depletion from their units to replace our gear.

Pfc MIKE DeLANEY
Echo Company, 2/26 _____

April 18, 1968

Dear Mom and Dad,
What are you guys doing? Well, I'm not at Khe Sanh now, or on Hill 861A. We're at Camp Carroll, a Marine base by Dong Ha. I sure am glad to be off that hill and out of Khe Sanh. We lost better than 200 men there. It was just a living hell.

Cpl DENNIS MANNION
Charlie Battery, 1/13 _____

Quang Tri, April 18, 1968

Dear Joe,
I'm out! Khe Sanh has been left behind! Don't get me wrong. I'm not being cocky. Only the lucky get out of Khe Sanh alive. Being good or talented doesn't help there.
From Hill 881N, we were helilifted to Khe Sanh, where I was detached from 3/26 and sent back to

Charlie Battery. Meanwhile, Kilo and the rest of
3/26 were choppered out of Khe Sanh. On the third
day, they decided to cut Charlie Battery some slack
and decided to send us back to the rear with 3/26.
Twenty-four hours later, I'm stepping off the
chopper at Quang Tri, abandoning my gear and
clothes, and stepping into a hot shower.

I got new clothes, a steak dinner, root beer, and
Black Label beer. So fantastic! Like being brought
to a new world. Today and tomorrow we'll be
sitting on our asses.

1stLt JOHN KAHENY
1/26 Combat Operations Center _____

When we went down to the airstrip for the extract from Khe
Sanh, the new battalion commander, LtCol Frederick McEwan,
asked me to stay with the tactical air control party that was
running the helilift. I was to ensure that everyone got out
okay and to check out with Regiment. There were just the
four of us sitting on the airstrip.

We ran out of helicopters. We filled them all up, but the air
officer, our two radio operators, and I were left. The air
officer got on the radio and complained bitterly that none of us—
especially me—wanted to stay another night at Khe Sanh. I had
gotten there just short of a year earlier. Well, a lame CH-46
came around; its rear ramp would not come down, but he said
if we could catch him on the runway he would let us pile in.

He came down and we ran out. First we threw the radios in,
then the radio operators, then the air officer. Someone gave the
"up" sign to the crew chief, indicating that I was aboard. But
I hadn't really gotten over the edge of the ramp yet. As they
started to pull me in, the helicopter took off and banked
sharply to avoid enemy fire. My cartridge belt and trousers
caught on the lip of the ramp, so the harder they pulled the
more my pants went down. I was finally rolled into the aircraft
with my cartridge belt and trousers around my ankles.

I've always thought it was very fitting to leave the combat
base that way—mooning two divisions of the North Vietnamese
Army.

Epilogue

The Khe Sanh Combat Base was razed to the ground approximately three months after the siege was lifted. Khe Sanh's traditional screening and surveillance missions were shifted approximately twelve kilometers east, to Ca Lu, because LZ Stud—renamed LZ Vandergrift by its Marine tenants—could not be reached by North Vietnamese 130mm and 152mm artillery emplaced in Laos. Over the next seven years of war, the ruins of the old combat base and its airstrip were occupied from time to time by both sides, but not permanently.

Capt HARRY BAIG
26th Marines Target Information Officer _____

Throughout the siege, there were three phases of combat. The first was the face-to-face confrontations of Marines and North Vietnamese as they met at the wire or in the vicinity of the Khe Sanh Combat Base. The second was the daylight attacks by supporting arms on known targets or on targets of opportunity. Air, artillery, and mortars, during this phase, were controlled by forward observers, by aerial observers, or by forward air controllers under the overall management of the Regimental Fire Support Coordination Center. The third and, to my mind, the most important phase was the planned nightly schedule of fires of artillery, the schedule of radar-controlled aircraft and B-52 Arclight strikes, all employed together for the saturation bombardment of enemy fortifications, weapons positions, and troop concentrations, and all under the closest control of the Fire Support Coordination Center. In addition, there were many nighttime targets of opportunity.

The actual battle plan for the reduction of KSCB and its surrounding outposts was revealed by Lieutenant La Thanh Tonc on January 20, 1968. The enemy never deviated from that plan. Tonc's revelation of the concept of operations, prior and detailed knowledge of the NVA methodology, the requirements or siege warfare, and the lessons of Dienbienphu and Con Thien, gave the intelligence and target team all the information we needed to plan the nature of the supporting-arms countermeasures. though on occasion I had cause to question the accuracy of my assumptions, nevertheless events tended to prove that we were correct. The manner in which Colonel Lownds assimilated his intelligence and welded together his fighting assets, from private to pilot, speaks volumes about the effectiveness of the Marine response to General Giap. In a sentence, Colonel Lownds employed traditional Marine tactics and doctrine of the twentieth century against an enemy who chose to put his faith and fortune in usages of the eighteenth.

Throughout the siege, our main concern was with the south-eastern sector. Here, in an area some five kilometers square, the Fire Support Coordination Center coordinated a good proportion of the supporting arms; here was felt the weight of the Mini and Micro Arclights; here were fired the majority of the artillery clearance fires. Throughout this area, too, the enemy prepared his siegeworks, bunker complexes, trenches, parallels, saps, and connectors. So intensely did the NVA prepare the ground that targets ceased to be regarded individually; instead, ground, and that which lay within it, was the target.... From a distance of 500 to 1,500 meters outside the perimeter, the ground was subjected to saturation bombardment. The fact that the enemy never altered his intentions for this area is a further indication of his inflexibility and rigidity. . . .

There is no question that to Colonel Lownds goes the credit for the successful defense of Khe Sanh and for the destruction of two NVA divisions. To my mind, his greatest gift lay in his ability to use his staff. Recognizing that his offensive capability lay with his supporting arms, Colonel Lownds called upon the Fire Support Coordination Center for more and greater efforts. Given enough supplies, he could have held indefinitely. This was not only his view, but the opinion of everyone, too.

But some of the credit must go to General Giap and the NVA. They gave us a good fight, and in the process they destroyed themselves. A man and a force, both known as past masters of guerrilla warfare, infiltration techniques, and siege tactics, were finally revealed as stolid, rigid, inflexible, and unbelievably foolish opponents. Our experience, during those seventy-seven days, legitimately raises the question, "Who besieged whom?" For a man who in civil life was alleged to have been a teacher of mathematics, General Giap had not studied his Vauban very closely. Had he profited from the teachings of the eighteenth-century French master of siegecraft, Giap could have caught us in the "toils of Euclid"—to our possible discomfort.

Newspaper correspondents never knew of the total weight and effectiveness of our artillery. . . . Inexperienced as they were, they magnified the volume of the enemy incoming rounds and disregarded the relative ineffectiveness of the enemy artillery. Had the NVA been capable of our artillery techniques, they could and would have blown us out of Khe Sanh. The siege clearly established not only the bankruptcy of the NVA master plan, but also the ineptitude of their vaunted artillery. And the press never saw this clearly.[1]

BOB BREWER
Quang Tri Province Senior Advisor _____

What we should have done was go right back in immediately and retake Huong Hoa District Headquarters after we lost it on January 20-21. But, by then, our military leaders had embraced the idea of the set-piece battle, which they expected to win. My several meetings with Colonel Lownds, General Tompkins, and General Truong [1st ARVN Division Commander] at Khe Sanh Combat Base in late January and February revolved around this issue. Truong wanted to retake Huong Hoa. In fact, he always resented the fact that I had ordered Capt Bruce Clarke to abandon the district headquarters and fight his way to KSCB on January 21. I felt after the eventual failure of the Tet Offensive that the Communists around Khe Sanh were just playing games, and that a breakout and reestablishment of order in what was left of Huong Hoa District were of paramount importance, but the U.S. military wanted to *operate*. That mentality, in the end, broke our support at home, in Vietnam, and elsewhere. We lost the war because too much was made of military victories and too little of day-to-day civil-political losses.

Capt EARLE BREEDING
Echo Company, 2/26 _____

The NVA we killed on Hill 861A on February 5 were clean-cut, and they had good haircuts. Their gear was in immaculate condition, hardly worn at all. It was all good stuff, all new. The clothing was all good. They were young, most of them. I believe they were the last of the NVA's hard-core troops, the last of their home reserves, the last of their young generation of soldiers. I think they went for broke—and lost. They didn't launch another major offensive like Khe Sanh or Tet until they went down and took Saigon in 1975. But that was the next generation. In 1968, they lost the last of their best new troops during Tet and at Khe Sanh.

Capt HARRY JENKINS
Mike Company, 3/26 _____

The United States had men in space while we were at Khe Sanh, yet we couldn't get the basic essentials like toothbrushes and soap to the troops manning the combat outposts without a great amount of difficulty.

1stLt FRED McGRATH
Bravo Battery, 1/13 _____

There are many accounts in existence concerning the pros
and cons of defending Khe Sanh. Those concerns never
entered our minds on the ground. The Marines I dealt with
saw Khe Sanh as a chance to grapple with Charlie in a set
piece. This did not happen very often in Vietnam, so the
chance to do so was exciting. As time wore on, that
enthusiasm did not wane. It was always the case that
"Charlie is out there. Let him come and get it!" Marines
tend to be apolitical. We couldn't have cared less whether
General Westmoreland had ulterior motives in assigning the
defense of Khe Sanh to the Marines. We had a mission. No
sweat.

Maj JIM STANTON
26th Marines Fire Support Coordination Center _____

One school of thought has it that the NVA opened the siege
in order to fix a reinforced regiment of Marines in an
unimportant corner of the country and oblige us to divert
thousands of sorties away from the real Tet objectives, such
as Hue City and Saigon. That is a legitimate observation
from a strategic point of view. Another school of thought
has it that we wanted to be there because Khe Sanh lay
astride their major infiltration route from North Vietnam. In
fact, they were going around us, but if we had been able to
patrol actively out of the combat base, we would have been
able to raise havoc on the infiltration routes. So this school
of thought feels that the NVA pinned us inside Khe Sanh to
relieve pressure on the infiltration routes.

About midway through the siege, I was privy to a heated
debate between Colonel Lownds and MGen Ray Davis, a
Marine who was then serving as the deputy commander of
the provisional Army corps operating in I Corps. General
Davis was furious with Lownds for sitting inside the base,
for not aggressively attacking the NVA. I knew that Lownds
wanted to be out there moving—Marines hate to be cooped
up—but he was under orders from the division commander,

General Tompkins, to sit and take it. So there was Lownds,
defending a strategy I don't really think he believed in to a
general whose views coincided with his own but who had no
authority to change things. Later that year, when General
Davis got commanded of 3rd Marine Division, Khe Sanh
and a lot of other fixed bases were dismantled and the
division's battalions and regiments were sent out to the field
to operate.

MGen JOHN TOLSON, USA
1st Cavalry Division Commanding General _____

On my visits to Khe Sanh Combat Base during the latter
part of March and the first half of April, I always felt that I
had been to the most depressing and demoralizing place I
had ever visited. It was a very distressing sight, completely
unpoliced, strewn with rubble, duds, and damaged equipment, and with troops living a life more similar to rats than
to human beings.[2]

LCpl PHIL MINEER
Bravo Battery, 1/13 _____

The news clippings we got kept referring to Dienbienphu.
There we were, 5,000 Marines in this little base, surrounded
by twenty times as many NVA led by General Giap. They
had us written off. But it wasn't that way inside the combat
base. Nobody gave up. It was shitty—really bad—but all we
wanted to do was go out after them. But they wouldn't let
us. We were ready. All we wanted to do was kick ass. We
had had enough of it.

I got home on Mother's Day, 1968. Sometime later, I was
watching the news when I heard they were folding the
combat base, destroying the bunkers, and pulling out of
there. It burst my bubble. It made no sense. I knew the
blood that went down there. I knew what guys went through
to hold on to that place. And they just folded it up. All
along, everyone was saying it was so political. That confirmed it.

LCpl CHARLIE THORNTON
Lima Company, 3/26 _____

The worst part of the duty at Khe Sanh was our inability to fight back effectively. We had to sit and endure the constant shelling without a way of striking back except for the response of our own artillery shelling. There were many times when we wished for an opportunity to move outside the perimeter to seek out the NVA. We ultimately did exactly that. However, it was not until April, when the siege was ending, that we were allowed to move into the mountains surrounding the base.

This was, of course, the end of the siege. We just packed up and left like nothing had ever happened. We certainly did not think at the time that it would be an event that would gain such notoriety. We were completely unaware of the detailed news coverage that was being broadcast to the States. The shame of it all is that we lived and died through such dreadful times just to give it all back.

During Khe Sanh and the rest of my thirteen-month tour of duty, I became close to men from all walks of life and cultural backgrounds. We became comrades and brothers because of common desires—not to defeat an enemy, but to survive thirteen months and go home alive. There was very little patriotism left in anyone after a tour of duty in Vietnam. We all loved our homeland, but we knew this war only served to bolster some general's ego in Washington as he recorded the daily body counts.

LCpl ARMANDO GONZALES
Bravo Company, 1/9 _____

No country, no government, no military has the right to do what our government, country, and military did to us. Without any intention of winning, they put us out as bait. That was totally wrong.

HN ROD DeMOSS
1st Battalion, 26th Marines _____

We had held Khe Sanh, which earned us a Presidential Unit

Citation, but we also just abandoned Khe Sanh, which really disillusioned me. We had risked our lives to hold this place, and then we just walked off and left it.

MGen TOMMY TOMPKINS
3rd Marine Division Commanding General _____

What was my reaction? Nothing. Khe Sanh had served its purpose. Now they were going to do something else.[3]

1stLt JOHN KAHENY
1/26 Combat Operations Center _____

Being home on emergency leave during late February and all of March was an interesting experience. The press had built up the siege at Khe Sanh to the point where people I met couldn't believe that I had just been there, much less that I was going to be going back, or that it was so easy—relatively speaking—to get in and out of there. I was much distressed while watching news accounts on television when I first got home, because I was catching up on incidents that had occurred while I was still at Khe Sanh. There seemed to be a general sense in the United States of doom and gloom about the siege that I found hard to believe. I was most distressed when I picked up the March 24 issue of *Newsweek* and found that the centerpiece of the Vietnam news was devoted to showing the results of the incident in which the platoon from Bravo Company had gotten ambushed on February 25. What disturbed me most was that the platoon commander, Don Jacques, whom I knew quite well, was shown with his groin shot out and being dragged through the wire. The editors lacked common sense and feeling toward Don's parents. There was no reason to show him the way they did. The general thrust of the article—and everything else in the press—was that the Marines were hopelessly outnumbered, that it was another Dienbienphu. We used to joke about *Hell in a Very Small Place* because we had a copy of it in our operations center, but we knew we were not in such dire straits as the French had been. As a matter of fact, the general attitude of most

Marines was that they couldn't wait to get going back out there to drive the enemy away from Khe Sanh.

If President Johnson had had one-tenth the courage of the Marines at Khe Sanh, the siege wouldn't have lasted as long as it did.

2ndLt SKIP WELLS
Charlie Company, 1/26 _____

When I got home in August 1968 and read the articles that my wife had saved, I realized that those articles were universally either untrue or completely out of line with the actual events.

I never felt any threat of a ground attack. I wanted it because I believed we would defeat it and because the *constant* artillery, mortars, rockets, and snipers were really a pain.

I still feel a certain bitterness about Khe Sanh. Not the actual fighting or being there. I'm very proud of that and of the Marines I served with there. I guess I'm still bitter about the whole Vietnam experience. It seems that it was such a waste, and to me, Khe Sanh is the classic example of that waste.

I recall talking to one of the fire-team leaders about "why we were in Vietnam." He said it was to "help the people stay free," and that he was prepared to die for that cause. Right or wrong, he was a brave and noble person, like most of them, and deserved a whole lot better than he got.

Pfc ELWIN BACON
Kilo Company, 3/26 _____

I guess the worst part of the whole deal of being up at Khe Sanh came to me at a much later time, when I realized that Khe Sanh as well as the rest of the war was, from the beginning, a waste of blood and time. Even though we had intentions of doing the best job possible and doing it for the idea of freedom, those who were our leaders, it seemed to me, knew from the start we were not to win this one. No matter what actually was achieved through our efforts, the final reasoning and justification for Khe Sanh and the

Vietnam War was not in the hands of the military, but in the politicians who ordered us there. God help them when they meet their Maker!

If nothing else was gained by the Vietnam experience, at least let it be a warning not to let it ever happen again. If this becomes a reality, then and only then Vietnam will have its value.

Pfc LIONEL TRUFANT
106mm Platoon, 3/26 _____

I think Khe Sanh will always be part of me, but I'm not the type of person who still lives with Vietnam. It's just a memory, it's in my head sometimes, but I don't let it restrict me in my functioning as a person.

Was Khe Sanh worth it? I ponder that question every time I think about Khe Sanh. It has to be worth it to me because of my experience there, because of what I had to give up as a person—the stress, the strain, the hurt, the emotional burden—because of what I saw my fellow Marines give up—friends of mine, guys I didn't know. It had to be worth it. Militarily, I assume it was worth it because we were supposed to have pinned down two crack North Vietnamese divisions, which, through the bombing, we helped decimate. It makes me wonder when I realize that a few months later they just flattened the whole place out. It makes me wonder why they didn't do it six months sooner.

Cpl BERT MULLINS
Bravo Company, 1/9 _____

I lost a lot of good friends at Khe Sanh. I remember all of them to this day. A lot of people died needlessly up there. At the time I did not realize I was participating in a battle of the magnitude we know today. I can discuss it somewhat dispassionately, but I think about my friends who died there, and I'm not sure it accomplished much.

NOTES

CHAPTER 1

1. Col William H. Dabney, Marine Corps Historical Division [MCHD] Oral History Interview. Hereafter, *Dabney MCHD Interview*.
2. Ibid.
3. Col Frank E. Wilson, comments on Marine Corps Khe Sanh Monograph, January 6, 1969.
4. *Dabney MCHD Interview*.
5. Ibid.
6. Ibid.

CHAPTER 3

1. Lt Col Johnny O. Gregerson, comments on Marine Corps Khe Sanh Monograph, January 3, 1969.
2. Kashiwahara, Capt Ken, "Lifeline to Khe Sanh," *The Airman*, July 1968.
3. Ibid.
4. Ibid.

CHAPTER 4

1. Maj Mirza M. Baig, comments on Marine Corps Khe Sanh Monograph, December 23, 1968. Hereafter, *Baig Comments*.

CHAPTER 6

1. MGen Rathvon Tompkins, MCHD Interview. Hereafter, *Tompkins MCHD Interview*.
2. Spencer, Ernest, *Welcome to Vietnam, Macho Man* (Walnut Creek, Calif.: Corps Press, 1987).
3. Ibid.
4. Ibid.
5. Ibid.
6. *Baig Comments*.

CHAPTER 7

1. *Dabney MCHD Interview*.
2. *Baig Comments*.
3. Ibid.
4. LtCol James B. Wilkinson, comments on Marine Corps Khe Sanh Monograph, December 19, 1968. Hereafter, *Wilkinson Comments*.
5. *Baig Comments*.
6. *Wilkinson Comments*.

CHAPTER 10

1. *Dabney MCHD Interview*.
2. Ibid.

CHAPTER 11

1. *Baig Comments*.

CHAPTER 12

1. *Baig Comments*.
2. Ibid.

CHAPTER 13

1. Tolson, LtGen John J., III, "Pegasus," *Army,* December 1971.
2. Ibid.
3. Ibid.
4. Ibid.
5. Ibid.
6. Ibid.
7. Ibid.
8. Ibid.
9. Ibid.
10. Spencer, *Welcome to Vietnam.*
11. *Dabney MCHD Interview.*
12. Tolson, "Pegasus."
13. Ibid.
14. Ibid.
15. LtGen John J. Tolson, III, comments on Marine Corps Khe Sanh Monograph, January 2, 1969. Hereafter, *Tolson Comments.*
16. Tolson, "Pegasus."
17. *Tompkins MCHD Interview.*
18. Col Bruce Meyers, Oral History Interview 2777, April 15. 1968. Hereafter, *Meyers Interview.*
19. *Tompkins MCHD Interview.*
20. *Meyers Interview.*

CHAPTER 14

1. Studt, LtCol John C., "Battalion in the Attack," *Marine Corps Gazette*, July 1970.
2. Ibid.
3. Ibid.
4. Ibid.
5. Ibid.
6. Ibid.
7. Ibid.
8. Ibid.
9. Ibid.
10. Ibid.

11. Ibid.
12. Ibid.

CHAPTER 15

1. BGen Jacob Glick, Oral History Interview 2777, April 15, 1968.
2. *Meyers Interview.*
3. Ibid.
4. Spencer, *Welcome to Vietnam.*

EPILOGUE

1. *Baig Comments.*
2. *Tolson Comments.*
3. *Tompkins MCHD Interview.*

BIBLIOGRAPHY

BOOKS

Camp, Richard D., Jr., with Eric Hammel. *Lima-6: A Marine Company Commander in Vietnam*. New York: Atheneum Publishers, 1989.

Nalty, Bernard C. *Air Power and the Fight for Khe Sanh*. Washington, D.C.: U.S. Air Force, 1973.

Pisor, Robert. *The End of the Line: The Siege of Khe Sanh*. New York: W. W. Norton & Company, Inc., 1982.

Shore, Capt Moyers S., II, USMC. *The Battle for Khe Sanh*. Washington, D.C.: U.S. Marine Corps, 1969.

Spencer, Ernest. *Welcome to Vietnam, Macho Man*. Walnut Creek, Calif.: Corps Press, 1987.

PERIODICALS

Dabney, Col William H. "Under Siege." *The Elite*, Orbis Publications (Vol. 2, No. 13).

Kashiwahara, Capt Ken, "Lifeline To Khe Sanh." *The Airman*, July 1968.

Pipes, Maj K. W. "Men to Match Their Mountains." *Marine Corps Gazette*, April 1974.

Studt, LtCol John C. "Battalion in the Attack." *Marine Corps Gazette,* July 1970.

Tolson, LtGen John J., 3rd. "Pegasus." *Army,* December 1971.

Watts, Maj Claudius E., III. "Aerial Resupply for Khe Sanh." *Military Review,* December 1972.

UNPUBLISHED MANUSCRIPT

Seavy-Cioffi, L.J. *Our Victory for Alpha One.*

OFFICIAL SOURCES

Various and voluminous official documents were used in piecing this story together. Among them were the Command Chronologies and After Action Reports submitted for the siege and breakout periods by the 26th Marine Regiment; the 1st, 2nd, and 3rd Battalions, 26th Marines; the 1st Battalion, 9th Marines; and the 1st Battalion, 13th Marines. Also, many of the letters by participants commenting on draft copies of Capt Moyers Shore's official Marine Corps Khe Sanh monograph are quoted, as cited, throughout the text. All of the documentary materials are archived at the Marine Corps Historical Center, located at the Washington Navy Yard in Washington, DC.

PRIVATE SOURCES

The bulk of this book is composed of excerpts from taped accounts and interviews and letters collected by the author from siege participants. It is safe to assume that any undocumented entry was obtained from the person cited at the head of the quote. The author has donated this collection to the Marine Corps Historical Center.

EDITORIAL NOTE

For purposes of clarity, style, and consistency, many—perhaps most—of the passages appearing in this book have been edited or corrected by the author. However, the substance of the edited quotes has not been altered except in the case of errors of fact corrected by the author.

Index